MEN IN LOVE

→ ←

Masculinity and Sexuality in the Eighteenth Century

GEORGE E. HAGGERTY

D1526735

COLUMBIA UNIVERSITY PRESS

COLUMBIA UNIVERSITY PRESS

Publisher Since 1893

New York   Chichester, West Sussex

Copyright © 1999 by Columbia University Press

All rights reserved

Library of Congress Cataloging-in-Publication Data

Haggerty, George E.   Men in love : masculinity and sexuality in
the eighteenth century / George E. Haggerty.

p.   cm. — (Between men—between women)

Includes index.

ISBN 0–231–11042–1 (cloth : alk. paper). —
ISBN 0–231–11043–x (pbk. : alk. paper).

1. English literature—18th century—History and criticism.

2. Homosexuality and literature—Great Britain—History—18th century.

3. English literature—Male authors—History and criticism.

4. Gay men's writings, English—History and criticism.

5. Masculinity in literature. 6. Gay men in literature. 7. Love in literature.

8. Sex in literature. I. Title.   II. Series.

PR448.H65H34   1999

820.9'353—dc21   98–47095

designed by Benjamin Farber

Casebound editions of Columbia University Press
books are printed on permant and durable acid-free paper.
Printed in the United States of America

c 10 9 8 7 6 5 4 3 2 1
p 10 9 8 7 6 5 4 3 2 1

BETWEEN MEN~BETWEEN WOMEN

Lesbian and Gay Studies

Lillian Faderman and Larry Gross, Editors

ADVISORY BOARD OF EDITORS

Claudia Card

Terry Castle

John D'Emilio

Esther Newton

Anne Peplau

Eugene Rice

Kendall Thomas

Jeffery Weeks

Between Men~Between Women is a forum for current lesbian and gay scholarship in the humanities and social sciences. The series includes both books that rest within specific traditional disciplines and are substantially about gay men, bisexuals, or lesbians and books that are interdisciplinary in ways that reveal new insights into gay, bisexual, or lesbian experience, transform traditional disciplinary methods in consequence of the perspectives that experience provides, or begin to establish lesbian and gay studies as a freestanding inquiry. Established to contribute to an increased understanding of lesbians, bisexuals, and gay men, the series also aims to provide through that understanding a wider comprehension of culture in general.

For Philip

CONTENTS

ACKNOWLEDGMENTS

➜ ᗉ

I have had wonderful support on this project from the beginning, and I would like to thank a number of different people and institutions. The people first: colleagues at the University of California, Riverside, who have read portions of the manuscript and encouraged me to complete a booklength study include: Steven Axelrod, Jennifer Brody, Joseph Childers, Carole Fabricant, Richard Godbeer, Stephanie Hammer, Katherine Kinney, and Traise Yamamoto. Even more specific support has come from an amazing group of students: Jon Adams, John Beynon, Doug Eisner, David Gere, Julie Gardner, John Ison, John Jordan, and Ashley Stockstill. I would also like to thank my colleague Robert Essick, who provided the cover illustration.

Colleagues in eighteenth-century studies and the history of gender and sexuality have helped in similar ways: Jill Campbell, Andrew Elfenbein, Shawn Maurer, Kristina Straub, Hans Turley have all taken an active interest in the progress of this manuscript, and others, such as Tom DiPiero, Pat Gill, Daniel Newman, and James Thompson, have helped me to get the word out in the form of essay publications.

The University of California, Riverside, has offered me sabbaticals from teaching during two different terms while I was at work on this project, and the award of a term at the Center for Ideas and Society helped me bring the project together.

I have benefited from helpful librarians at the University of California libraries in Riverside, Berkeley, Irvine, and Los Angeles, as well as at the

Clark and Huntington Libraries, the Cambridge and London University Library, and the library at the University of East Anglia.

Ann Miller and Alexander Thorp at Columbia University Press have been an author's dream: encouraging and helpful from the first, they have been a positive influence at every stage of the publication process. I would also like to thank Susan Heath for her astute manuscript editing.

Portions of chapters have appeared in the following journals and collections: a very different version of part of chapter 3 in *The Eighteenth Century: Theory and Interpretation*, and another section in Donald Newman, ed., *James Boswell: Psychological Interpretations* (New York: St. Martin's, 1995); one section of chapter 4 in *Eighteenth Century Studies*; an earlier version of another section in *The Journal of Homosexuality*; and part of chapter 5 in Thomas DiPiero and Pat Gill, eds., *Illicit Sex: Identity Politics in Early Modern Culture* (Athens: Georgia University Press, 1997). I am grateful for permissions to reprint material that originally appeared in these places.

Finally, I would like to thank a few people who offered more support than colleagues and friends can ever expect. They are my sister, Pat De Camp, friends Bob Glavin and Bill Kinnucan, colleagues Sue-Ellen Case and Susan Foster, and my partner, Philip Brett. Philip has been my model for the study of male love for the last twenty-five years or so. This book is dedicated to him.

MEN IN LOVE

INTRODUCTION

Masculinity and Sexuality

I link gender and sexuality in the title of this study because eighteenth-century gender studies have only begun to examine the varieties of masculinity and the ways in which gender determines—pre-determines, as it were—sexual behavior. Those of us involved in the history and theory of sexuality may all have experienced the relentless attempts of colleagues and administrators to euphemize lesbian or gay studies as gender studies—in class assignments, in hiring, and in promotion letters. In eighteenth-century studies, however, gender is at least as rich and promising a rubric under which to study the codification of cultural roles as any. As various recent critics have shown, gender is a contested concept throughout the eighteenth century, and a great deal of cultural complexity can be unraveled as questions of gender construction are answered. As Julia Epstein and Kristina Straub say in their introduction to *Body Guards*, "the boundary between biological sex, gender identity, and erotic practice" is "unsettlingly fluid."[1]

The term *sexuality* itself had no currency in the eighteenth century;[2] and most historians of sexuality now accept Foucault's much discussed observation that: "the psychological, psychiatric, medical category of homosexuality was constituted from the moment it was categorized—Westphal's famous article of 1870 on 'contrary sexual sensations' can stand as its date of birth—less by a type of sensations than by a certain quality of sexual sensibility, a certain way of inverting the masculine and feminine in oneself."[3]

Foucault's own study of Enlightenment sexuality notwithstanding, other histories of sodomy, such as those by Alan Bray, Gregory Bredbeck, Jonathan Goldberg, David Halperin, Cameron McFarlane, Stephen Orgel, G. S. Rousseau, Alan Sinfield, Randolph Trumbach, and others, have begun to suggest the range and function of male-male desire before 1870.[4] According to Trumbach, the adult male "mollie" who was exclusively attracted to other males only emerged in the mid-eighteenth-century, and even then without as clearly delineated an "identity" as some historians have suggested. Be that as it may, a certain sexual sensibility emerges in the eighteenth century that begins to have recognizable contours. "Hermaphrodism of the soul," moreover, a formulation that Foucault quotes as a contemptible misunderstanding of sexuality, fails to acknowledge the very real process of gender codification that was going on throughout the early modern period of cultural formation, most energetically and at times virulently, of course, in the eighteenth century. The very notions of "masculine" and "feminine" were sites of cultural conflict throughout the century. As various feminist critics have argued, moreover, only gradually did "feminine" behavior become the exclusive domain of the female; even less obviously, I would argue, did notions of "masculinity" become the property of individual "males," and not without a great deal of unresolvable conflict about what constituted masculinity and how it could function most effectively as a cultural determinate.[5]

Masculinity, then, is as much a cultural construct as femininity is. Recent theorists of masculinity, such as Kaja Silverman and Slavoj Žižek, have argued that male subjects are as thoroughly determined by Lacanian "lack" as female subjects and that male subjectivity itself is a site of the struggle of cultural determination most crucial to hegemonic control. In her attempt to read Althusser through Freud and more particularly Lacan, Silverman reopens the concept of "interpellation" to include the notion that the "state apparatus" itself is only a "dominant fiction," rather than anything "real."[6] Silverman also argues, with the help of Lacan and other French theorists such as Laplanche and Pontalis, that the dominant fiction is in any case more real than any details of concrete reality. I think that it is helpful to consider how "dominant fictions" are created through processes that the writers of fiction—among whom I include novelists, poets, and historians—implicitly understand. That is why the cultural resonance of certain fictional constructs offers a way of understanding more clearly the role of masculinity in eighteenth-century culture. Male-male desire, I will claim, is as much a part of the "dominant fiction" of the eighteenth century as other seemingly more socially acceptable constructs. As theorists of homosocial desire have made clear, culture has a stake in eroticizing male relations and making women the object in a system of exchange.[7] Restoration and eighteenth-century English literature offers so many examples of male-male desire that it is reasonable to imagine that the spectacle of male love was an essential ingredient in the codification of gender difference that took place at this time.

If gender and sexuality are fluid concepts throughout the long eighteenth century, fluid too is the concept of masculinity itself. After all, for the rake and the fop to stand together on the Restoration stage and move in alternating chapters in countless novels, a fairly flexible notion of recognizable, if not sanctioned, male behavior would have to be in place. Indeed, the anxiety about the role of masculinity in emerging individualist culture is at the heart of a number of these ritualistically repeated dramatic and novelistic contrasts. If Sir Fopling Flutter (in the 1670s) and Beau Didapper (in the 1740s) have to be expelled in order for the consolations of comedy to take effect, the same fate awaits rakes such as Fainall (1700) and Sir Clement Willoughby (1770).[8] Indeed, I think it is fair to say that every fictional or dramatic representation of a male figure throughout the century is a comment on masculinity, and each of the representations that I will discuss can serve to unravel a complex set of social assumptions that these very characters helped to formulate.

In the *Spectator* Addison and Steele introduce a range of men who are meant as caricatures of contemporary figures. The role of the *Spectator* in emphasizing domestic relations and the function of masculinity in the private sphere has been richly documented by Shawn Maurer.[9] "Models" such as Sir Roger de Coverley, Sir Andrew Freeport, Captain Sentry, and Will Honeycomb fulfill a political agenda, to be sure; but they also function culturally to outline the range of possibilities for masculinity itself. Unlike the more extreme representatives of masculinity in Restoration drama, that is, they work to domesticate masculinity and render it serviceable to a mercantilist agenda. Addison makes the point that "Men and Women ought to busie themselves in their proper spheres," and he offers the negative example of "a Young Gentleman, who has passed a great Part of his Life in the Nursery, and, upon Occasion, can make a Caudle for a Sack Posset better than any Man in *England*."[10]

This connection between aristocratic privilege and a very specific kind of gender confusion becomes a commonplace throughout the century and functions politically in crucial ways.[11] I am interested in the aristocratic or near aristocratic extreme, as in the case of Hervey, Walpole, and Beckford; and in the ways in which the privileges that such figures enjoy come to include the "luxury" of male-male desire. A few overly privileged individuals might not warrant such careful attention; but if in their private correspondence and published writings—to the extent that these two can be distinguished—we can find a model for male-male relations that in later generations becomes the ideal of a middle-class majority, then to consider the language of their devotion to one another in detail may be more culturally revealing than their elitist positions would imply. That these few individuals also composed some of the most fascinating and best loved poetry, fiction, and drama of the age would for some, of course, warrant their inclusion in a study such as this. More to the point may be that their role in the discussion of eighteenth-century "sexuality" has long been recognized if never fully developed.[12]

The middle-class intellectual, in mid-century most commonly identified as the "man of feeling," is equally compromised in the public imagination. Fictional figures such as Sterne's Yorick and Mackenzie's Harley are also feminized in intriguing ways. Sedgwick notes the "ideological use of male 'androgyny' . . . to express and assuage the specific homosocial anxieties of the male middle-class intellectual." She also points to a "newly emerging 'universal' literary consensus based on the normative figure of the pseudo-androgynous, sexually highly valent male intellectual within the content of an increasingly eroticized and family-dominated public discourse."[13] One of the challenges I set myself in this study is to understand the role of such gentle men in the construction of domesticated masculinity that is going on in mid-century and beyond. Claudia Johnson is not alone in noting that the "man of feeling" usurps female prerogative in almost brutalizing ways. "Under the sentimental dispensation contemptuously referred to by Wollstonecraft as the 'manie of the day,'" she says, "gender codes . . . have been fundamentally disrupted. . . . [T]he conservative insistence upon the urgency of chivalric sentimentality fundamentally unsettled gender itself, leaving women without a distinct gender site."[14] I agree with this assessment, but I would also insist that men are not more enabled simply because the codification of male behavior seems so all-encompassing. The ubiquity of "chivalric sentimentality" late in the century made it as difficult for men to function culturally in any but the most circumscribed ways. If men are allowed to cry, that does not mean that they are any freer to express erotic longing, especially for other men. That a wide range of men do manage this expression in terms that have always been celebrated is one of the topics that interests me here. I address these concerns at length in chapter 3.

Masculinity is not one thing in the eighteenth century, any more than it is one thing in the twentieth. Alan Sinfield reminds us that "it is not necessary to assume an even development, whereby one model characterizes an epoch and then is superseded by another."[15] After all, a rake, a fop, a merchant, an apprentice, a husband, or any individual man might feel love for another man. If he is a molly and expresses this love physically, in a molly house, he may find himself tried and executed. If he is a libertine, and he expresses desire for a boy that is as powerful as his desire for a woman, he may be publicly celebrated. A middle-class gentleman may seduce a younger man and find himself in trouble (although only rarely and then he is usually acquitted), but a man of lower station may be executed for similar behavior. In fiction these figures are caricatured at best. In letters and journals they are ridiculed. In broadsides they are viciously maligned. I will consider cases—legal, fictional, and sensationalistic—in which male-male desire is expressed and codified in these various ways. But at the same time, even more central to this book are those instances in which male-male desire is expressed and publicly celebrated. If male-male love is given a voice and the ideals of friendship are described so as to make them indistinguishable from erotic love, then what does this tell us about the parameters of public discourse in the eighteenth century?[16] It would be a mistake to dismiss this love as "simple friendship," not only because in certain cases (such as between Gray and Walpole) it is definitely more, but also because there is no such thing as the "simple friendship" the phrase implies. Friendship can be animated by many things, including rivalry, jealousy, desire, and love. As I discuss below, making these distinctions is never easy. At the same time I am not claiming that these are "gay relationships" or that every expression of male love is akin to our notion of the "homoerotic." Rather, I am interested in the phenomenon of these public expressions of love, and I hope to discover what they say about a culture that in all its other public discourse condemned the sodomite. In fact, this striking contrast—between

sodomitical behavior, which is punishable by death, and love, which is idealized—animates this entire study.

The questions I am going to address at length in this project include the
following: what is male-male desire in the eighteenth century; how is it represented in literary and historical documents; and what does it have to do
with notions of "femininity" and "masculinity" as they were being formulated throughout the century. I will consider, moreover, how "love" between
men is expressed, to what degree it can be categorized as erotic, and whether
even the most erotic male-male interaction has anything to do with what we
think of as homosexuality today.

The Limits of Libertinism

The discussion of sexual relations between men in the later years of the
seventeenth century has been almost exclusively concerned with the question of libertinism. The open sexual bravado of the libertine stance, as
well as the ease with which male and female love objects can be inter-
changed, have made figures like Rochester and others immediately accessible to historians of sexuality. Rochester has in fact been the body over
which the very battle over "homosexuality" in the Restoration has been
fought.[17] Rochester was notorious as a libertine in the court of Charles II,
and his famous deathbed conversion does nothing to undermine the
breathtakingly clear power dynamics at work in the so-called libertine
ethos.

Writers such as Harold Weber and James Turner have written extensively about the qualities of libertinism. Turner reminds us of the complexities of such a culturally malleable term when he says that "the libertine is sometimes interchangeable with, and sometimes distinguished
from, the Priapean, the spark or ranter, the roaring blade, the jovial athe-
ist, the cavalier, the sensualist, the rake, the murderous upper-class hooli-
gan, the worldly fine gentleman, the debauchee, the beau, the man of
pleasure, and even the 'man of sense.' "[18] All of these possibilities are evident in late seventeenth- and early eighteenth-century depictions of the
figure, in poetry, in drama, in letters, and in various other forms of public
discourse. At work behind libertine ideals was of course a political and ideological framework that was carefully articulated and in some cases brilliantly persuasive. More often than not, however, it is the sexual freedom
that is given most play in the libertine creed, and Rochester does nothing

to dispel the notion that the chief license that these careless aristocrats seek is sexual.[19] If I look at a few of his poems here, it is not to connect him to a "homosexual' tradition but rather to show how little he qualifies for such a role.

In his famous poem about premature ejaculation, for instance, "The Imperfect Enjoyment," Rochester articulates the aristocratic position precisely:

> Naked she lay, claspt in my loving Arms,
> I fill'd with Love, and she all over charms,
> Both equally inspir'd with eager fire,
> Melting through kindness, flaming in desire;
> With *Arms*, *Legs*, *Lips*, close clinging to embrace,
> She clips me to her *Breast*, and sucks me to her *Face*. (1–6)

As the title of the poem suggests, however, all is not well in this bower of bliss, and in just a few lines before it is seemly to do so and to the certain disappointment of his mistress, the poet ejaculates:

> But whilst her busie hand, wou'd guide that part,
> Which shou'd convey my *Soul* up to her *Heart*,
> In liquid *Raptures*, I dissolve all o're,
> Melt into Sperme, and spend at ev'ry Pore:
> ....
> Smiling, she chides in a kind murmuring *Noise*,
> And from her *Body* wipes the clammy joys; (13–19)

What follows is a lament over the loss of power in his penis, which builds to a celebration of past prowess in the phallic domain. What I find particularly interesting, for the purposes of this discussion, is the following crescendo:

> The *Dart* of love, whose piercing point oft try'd,
> With Virgin blood, Ten thousand Maids has dy'd;
> Which *Nature* still directed with such *Art*,
> That it through ev'ry *Cunt*, reacht ev'ry *Heart*.
> Stiffly resolv'd, twould carelessly invade,
> *Woman* or *Man*, nor ought its fury staid,
> Where e're it peirce'd, a *Cunt* it found or made. (37–43)

I don't imagine that anyone would choose to label this behavior "homosexual" or even homoerotic.[20] What interests me however is the libertine ability to "make a cunt" wherever he chooses. Like Halperin's Greek love, libertine love seems to be more about power than it is about desire.[21] Cunt-making after all is a process of subordination, and it is a process that depends on a functioning organ alone. Of course, the anxiety about the ability of that organ to function is an anxiety about the construction of masculinity. As the increasingly hysterical tone of the poem suggests, male subjectivity itself is threatened when the penis is flaccid: if it can't make cunts, it might as well become one.

In "The Disabled *Debauchee*," an aging rake tells of past conquest in these familiar lines:

> I'll tell of *Whores* attacqu'd, their Lords at home,
> *Bawds Quarters* beaten up, and *Fortress* won,
> *Windows* demolisht, *Watches* overcome,
> And handsome ills, by my contrivance done.
>
> Nor shall our *Love-fits Cloris* be forgot,
> When the well-look'd *Link-Boy*, strove t'enjoy,
> And the best Kiss, was the deciding *Lot*,
> Whether the *Boy* fuck'd you, or I the *Boy*. (33–40)

Again, the power dynamic seems what is most important here, and it would be unwise to make any claims about Rochester's "sexuality" on the basis of this kind of remark. Harold Weber, writing about "Homosexual Economies in Rochester's Poetry," talks about the implicit fear of female anatomy in both these poems—as well as in such poems as "Signior Dildo" and "Fair Cloris in a Pigsty Lay"—and Rochester's inability, for all his polymorphous perversity, to imagine sexuality between two women. But surely that is not surprising when even the sexual relations between "men," as these poems suggest, is so rigidly hierarchical as to insist on power relations before any kind of desire can be articulated. This is not even the kind of homosocial bonding that Eve Sedgwick describes so effectively in *Between Men*. This is a sexuality of every "Man" for himself—a libertinism, as Weber argues, that "flaunts a provocative self-fashioning that depends on a conventional misogynist understanding of hierarchical relations between the sexes."[22] Bisexuality understandably offers itself as a way to characterize the sexuality of the licentious libertine. I would like to reject the "bisexual" label as energetically as I reject the "homosexual" one. Whatever bisexuality is, it is not the careless interchange of sexual object that the libertine ethos seems to foster. Bisexuality of course presupposes a notion of sexuality that allows for an articulation of desire in terms of personal identity. The libertine would have seen his predilection for sexual congress with boys, servants, or even "passive" adults as an activity granted him by social position and personal philosophy, if that is not too exalted a term, and he would therefore have resisted any attempt to label his sexual identity. If the term *bisexuality* is to have any meaning at all, it cannot be indiscriminately applied to historically complex sexual activity, as the next example can help to explain.[23]

In another moment of libertine extravagance, here is Sir Charles Sedley, as reported by Pepys:

> coming in open day into the balcone and showed his nakedness—acting all the postures of lust and buggery that could be imagined, and abusing of scripture and, as it were, from thence preaching a Mountebank sermon from that pulpitt, saying that there he hath to sell such a pouder as should make all the cunts in town run after him—a thousand people standing underneath to see and hear him.
>
> And that being done, he took a glass of wine and washed his prick in it and then drank it off; and then took another and drank the King's health. . . . Upon this discourse, Sir J. Mennes and Mr. Batten both say that buggery is now almost grown as common among our gallants as in Italy, and that the very pages of the town begin to complain of their masters for it.[24]

Again, sexual activity between men seems to be at issue here, but Sedley's defiance of social norms and his flaunting of aristocratic privilege, as well as so much else, places him apart from his observers, who may even connect this behavior, as Pepys's friends do, to sodomitical practice. Sedley's sexual "performance" becomes a celebration of his penis, in opposition, perhaps, to Rochester's satire of condemnation. But both Sedley's performance and Rochester's poem center on the organ that gives the libertine his identity. Same-sex desire falters before the need to exhibit one's own prowess. As Vincent Quinn argues, "some of the same-sex behavior associated with libertinism probably originated from a desire to repudiate middle-class respectability rather than from a true alliance with homosexual sub-cultures. Moreover the freedoms that libertines claimed were available only to a small minority. Far from being egalitarian, their stance was reliant on their class position and their gender—libertines were aristocratic men not working-class women. Indeed working-class women were frequently their victims, and the language used in libertine texts . . . is often misogynistic."[25]

In George Etherege's play, *The Man of Mode* (1676), Rochester (as Dorimant) and Sedley (transformed into Medley) are world-weary rakes who cannot quite carry off their intrigues without giving in to the desires of the women with whom they are involved. Both of them move easily in any social situation and have command of enough wit to make them the center of any social gathering. They are neither ostracized nor even maligned, except by country characters who do not know any better. In other words, these are not figures of opprobrium. In fact, they seem vaguely titillating to most women in the play, and their sexual attractiveness is directed almost exclusively to members of the opposite sex. The one important exception to this sexual dynamic is of course, Sir Fopling Flutter himself, who so much wants to be one of the boys that he seems to be expressing desire for them. I discuss these relations at greater length in chapter 2, but I would like to reiterate here my claim that the libertine himself is not the most important figure to consider in a discussion of male-male desire in the eighteenth century. Rather than challenge the substance of these discussions directly, I would like to suggest that the spectacle of male friendship resists the explanatory power of the libertine model and offers a different understanding of male-male desire in early modern culture.

One recent attempt to explain the development of masculinity in eighteenth-century bourgeois culture is that proposed by Michael McKeon, who points out that "the normative model of male aristocracy traditionally shared some of the standard markers of femininity—not only a fine luxuriance of dress, but also a softness and whiteness of complexion. By the mid-eighteenth century, however, these traits were being derided with reference both to the effete aristocrat and (in an almost insensible extension) to the depraved sodomite."[26] This "extension" is of concern to me throughout this study, and I would hope that the work I am doing here can be seen to complicate this interesting analysis of the relation between sodomy and aristocracy. I should note, however, that while I look at many of the same documents that McKeon discusses, I often read them differently. I disagree, moreover, about the value of much of the historical work that McKeon cites. These differences and disagreements will become more apparent as I proceed.

Greek Love

One of the several *Spectator* papers on friendship offers a different reading of male-male relations, one that sounds more like a description of companionate marriage than anything else: "Friendship is *a strong and habitual Inclination in two Persons, to Promote the Good and Happiness of one another.*" Further: "Love and Esteem are the first Principles of Friendship, which always is imperfect where either of these two is wanting. . . . There is something in Friendship so very great and noble, that in those fictitious Stories which are invented to the Honour of any particular Person, the Authors have thought it as necessary to make their Hero a Friend as a Lover. *Achilles* has his *Patroclos* and *Aeneas* his *Achates.*"[27]

In *Between Men*, the now classic study of such homosocial bonds in the eighteenth century, Sedgwick raises a number of crucial questions about the nature of friendship in a homosocial culture, and she describes the ways in which male-male bonds could be used to organize masculinist ideology. At the same time she argues that male homosocial and homosexual bonds are not always to be so vividly distinguished. "[I]n any male dominated society," she says, "there is a special relationship between male homosocial (*including* homosexual) desire and the structures for maintaining and transmitting patriarchal power." Male friendship and erotic male relations, that is, are not necessarily different, according to Sedgwick's scheme, in either the ways they are expressed or the ways they are culturally interpreted: "For historical reasons," she says, "this special relationship may take the form of ideological homophobia, ideological homosexuality, or [as in the case of much of the material I discuss] some highly conflicted but intensively structured combination of the two."[28]

Many of Sedgwick's observations about post-Renaissance male relations are based on a reading of Alan Bray's *Homosexuality in Renaissance England*, which still ranks among the most trenchant historical descriptions of premodern male "sexuality."[29] More recently, Bray has written briefly but suggestively on the question of Renaissance male friendship itself, and in doing so has helped to articulate a reading of friendship that both acknowledges its homoerotic content and explains how friendship could function culturally to foster bonds in outwardly homophobic cultural situations. Bray discusses "two images that exercised a compelling grip on the imagination of sixteenth-century England": the masculine friend and the sodomite.[30] He argues that although these figures occupy almost diametrically opposed positions in the public imagination—one universally admired, the other universally vilified—in their very opposition they create a symmetry that is of deep cultural significance. He goes on to show that the two figures not only frequently parallel one another in interesting ways but also, at signal moments, become mutually indistinguishable. As I hope to demonstrate, Bray's analysis offers an invaluable interpretive tool for discussing male relations in the long eighteenth century in general.

The sources of such male-male devotion exist in many of the classical models of friendship that literary historians usually cite in this context: besides Palamon and Arcite, there are, for example, David and Jonathan, Orestes and Pylades, Nisus and Euryalus, Achilles and Patroclus, Aeneas and Achates.[31] These same historians, however, are ready to try various measures for explaining away examples of male affection, no matter how fraught with the exigencies of the libidinal.[32] In *Epistemology of the Closet*, Sedgwick explains this fact of silencing as a high priority of homophobic culture and articulates its usual set of reasons among her list of "excuses" for not addressing homosexuality—"Passionate language of same-sex attraction was extremely common during whatever period is under discussion—and therefore must have been completely meaningless. Or . . . Same-sex genital relations may have been perfectly common during the period under discussion—but since there is no language about them, *they* must have been completely meaningless." Her gesture should at the very least encourage critics of eighteenth-century literature and culture to address these questions directly.[33]

Critic Robert Aldrich has recently attempted to explain the cult of classical learning in the eighteenth century. In *The Seduction of the Mediterranean* he states boldly that "[t]he 'homosexual' heritage of Greece (and to a lesser extent, of Rome), in poetry and philosophy, art and history was the most powerful and most positive image of sexual and emotional relationships between men (or men and boys) available to succeeding generations. . . . At times when 'homosexuality' was condemned as sinful, dangerous, and unmanly, the Greek prototype provided an unparalleled and glorious image of man's desire for other men." Aldrich argues that throughout the eighteenth century this attitude toward the classical tradition was increasingly codified. "In 1764," he reminds us, "Voltaire's dictionary discussed love between men as 'amour nommé socratique.'"[34] Although Aldrich's study focuses in the eighteenth century on Johann Joachim Winckelmann, I will show various ways in which an awareness of this feature of the classical tradition is articulated and revised throughout eighteenth-century England. The culture of classicism at that time is so pervasive as to be almost unrecognizable. Throughout the century, however, it becomes suffused with a glow of Eastern exoticism that renders its most rigid dicta shimmeringly indistinct. This is most obvious, of course, in the work of Beckford and other Gothic writers. But the language of Orientalism appears in works as various as the *Spectator* and *Rasselas* as well as in Gray and Walpole's correspondence and in the drama of the Restoration. Greek love, that is, is often painted in Eastern colors in order to render it exotic and inaccessible. This is not perhaps as intellectually sophisticated as the rendering effected by classical scholars in the nineteenth century, but it was as imaginative a way to explain male-male desire as any attempted in that century.[35]

David Halperin has argued strenuously for a hierarchical model of male relations in ancient Greece. In *One Hundred Years of Homosexuality* he puts the case plainly: "What was approved, and (in certain circumstances) even celebrated, by free classical Athenian males was not homosexuality *per se*, but a certain hierarchical relation of structured inequality between a free adult male and an adolescent youth of citizen status—or a foreigner or a slave (the latter combination being considerably less glamorous)."[36] Of course, Halperin's opinion has not gone uncontested—the case for long-term love relationships between free adult males has been made most persuasively by John Boswell[37]—but it suggests a model of Greek love that is close enough to the libertine model to be suggestive in this context. At the same time, whether or not we accept Boswell's description of adult male long-term relations, the model that Halperin proposes excludes the more difficult model of adult male friends. I call this model difficult because it can as easily be confused with twentieth-century notions of friendship, which in themselves are more complex than is usually recognized. Boswell makes it clear that " '[f]riend' is . . . ambiguous in Greek."

In the *Phaedrus* [he tells us], Plato suggests that while the "lover" of
a young man is "in love," the beloved feels "friendly," and mistakes
his feelings, which are the same as the lover's, as friendship, though
in fact he desires to see, to touch, to kiss, to lie with or beside him—
feelings not characteristic of "friendship" as understood either then
or now. . . . A large part of the reason sexuality would complicate an
ancient friendship is that the primary and defining characteristic of
the friendship (as opposed to any other emotional commitment) was
its inherent equality: friendships had to take place between equals, or
the relationship itself had at least to entail a general equality.[38]

I find this argument persuasive, but I would add that although such relationships might well have been sexual, the emphasis in the available
descriptions is on the love that friends share. Of course, as K. J. Dover
argues, "[s]trong sexual desire reinforces love, normally generates love, and
is sometimes generated by love."[39] Love as *eros* and love as *philia* cannot
readily be distinguished in any culture, or indeed in many social situations,
as well today as in the eighteenth century; but as Dover and Boswell both
argue, it is too easy to eliminate the erotic when dealing with relations
between men. Dover goes even further: "The long-standing Western
European assumption that homosexual eros is essentially diabolical may be
responsible for a certain reluctance, even on the part of those who would
immediately reject moral condemnation of homosexuality *per se*, to recognize that homosexual eros can inspire as much unselfish devotion as heterosexual."[40] Dover's terms may be anachronistic, but his observation is crucial. It seems to me that the classical world is as important to the eighteenth
century for its model of erotic male friendship as for any model of inter-
generational seduction. For what animates the century as an alternative to
the hierarchical libertine model turns out to be again and again a model of
erotic friendship.

   Halperin discusses the friendship model as well. In a brilliant chapter,
he shows how friendships like those between Achilles and Patroclus and
David and Jonathan are subject to rewriting and reinterpreting throughout
the classical age:

The ideology implicit in this peculiar and distinctive mode of constructing and representing friendship can be briefly described.

Friendship, it seems, is something that only males can have, and they can have it only in couples. . . . The male couple constitutes a world apart from society at large, and yet it does not merely embody a "private" relation, of the sort that might be transacted primarily in a "home." On the contrary, friendship helps to structure—and, possibly, to privatize—the social space; it takes shape in the world that lies beyond the horizon of the domestic sphere, and it requires for its expression a military or political staging-ground. This type of friendship cannot generate its own *raison d'être*, evidently: it depends for its meaning on the meaningfulness of social action.[41]

Such careful and discriminating readings of classical "friendship" are welcome, not only because, as Halperin says, "a somewhat more loosely defined modern concept called 'friendship' " hardly functions as a universal sociological category; but also because "Greek love" is confusing enough without throwing mere "friends" into the mix. At the same time, however, it is important to recognize that if the public/private couples that Halperin has mentioned, and many others like them, were reinterpreted within the classical age, then they have also been re-reinterpreted for every age. In the eighteenth century itself they represent, for educated upper-class gentlemen, as well as their middle-class associates, a model of love between men.

Richard Dellamora, Christopher Craft, and Linda Dowling have all written extensively on the "classical" quality of male homoerotics in nineteenth-century England. As they do so, they explain the variety of ways in which notions of "Greek love" were reimagined at the close of early modern culture. Dellamora points out a significant feature of English classical education by quoting from Arthur Hallam's prize undergraduate essay on Greek love, in which Hallam offers "an intense idealization of friendship/love." Dellamora explains that Hallam "attempts to bridge the necessary anxieties with a positive account of 'the sublime principles of love.' "[42] Craft discusses how John Addington Symonds describes his own sexual and intellectual awakening after reading the *Phaedrus*, the *Symposium*, and ultimately and more immediately the poetry of Whitman, all of which resulted in the desire "to write the history of paiderastia in Greece and to attempt a theoretical demonstration of the chivalrous enthusiasm which seemed to me [Symonds] implicit in comradeship."[43] (That Whitman could be connected with the classics in this way is of course provocative.) Dowling explains how Symonds and Walter Pater "would deduce from Plato's own writing an apology for male love as something not only noble but infinitely more ennobling than an exploded Christianity and those sexual taboos and legal proscriptions inspired by its dogmas." She goes on to explain that, "[t]he single most revolutionary consequence of this hidden or 'coded' counterdiscourse was conclusively to sweep aside the deep fear of 'corruption' and 'effeminacy' associated with male love by a classical republican discourse that . . . had exercised a powerful hold over the English cultural imagination for over two hundred years."[44]

One of the purposes of my study is to show that this cultural shift was in a considerable measure prepared/prefigured in a wide range of individual cases throughout the eighteenth century. Writers who were privileged enough to receive a formal classical education often found in it the resources for the expression of transgressive desire. If this is true for cases like Gray, West, and Walpole, which we know because of the publication of their private letters, how many more unpublished accounts of such love must have flourished between schoolboys and young adults. Linda Dowling makes the helpful point that "[t]he *effeminatus* in classical republican theory is . . . always a composite or protean figure, the empty or negative symbol at once of civic enfeeblement and of the monstrous self-absorption that becomes visible in a society at just the moment at which . . . private interest has begun to prevail against those things that concern the public welfare."[45] Such monstrous effeminate figures appear throughout the eighteenth century, of course, and, as I discuss in chapter 2, their cultural function is extensive and complex. At the same time it is important to recognize that the friendship that exists at the heart of republican classical theory, as spokesmen such as Addison and others attest, is celebrated as an ideal in many cases precisely because it places private interest in a public context, as Halperin has suggested.

The spectacle of male friendship in the eighteenth century has been the subject of a variety of studies.[46] Raymond Stephanson makes the point that "erotic" and "sexual" expressions need to be distinguished and that "the difficulties of understanding the emotional drift of desire in actual letters between men can be formulated around three specific questions: what to make of letters in which the languages of love and friendship are indistinguishable? how to understand the widespread epistolary gesture which projects one or both of the male correspondents as a female of erotic or sexual interest? how to explain references to the male body?" These are welcome areas of investigation, and Stephanson is so astute in his reading of individual letters that his claim that "one cannot easily distinguish the impassioned language of predominantly heterosexual men from bisexual libertines or from homosexually-inclined writers" seems eminently reasonable. Stephanson is nonetheless able to distinguish between "erotic role-playing," as in the case of the correspondence between Pope and Wycherley, and actual expressions of "homosexual desire," as in the case of the effeminate Lord Hervey. He says further that "transvestite gestures" in letters between men "appear to constitute an erotic component between male friends which was not necessarily genital — an eroticized psychosexual space, in other words, whose verbal gestures were still normative within an older paradigm of masculinity and friendship, and not yet the signs of the new-style homosexual." Later, he explains that "we would be mistaken to describe such desire as necessarily 'homoerotic' in our modern sense of 'latent homosexuality' or some underlying genital desire." And after articulating the obvious question, "what are we to call such a component?" he answers by "proposing a paradigm for this discourse of this subjectivity[:] . . . epicœne friendship." "Until later in the eighteenth century," he says, "there existed a *public* discourse which encouraged [predominantly heterosexual men] to imagine their friendships with men in ways similar to their experience of affection for wives or female lovers."47

I say that this argument "seems" reasonable only because in the end it leaves us where we began. In this almost tautological logic, "hetero" males may play at same-sex desire, while "homosexually-inclined" figures, or even "bisexual libertines" must have meant what they said in erotically coded missives. Aside from assuring us that public discourse allowed erotic language between men, Stephanson succumbs to many of the anachronisms he would contest. For his range of sexual identities is riddled with late twentieth-century assumptions. He writes, moreover, as if the homosexuality of those writers whom he classes as such, Lord Hervey and Thomas Gray, for example, has always been acknowledged and recognized; but the sexual interests of even these figures has been an open secret at best. Later I discuss both men at length, but in the meantime I would only ask what we gain by a theory of friendship that offers us only the most outrageously effeminate figures as "homosexual" and claims that other, perhaps more important figures, are just good at role-playing.

I would like to avoid the pointless categorizing that goes on in Stephanson's and other essays about male-male relations by offering a different perspective from which to look at these relations. In the discussion that follows, I use an often misunderstood four-letter word to discuss male relations. Like the word *sodomy*, this word did have currency in the eighteenth century and could frequently be used to express various degrees of same-sex desire. Unlike *sodomy*, however, the word does not call up monsters of sexual transgression. If anything, it in fact regularizes desire in a publicly unthreatening way. At a recent meeting of the Group for Early Modern Cultural Studies, I organized a panel to discuss the problem of talking about *sexuality* in a time when the term had no currency. One member of the panel, a colleague interested in examining the dynamics of female-female relations, described a peculiar kind of desire: "I want to find a way to describe this 'romantic friendship,' " she said, "but to include the element of lust that is clearly often a part of it."[48] I said, in response, that I thought Western culture already had a word for that, and that the word was "love." There was a lively response to this idea, not least of all the urgent rejection of a concept that has been responsible for so much ill-treatment of women in our culture. But as I tried to point out then, and as I articulate throughout this study, love has functioned in Western culture precisely because of the ways in which it euphemizes desire (lust), and a heteronormative culture has always been able to use it to short-circuit, as it were, questions of sexuality and/or same-sex desire.

In place of "epicœne friendship," then, I would propose the use of the word *love*, as a way of talking about the emotional bond between the pairs of friends that Stephanson describes. He would protest that I am not discriminating between emotional love and genital love. But I do not want to make that distinction; nor do I think it necessary. In the first place, the constant insistence that we look for the "genital" in erotic relations is like searching for keyhole testimony in a sodomy trial. What does it prove or disprove? "Rochester" with his page: genital. Gray and Bonstettin: not genital. Which says more about male-male relations in the eighteenth century? I would claim the latter, precisely because it involves love and a degree of personal commitment that has a quality close to what we would call "identity." If it is suggested that a man "loves" a woman, or that woman "loves" a man, in early modern culture and beyond, who would ask "is it genital love or emotional love?" If the answer to my question is "no one," then I think I have begun to demonstrate why even as careful an examination as Stephanson's is problematic. "Love" is used (and misused) in Western culture to describe an erotic and emotional bond between two people.

If an eighteenth-century gentleman were to say that he loved his (female) servant, news would quickly spread of his transgressive desire. If he were to say he loved his wife, eyes would perhaps roll, but at least some "desire" would be interpreted as part of this uxorious expression. If he says that he loves his male friend, however, desire disappears and a new "noble" version of affection is put in its place. But love between men is as likely to take the first or the second of these forms as it is to take the desexualized form that in literary criticism at least has always been assumed.

Expressions of love between men in the eighteenth century, then, can be read as expressions of a complex cultural interaction that do more than "queer" the works or writers involved. I am interested in love in all its cultural as well as personal complexity. The purpose of my project is to rewrite our understanding of male-male desire, not only in terms of sodomy and sodomitical relations but also in terms of love. In this, my proposal is radical. For in discussions about male-male desire in early modern culture, love has rarely found a place.

Throughout this study, I consider male-male relations and "identities" of the following kinds: friends, both heroic, as found in seventeenth-century French romance and Restoration tragedy, and personal, as in the classically modeled friendships of Gray and his friends Walpole and West; fops and beaus, as depicted in Restoration and early eighteenth-century comedy and various satirical portraits; and effeminate sodomites, as represented in the literature of the mid-eighteenth century; mollies, as presented in social satire throughout the eighteenth century as well as sodomy trial accounts throughout the period; men of feeling and other figures in which sensibility and sexuality are vividly interconnected. I also discuss various other sodomites, libertines, pederasts, and sexual aggressors, especially as they are depicted in the pages of Gothic fiction.

What connects these discussions is an interest in the codification of gender and the increasing pathologization of love between men. From Antony's erotic celebration of Dolabella to Beckford's exotic expressions of erotic devotion to his cousin Courtenay, more than a shift in literary taste has transpired. Sexual desire itself has been policed, as Foucault would explain, in order to render some forms of erotic expression more transgressive than others.[49] If this almost goes without saying, it remains to be emphasized that sodomy is as much a social construction as the domestic dyad that it so insistently threatens. What the monstrous figure of the sodomite has so often excluded is the love he shares with the men with whom he is sexually intimate. The "love" cannot be expressed — "dare not speak its name" — because that is what is really threatening. Two men having sex threatens no one. Two men in love: that begins to threaten the very foundations of heterosexist culture.

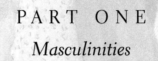

PART ONE

Masculinities

CHAPTER ONE

Heroic Friendships

The erotics of male friendship are rarely more vividly represented than in the heroic tragedies of Restoration and early eighteenth-century England. In almost every tragedy by Dryden, Lee, Banks, or Otway a complicated dynamic of male relations is central to the plot and instrumental to dramatic resolution. Before "she-tragedy" swept the Restoration stage, much of the dramatic interest in tragedy revolved around relations between men.[1]

The erotics of the Restoration theater has been discussed largely in terms of actresses, their relations with members of the Court audience, and the air of prostitution with which the entire theatrical apparatus was suffused. Critics such as Paula Backscheider, Kristina Straub, and Elin Diamond have been especially convincing in their examination of the theatrics of prostitution and the possibilities of female transgression, both in terms of cross-dressing and female-female desire.[2] Recent discussions of heroic drama, such as those by Joseph Roach, have begun to address the "Orientalist" qualities of plays such as *Aureng-Zebe* (1675) and *The Indian Emperor* (1665) and to explain the role such plays might serve in the theatrics of global expansion.[3] No one has adequately explained the presence in all these plays of eroticized male-male affection, central enough both to dramatic plot and to the self-projection of a culture in search of ways to construct a global authority. Nor has the Restoration theater itself been considered as a site of male-male desire. Although we have a great deal of information about the theaters, managers, and players, no one has brought to it the careful consideration of male sexual practice that scholars of earlier periods have brought, to, say, Elizabethan and Jacobean theater. As I attempt here to make a claim about the quality of male-male affection in a number of plays, I hope to be able to extend this discussion to the theater itself, because only in the workings of what Diamond calls the "theater apparatus" can the full content of these suggestive scenes be explored.

Harold Weber begins to establish such a context in his discussion of *Sodom*, the infamous play about a world of male-male sexual activity set in a court that mimics that of Charles II. Weber explores the "dangerous political implications" of the play and hints at the sexual atmosphere of the theater itself.[4] Weber says that the play "generates an unusual literary world of homosexual machismo in which male virility grounds and proves itself on the male body."[5] *Sodom* of course proves nothing about audience expectation or the ethos of the theater, but it does suggest that issues of male-male desire were as available in the Restoration as they were in the early seventeenth century.[6] Kristina Straub makes the point even more forcefully. In "Actors and Homophobia," she argues that "[f]rom the late seventeenth to the late eighteenth century, the image of actors as represented in the British popular press is that of sexual suspects, men who are in some way outside the boundaries of culturally dominant definitions of masculinity."[7] She shows, further, the ways in which "men . . . are unmanned on the Stage," and why an actor could not be "a full-fledged member of the aristocratic, homosocial culture based on the exchange and ownership of women."[8] The plays themselves suggest a very different attitude about masculinity, at least to the extent that they hold up erotic male friendship as an ideal. Their conservative, Tory agenda seems to demand that in order for the friendship model to function soundly it needs a clear erotic as well as a political valence. "Aristocratic, homosocial culture," then, is about more than the exchange of women.

In Dryden's *All for Love* (1677), for instance, among the series of Romans who are to convince Antony to give up his Egyptian diversion and return to the straight path of virtue—including his general, Ventidius, who lures Antony with his troops, and his wife Octavia, who lures him with his children—is the momentarily incongruous figure of Dolabella, his friend. Dolabella is described as one "whom Caesar [Octavius] loves beyond the love of women," and he uses this lovability to seduce the wavering hero from the pleasures of Alexandria. Antony becomes wistful when Dolabella's name is mentioned in this context:

> He loved me too:
> I was his soul, he lived not but in me.
> We were so closed within each other's breasts,
> The rivets were not found that joined us first.
> That does not reach us yet: we were so mixed
> As meeting streams, both to ourselves were lost;
> We were one mass; we could not give or take
> But from the same, for he was I, I he. (3.90–96).[9]

Antony's hymn of praise, straining at language as it does and stretching to "reach" the expression of their love, encodes in almost blatant terms an affection that is more than "platonic." "The rivets were not found"; "We were so mixed / As meeting streams"; "We were one mass": male-male desire is at work in passages such as this, even if they function culturally in other ways as well. All these images stress physicality, fluidity, and bodily identification in a way that belies any simple "friendship" interpretation; even if the attempts to dissolve the distinction between the two individuals here could be read as metaphorical, the tenor of these tropes amounts to more than spiritualized affection. Moreover, this is not the poetry of frustrated desire: it recounts a love that is more than lack, an other that could be experienced as the self, a marriage of body and soul without impediments, an attempt at expressing an identity. "[F]or he was I, I he": this expression shimmers with the possibility of a different kind of subjectivity, physically as well as spiritually different, from that which was being articulated, already in the late seventeenth century, as isolation and tragic separateness. This outburst of male love, moreover, is not a quiet aside that takes place on the margins of the literary; it is instead one of the definitive speeches of one of the most popular tragedies of the period. This sexualized male relation, in other words, helps to define the heroic.

Such heroic statements of male love are a far cry from the declarations of libertine ethos that I quote in my introduction. As I say there, the libertine model offers little to explain these intimate physical bonds. Libertines are "homosocially" united, of course, but theirs is a homosociability of satiric individualism. The eroticized friendship that is foundational to Restoration tragedy has a different rationale. In considering the malleability of terms such as "friend" and "sodomite," Alan Bray makes it clear that accusations of "sodomy" are most often politically motivated and that those of friendship are by definition free of the sodomitical taint.[10] By looking at a few figures who shift from the role of friend to that of sodomite, Bray is able to suggest that the terms themselves are virtually without substance, what a twentieth-century sociologist might call identity. Restoration tragedy is a largely untapped source for the acculturation of sodomitical relations. Friends are physical, emotional, and psychological partners, who love and are loved in ways that heteronormative culture has always reserved for cross-gender relations. What fascinates me, however, is not the transgressive potential of this love, but rather its own seeming normativity.[11]

In this context it is helpful to look at an earlier play that took eroticized male relations as its central subject. If Marlowe's *Edward II* (1594) is in many ways the early modern original for heroic tragedy, then it also problematizes the heroic model. *Edward II* both sexualizes its central friendship with unapologetic male-male desire and politicizes it by showing how erotic friendship can pose a threat to the cultural status quo. In that play the king repeatedly defies aristocratic control in speeches to his beloved Gaveston:

> Now let the treacherous Mortimers conspire,
> And that high-minded earl of Lancaster;
> I have my wish, in that I joy thy sight,
> And sooner shall the sea o'rewhelm my land
> Than bear the ship that shall transport thee hence.
> I here create thee Lord High Chamberlain,
> Chief Secretary to the state and me,
> Earl of Cornwall, King and Lord of Man. (1.1.148–155)[12]

Following Bray, Jonathan Goldberg argues that "[t]he sexual relations cannot go unnoticed in *Edward II*, and the radical move in the play lies in having the Mortimers contend that although Gaveston has not remained in his proper place, there is nothing improper in his sexual relationship with the king." Sodomy does not emerge from the sexual relations between the two men. Goldberg argues that Edward establishes a "sodomitical" regime at the moment that he refuses paternal law and order for the sake of the indulgences of friendship. The king commits sodomy, not by sleeping with Gaveston but by his act of *preferment* in raising Gaveston to the level of the aristocracy. In Foucault's terms, as Goldberg reminds us, "*sodomy* is the word for everything illicit, all that lies outside the system of alliance that juridically guarantees marriage and inheritance, the prerogatives of blood, as the linchpin of social order and the maintenance of class distinctions."[13]

Later heroic tragedy, although by no means "sodomitical" in this political sense, does address the sexuality of power, or rather the ways in which authority is expressed in terms of physical desire; and like its most important early modern predecessor, *All for Love* sees male-male desire as a potential attribute of royal authority and a prop to kingly prerogative.

When Dolabella actually walks on stage in *All for Love*, the raptures that he and Antony express are vividly suggestive:

ANTONY: 'Tis he himself, by holy friendship!
           (*Runs to embrace him*)
           Art thou returned at last, my better half?
           Come, give me all myself!—Let me not live,
           If the young bridegroom, longing for his night,
           Was ever half so fond.

DOLABELLA: I must be silent, for my soul is busy
           About a nobler work: she's new come home,
           Like a long-absent man, and wanders o'er
           Each room, a stranger to her own, to look
           If all be safe. (3.119–127)

This imagery of the wedding night and of mutual physical exploration gives substance to the erotic suggestions of the earlier speech, but it also subtly feminizes Dolabella, whose soul is female and whose relation to Antony's young bridegroom can be nothing other than the young bride. (Later, Dolabella admits that "nature has cast me in so soft a mold / That but to hear a story feigned, for pleasure, / Of some fond lover's death moistens my eyes, / And robs me of my manhood" [4.12–15]). "Feminization" is of course a crude way of describing what happens to Dolabella, relying as it does on a rigid gender binary that the play defies. Dolabella is not female; he is a different kind of male. Like a prototype of the "man of feeling," that is, Dolabella is soft, tearful and somehow not the man, say, that the soldier

Ventidius is. Yet this redefinition of masculinity in the object of Antony's affections does nothing to diminish the power of the heroic stance; rather, it increases it. What is so surprising in this context is that the power of Dolabella's attractions for Antony seems understood by all characters concerned, not least of all by Dolabella and Antony themselves. This situation contrasts with that in *Edward II*, in which an unsuitable favorite is being pampered at the expense of the realm. Rather, Dolabella is introduced in an attempt to wrench Antony's attentions away from Cleopatra and back to their "proper" subject, his position in the Roman empire.

As Bray argues, however, this form of male intimacy—eroticized friendship that functions to maintain legal authority and hegemonic control—is impossible to distinguish from those friendships that are labeled sodomitical throughout the early modern period. As Goldberg says, "friendship and sodomy are always in danger of (mis)recognition since what both depend upon physically—sexually—cannot be distinguished."[14] Dryden insists that friendship is erotic and that such "(mis)recognition" is a fundamental feature of Roman, that is Western, culture. Dryden sexualizes the relationship between Antony and Dolabella as a way of increasing its dramatic force, and he hints at a physical intimacy as a way of suggesting the erotics of the male-identified Roman world. This is not to say that Antony and Dolabella are sodomitical partners, but rather that Dryden wants to make it clear that their love has a decidedly erotic power. Indeed, for Antony power and erotic power are synonymous, and that is why Dolabella not only succeeds where Ventidius and Octavia fail—succeeds that is in getting a rise out of the fallen hero—but also involves Antony in the three-way conflict that brings about the tragic denouement of the play.

Dolabella exerts a seductive power that is second only to that of Cleopatra in the play, and in many ways it is he, rather than Antony's wife, Octavia, who represents Cleopatra's greatest threat. As her eunuch Alexas tells Octavia: "he's handsome, valiant, young / And looks as he were laid for nature's bait" (4.80–81):

> The least kind word or glance
> You give this youth will kindle him with love;
> Then, like a burning vessel set adrift,
> You'll send him down amain before the wind
> To fire the heart of jealous Antony. (4.84–88)

Cleopatra understands Dolabella's burning desire and the danger that it holds both for her and Antony. She invokes it with a resigned and already defeated heart ("I must attempt it / But oh, with what regret!" [4.99–100]). That she cannot finally betray Antony in this way places her above Dolabella in the heroic scheme of the play. Dolabella's erotic intensity gives an heroic quality to his friendship with Antony, but it also makes him a victim to the irresistible charms of Cleopatra. The play does not condemn Cleopatra for her role in seducing Antony from his heroic duty, nor does it shy away from the presentation of the erotic friendship that might seduce him back into the Roman fold. Dolabella's erotic love for Antony is the clearest challenge to Cleopatra, and in the heroic scheme of the play, both have a claim to Antony's affection. If Dolabella offers the last hope for Antony, he does so by eroticizing duty, which elsewhere in the play has been stiffly military or dully domestic. At the same time Dolabella's erotic youth renders that hope as unstable as erotic attraction itself. When he falls for Cleopatra, the tragic denouement is assured.[15]

David Veith, the editor of the most widely available edition of *All for Love*, argues that "civilization . . . has never, since classical times, really condoned homosexuality."[16] Dryden depicts a moment in classical history when friendship held this erotic potential, and he does so without embarrassment. Veith seems unable to distinguish the friendship that Dryden describes from a sodomitical relation of the kind that both earlier and later generations had no trouble reading into male relations when they wanted or needed to.[17] Dryden does not see Dolabella's love for Antony as shocking, and the audience response to this scene has not been recorded, as it was for the scene between Antony, Octavia, and their children, which Dryden himself admitted almost lost him the sympathy for Antony that he had worked so hard to establish.[18] It is almost as if Dryden felt that his age was another that could condone erotic friendships between men, at least when they were articulated in the service of heroic cultural goals.

Antony's love for Dolabella is heroic by definition. It places him beyond any simple moralistic reading of masculine desire and celebrates aristocratic privilege at the same time that it documents the collapse of that privilege as a cultural possibility. Dolabella cannot save Antony, of course, and his own desire for Cleopatra makes this ideal of friendship seem particularly fragile and debilitating. Antony becomes the victim of his desires, the "shadow" that his opening speech had predicted. ("Lie there, thou shadow of an emperor. / The place thou pressest on thy mother earth / Is all thy empire now" [1l.216–218]). Bray makes the point that earlier in the century both physical intimacy and emotional commitment were a part of the convention of friendship, and he notes that "elaborate reflections . . . on the nature of one man's desire for another" are by no means unusual.[19] Antony and Dolabella represent an ideal of friendship that includes the physical as part of what gives that ideal its peculiar cultural force.

Usually, as Bray argues, the "civil" implications of friendship and the "subversive" implications of sodomy are kept distinct. Titus Oates offers an intriguing example of what we might call political sodomy. At the time of the Popish Plot, he was accused of sodomy by his opponents in court, but the charges were later refuted. As Rochester notes in a letter to Savile, "Mr. O— was tried two days ago for buggery and cleared. The next day he brought his action to the King's Bench against his accuser, being attended by the Earl of Shaftesbury and other peers to the number of seven, for the honour of the Protestant cause."[20] What I find interesting about this letter is the almost exclusively political valence of Rochester's discussion of this incident. It matches the examples that Bray discusses from the earlier seventeenth century almost exactly. Whatever Oates's crime may have been, male-male sexual activity cannot fully explain the accusation of sodomy. At the same time, Bray argues, "one can also come across a document that appears . . . to be putting the two [figures] together and reading a sodomitical meaning by such a monstrous image into just those conventions of friendship which elsewhere seemed protected from that interpretation."[21] One such document is the "record" of the sodomy trial of Mervin, Lord Audley of Castlehaven, which Bray discusses. Castlehaven was tried and executed in 1631, but the record was not published until 1699. This document recounts a debauched household in which male sodomitical relations are vividly described in a context of spousal abuse and group rape. The terrors of this account are, of course, politically motivated. Castlehaven was considered dangerous as a Catholic in the already religiously suspect court of Charles I, and his trial and execution were meant as a warning to the king, who was himself later beheaded.[22] "Sodomy" functions as an offense with a clearly political valence. At the same time the interest in the details of male-male sexual engagement belies a merely political end. Not only do Castlehaven and his servants represent a corrupt aristocratic domesticity, they also offer an almost pornographic touchstone for male-male physical desire. The publication of an account of this trial at the close of the Restoration suggests that such an understanding of sodomy was available to Restoration audiences and that aristocratic immunity from sodomy prosecution was again on the wane.

Dryden's interest in this topic was surely political as well as personal, and if he tries to make his depictions of friendships erotic, he does so in full awareness of how male-male eroticism can be used politically. Obviously, he thought that the depiction of male love was worth the risk of public censure, and he saw this love as ennobling rather than demeaning. Does that mean that the love is not sodomitical? Must it? The celebration of male love in his play, and others of the period, makes it impossible to generalize about how male-male desire was perceived and how it was protected.

In *Sexual Suspects* Kristina Straub persuasively argues that "[g]iven the ambiguous sexual legacy of seventeenth-century English players as surrogate women or 'sodomites,' discourse about actors' sexuality in the eighteenth century constitutes a site of visible, hegemonic struggle over how masculine sexuality and gender are to be defined. The ostensibly clear lines of gay and straight that organize our present, homophobic culture can be seen in the process of becoming 'natural' assumptions about male identity."[23] I agree, but I also think that while such concerns were circulating about players, a play like *All for Love* shows how far Restoration culture is from naturalizing a gay/straight dichotomy. When Antony and Dolabella profess their love for one another in that play, the hope of the Roman world depends on the intensity of this bond. Such love is the foundation upon which male sexuality is "constructed," I would argue, and the politics of male-male desire in these plays are as crucial to the emerging hegemony as are details of global conquest or female subjugation. Men must love men in a homosocial configuration in order for culture to function smoothly. That means that men must find in one another an erotic attraction in order to compete, as *All for Love* dramatizes, with the debilitating force of female desire. Dryden seems to be saying here that the female must be commodified as an object of exchange and not mistaken as a competing subject. Of course, such love is not always free from the debilitating effects of erotic intensity, as other plays make clear. But even when male-male desire is problematic, it exists in a different register from male-female bonds. If *Sodom* makes this misogynistic point grotesquely clear, heroic tragedy gives it a philosophical rationale.

One playwright who challenges this conservative agenda, at least in his earlier plays, is Nathaniel Lee. Lee's *The Rival Queens* (1677), which presents Alexander at the moment of his fall, can serve as an example of a different portrayal of erotic friendship. In this play two jealous wives, Roxana and Statira, are fighting for Alexander's attention, and a number of ill-wishers, Cassander among them, are conspiring to bring him down. Central to the action too, however, is the conflict between the young men Hephestion, Alexander's "favorite," and Lysimachus, Hephestion's rival for the hand of Statira's sister, Parisatis. Their duel begins the play, and when it becomes clear that Parisatis is in love with Lysimachus, Alexander's insistence that she be given instead to his favorite is one of the suggestions that his control of power is giving way to emotional irrationality. His preference for the young Hephestion threatens the social order. Alexander places the young man in positions of power over others with more experience, and showers him with affection in scenes such as this:

[Enter Alexander. All kneel but Clytus]

HEPHESTION: O son of Jupiter, live forever.

ALEXANDER: Rise all, and thou, my second self, my love,
O my Hephestion, raise thee from the earth
Up to my breast, and hide thee in my heart.
Art thou grown cold? Why hang thine arms at distance?
Hug me, or else, by heaven, thou lov'st me not.

HEPHESTION: Not love, my lord? Break not the heart you framed
And molded up to such an excellence,
Then stamped on it your own immortal image.
Not love the king? Such is not woman's love,
So fond a friendship, such a sacred flame
As I must doubt to find in breasts above. (2.96–108)[24]

This sounds much like Antony's devotion to Dolabella, but as the scene continues it becomes clear that Hephestion functions more like Cleopatra in this play than like Dolabella.[25] Alexander's devotion to him and his to Alexander, that is, quickly asserts itself as one of the play's problems. And as in Marlowe's play, the terms of the hero's downfall have to do with the quality of what he is willing to sacrifice for this "sodomitical" affection. In discussing *Edward II*, Goldberg claims that "One switching point for the proper intimacy between men to be called sodomy rather than friendship was . . . precisely the transgression of social hierarchies that friendship maintained, those transgressions of the kind for which Gaveston is accused when he usurps the privileges that the peers believe belong only to them."[26]

The Rival Queens examines such transgression in terms that Marlowe's play and Castlehaven's trial both suggest:

ALEXANDER: I'll tell thee, friend, and mark it, all ye princes,
             Though never mortal man arrived to such
             A height as I, yet would forfeit all,
             Cast all my purples and my conquered crowns,
             And die to save this darling of my soul.
             Give me thy hand, share all my scepters while
             I live; and when the hour of fate is come,
             I leave thee what thou meritest more than I,
             the world. (2.116–123)

This violation of social hierarchy marks Alexander's love as sodomical as clearly as any keyhole testimony of physical penetration would. One might ask what a scene like this is doing in the play, when not one but two wives (Statira and Roxana) are fighting over Alexander and when the politics of the court are complex enough to make the added complication of this particular love seem unnecessary. But perhaps that is just the point. Unlike the hero of *All for Love*, Alexander the Great had a reputation for loving his young officers, and that reputation is being depicted here, loosely and according to the conventions of Restoration tragedy, of course. Nathaniel Lee's attraction to this story needs no further explanation, for it fits the contours of heroic tragedy in its subject and its outline. His main source for the details of the plot was La Calprenéde's vast seventeenth-century romance, *Cassandra*, which was fully translated into an English narrative in 1661 (second edition 1676).[27] Sir Charles Cotterell's translation of *Cassandra* is a source of much of the overheated male affection as well as of the characters and action of the play. Indeed, the translation celebrates heroic friendship in even more explicit terms than the play does. In an early but representative scene, for instance, Artaxerxes greets Oroondates (Orontes):

[H]e threw himself into *Oroondates* armes, and hugg'd him between his with so much vehemence, that my Master found he truely and ardently loved him. *My dear* Orontes (said he, kissing him a thousand times) *is it possible that it is your self; and that I really see you, and embrace you? Good Gods, if it be a dream, grant that it may last eternally;* and interrupting these words with infinite expressions of kindness, he would not have given them over of a long time.[28]

Scenes such as this, as typical of French romance as they are difficult to explain, seem to cross and recross the boundaries between male friendship and the eroticization of male bonds so often as to make any such distinction meaningless. In any case, were Lee to have looked here for material that would heighten the aura of the erotic in and around the male relations in his play, he would surely have found it. Not only is Hephestion always mentioned as Alexander's "second self," he is also the subject of the most sustained male rivalry and one of the most bitterly expressed elegiac laments of the romance.[29]

Much of Lee's action in *The Rival Queens*, however, finds its sources in English historical drama, from Shakespeare as well as Jacobean playwrights. This tradition, of course, can be traced back to the work of Christopher Marlowe, and Lee's interest in the heroic implications of male-male desire, here and in his other great plays as well, suggests that he may have taken Marlowe as an important literary model.[30] Lee's own reputation for sexual license, so difficult to separate from other lurid tales that circulate around the question of his madness, adds a Marlovian analogy that is very tempting to accept.[31] Lee's drunkenness and his temper are perhaps not the only features of personality that he shared with Marlowe. And like Marlowe, he works very hard to make the male love that he depicts in his play a political rather than a personal outrage. Alexander's love for Hephestion leads him to make a number of irrational decisions and becomes to a certain extent his "flaw"—he always gives in to erotic emotion when clear thinking would win the day—but at the same time, in scenes such as that already quoted, that love is presented as rich, honorable, and defiant. It is celebrated in language that seems to be straining to express something about emotion that is inexpressible. "My second self"; "Hide thee in my heart"; "such a sacred flame"; "this darling of my soul": the language here, and in the passages from *All for Love* as well, seems to be

searching for ways to express male-male desire that does not simply repli-
cate the terms of male-female poetry of passion or the libertine hierarchy of
activity/passivity ("Whether the *Boy* fuck'd you, or I the *Boy*").[32] Cassander
does remark that Alexander's "flesh" is "as soft / And penetrable as a girl's"
(1.1.263–264), but this penetrability is precisely what qualifies Alexander for
the play's heroic interest. Indeed, his love for Hephestion is repeatedly con-
trasted to "woman's love," which the play presents as more violent and less
powerful than the relations among men. The women in this play are given
to spectacle, and their scenes, which become the model for tragic conflict,
tend toward the histrionic. Such scenes implicitly (and misogynistically)
pathologize female desire and allow it to consume itself. Masculine desire
becomes an alternative center of value here. When Lysimachus tries to
change Alexander's mind about his favorite, Alexander replies, "I here command you nourish no design / To prejudice my person in the man / I love,
and will prefer to all the world" (2.232–234).

The emphasis in these speeches is on education and formation; on a
quality of affection that is full of light and life; on an open public declara-
tion of a passion that functions in the world. Sexual desire between men
and women is seen as dishonest, scheming, and debilitating. But the love
that Alexander and Hephestion share is powerful, public, and intimidating.
Other characters in the play argue that because of his love for Hephestion,
Alexander's fate is doomed—the play begins with his rival's claims—but
they never argue that these expressions of male desire disqualify Alexander
for the heroic stance. In fact, such expressions help to define what is meant
by heroism in this play.

Paula Backscheider argues that "[in] the early Restoration, when the theater was identified so closely with the court and when the theater openly
accepted its function as a site of distribution and interpretation of news, the
theater was a hegemonic apparatus that was being used to influence a critical public in order to legitimate an ideology."[33] In Lee's hands, however,
the theater always threatens to subvert its putative ideological aims. No
Restoration playwright was more threatening to the establishment than
Lee. He condemned the excesses of the Restoration court and brooded on
human motivation in extreme states. One critic says that "moral depravity,
melancholy, and madness [are] the sources of conflict in all his plays."[34]
More to the point, it would seem, is Lee's willingness to tease friendship
with its sodomitical possibilities, expanding the ideal of friendship that

Dryden's heroic plays articulate with the obvious suggestion that male-male desire, male bonding, is always already erotically determined and that the consequences for culture are inevitably profound.

The word *bonding* leads to the obvious suggestion that what we are witnessing here is simply a homosocial tie, as Sedgwick would call it, that assures the smooth running of a patriarchal system. In this argument, we might say that the language expresses nothing more than straightforward male affection. The articulations of male-male desire in *The Rival Queens* (and Lee's other more overtly political plays as well) defy this reading. They make a political point that is moralistic in intent, to be sure. But, because of their emphasis on eroticized friendships, they also give center stage to a kind of male-male desire that challenges social convention. His case is a complicated one. Marlowe may have defended sodomy "not as idealized friendship or some spiritual relationship or as some self-integrative principle of identity," but as "*the proper thing to do*."[35] But Lee seems more than conventionally fascinated with Alexander's failure to control his own libidinal energy, and the political implications of irrational desire, elsewhere ritualistically contained within a love versus duty construction, in Lee's hands become a complex cultural critique. Erotic friendship solidifies cultural control at the same time that it begins the process by which culture must confront its own un-reason. Lee's own later mental breakdown may have found its source in the inherent contradiction of this stance. In any case, the friendship he idealizes here is in part responsible for the downfall of his deeply passive hero. But Lee makes no apology for this. In his unusually popular play, the erotics of male affection defy the cultural accommodation that "tragedy" would seem to imply. For Lee, that is, heroic friendship had meaning beyond the limits of tragic form.

In Restoration theater, spectacle and politics are so intimately related as to be indistinguishable.[36] Roach argues, for instance, that the Augustan theater functions "as an instrument, closely analogous to contemporary optical instruments, especially suited to the magnification of behavior. Used within a system of observation and implicit classification," he says, "such an instrument disseminates . . . powerful constructions of social and cultural difference."[37] The behavior that Roach discusses is that of an expanding empire: defining such figures as the "Noble Savage," the conquistador, and the priest all function in a play such as Dryden's *The Indian Emperor* to establish an ocular relation between the English audience and its dramatized "other." I would argue that male-male desire functions in such a theatrical milieu as the lens through which this bizarre otherness is viewed. Heroic male friendship underwrites the entire theatrical enterprise, in order to inscribe male-male desire into the cultural status quo.

The theater apparatus does not just objectify the actress for a male audience, as Elin Diamond so brilliantly argues, it also works to establish the erotic identity of the entire culture. Following Brecht, Diamond argues that certain "gestic" moments in performance can make "visible the contradictory interactions of text, theater apparatus, and contemporary social struggle."[38] If Diamond explains how the actress could be a figure of both admiration (for her craft) and calumny (for her sexual activity), then how similar is the representation of the friend/sodomite. A gestic moment of male-male love could bring together the forces of theatrical representation in order to make the sodomite visible to a culture that both celebrates heroic friendship and sees male-male love as monstrous. Restoration theater's spectacular elements–its elaborate sets and scenery, its costumes and lighting, the possibility of "discovered" scenes, everything that Diamond describes as a "new scopic epistemology" — could also be used to expose the cultural function of the scenes of male-male affection I have been describing. If I might return for a minute to Rochester, I would suggest that his *Valentinian*, a revision of a play by John Fletcher, contains a scene that offers a context for the placing of these other examples of male-male affection. Late in Rochester's play, after Valentinian has, with the help of his eunuch, Lycias, raped Lucina, the wife of his general Maximus, and after she has died in shame and self-contempt, the scene opens with the stage direction: "Valentinian *and the* Eunuch *discover'd on a Couch.*" Such a discovery suggests that we are moving to the heart of the play's meaning, just as Angellica's similar position in *The Rover* exposes the theatrical fetishization of the actress in Aphra Behn's play.

In *Valentinian*, however, a different erotic obsession is exposed:

EMP[EROR]:   Oh let me press these balmy Lips all day,
              And bathe my Love-scorch'd Soul in thy moist Kisses.
              Now by my Joys thou art all sweet and soft,
              And thou shalt be the Altar of my Love,
              Upon thy beauties hourly will I offer,
              And pour out Pleasure and blest Sacrifice. (V.v)[39]

Everything about this scene is "wrong": nothing in the play prepares an audience for this last-act embrace with the eunuch; this is not exactly the kind of friendship that Dryden and Lee depict, although it does share certain features with those friendships; and the play is by Rochester, already well-known as a libertine adventurer. Still, this moment has a gestic power that is impossible to resist. Valentinian's pledge of eternal love is clearly the most homoerotic expression in Restoration tragedy. Lycias's status as a eunuch should not disguise the fact that he is an attractive young man who offers the Emperor rich and lusty kisses in response to his own. This scenic moment seems to me to offer a great deal: all the admiration for the friend and all the horror at the sodomite are here combined in a single moment of dramatic intensity. The very contradictions of Restoration culture are brought exposed by this "discovery" scene, and more than a single emperor's sexual interests are being represented. Here at last is a moment that suggests that male friendship is more than platonic and that male-male love is more than sodomitical.

The theater itself encourages such a reading. *Valentinian* belongs to the same period as *All for Love* and *The Rival Queens*, and *The London Stage* tells us that the intended cast for the production, which was in fact postponed until 1684, included Charles Hart as the Emperor and Thomas Clarke as Lycias. Hart was of course one of the central actors of the King's Company, and he introduced roles as wide-ranging as Horner in *The Country Wife* (1675) and the "mad" partner of Nell Gwynn in James Howard's *All Mistaken, or The Mad Couple* (1667), as well as every other important part that the King's company presented. Interestingly, when he introduced the parts of Antony and Alexander in 1677, his young male partner was Thomas Clarke.[40] Montague Summers long ago noted the "uranian" features of the Restoration stage, and he lists Clarke among several actors whom he cites as "homosexual."[41] While Summers's work displays all the dangers of ahistorical research into the history of sexuality, it does strike a chord that the plays themselves echo. If Clarke and other actors such as Kynaston (whom Robert D. Hume and Judith Milhouse think would have made a better Dolabella than Clarke—"Dolabella is the sort of role in which Edward Kynaston specialized")[42] and Mountfort (whom Summers says was the subject of several scandals and who at nineteen played Lycias) were involved in sexual intrigues of various kinds, then the kinds of scenes I have been discussing would have a valence far different from that in which "homosexuality" is seen as a breach of decorum. *Valentinian* exposes the erotics of male friendship in unmistakable terms and at the same time it suggests that the language of heroic love is steeped in physical affection. The discovery scene in the last act of the play articulates in the clearest theatrical terms available that erotic affection between men is at the center of this homosocial culture.

It makes sense, then, that the most misunderstood play of the eighteenth century, George Lillo's *The London Merchant* (1731), should extend the tragedy of male affection into the common lives of London apprentices.[43] In terms of literary history, this play is important because it introduces a tragic hero who emerges not from the annals of classical heroics but from the folk ballad tradition. In the original ballad George Barnwell is an apprentice seduced by a "harlot," and in Lillo's dramatic version of the tale, his lowly status becomes the basis of his tragic fall.

Lillo does not mindlessly reproduce the terms of the ballad, of course, and in the play he problematizes issues of class and gender in ways that the poem does not. His Millwood is a startling villain, not least of all because she attributes her crimes to the position in which women have been placed in patriarchal culture. Stephanie Hammer has argued that Millwood's "rhetorical triumph [at the close of the play] reveals the dark side of Thoroughgood's enlightened realm, for the same virtuous commercialism that has made him rich has made a commodity of her virtue."[44] To be sure, Lillo was most interested in reaffirming the prerogatives of capitalist culture, and as a result it is the male relations that have most significance in the play. Barnwell's relation with his good master, his almost familial bond, is one of the clearest centers of value in the play, and when Barnwell's dark deeds are recounted, his embezzlements are taken almost more seriously than his murder of his uncle. The trust between a master and apprentice is of paramount importance here.

Important too from the point of view of mercantile success is the bond of friendship. Trueman is Barnwell's "true" friend, of course, but he is also the play's example of a good apprentice, one who is honest but who also knows that for the system to work, all grace as well as all judgment must emerge from within the system itself: the workplace, the master's office, the law—all have meaning only in terms of their function within an emerging capitalistic economy. Every apprentice's experience is the model of industry and responsibility—Barnwell is after all responsible for the accounts at

Thoroughgood's business—and one apprentice's "fall" threatens to expose the workings of the system itself.

It is not surprising, therefore, that friendship becomes an important theme of the play. Trueman tries to protect Barnwell at his own expense, and far more than Maria, Barnwell's devoted female friend, he exerts his influence to attempt to draw Barnwell back into the path of virtue. Millwood's deceptions are too much for Barnwell, however, and he carries out his crimes according to the directions of his mistress. Millwood's villainy makes Barnwell nothing more than a pawn.

Where he is not a pawn, however, is in his relations with the "good" world of commercial endeavor and hard work from which Millwood has parted him. All the value of this world is represented in the figure of Trueman. In this "middle-class" tragedy, just as in its heroic counterparts, male-male affection provides the key to the system of values that the play attempts to celebrate. Early in the play, when Barnwell is about to violate the trust that has been placed in him, Trueman accosts him in deeply moving terms:

TRUEMAN: I cannot bear this usage from a friend, one whom till now I ever found so loving, whom yet I love, though this unkindness strikes at the root of friendship and might destroy it in any breast but mine.

BARNWELL (*turning to him*):
I am not well. Sleep has been a stranger to these eyes since you beheld them last. . . .

TRUEMAN: You speak as if you knew of friendship nothing but the name. Before I saw your grief I felt it. Since we parted last I have slept no more than you, but pensive in my chamber sat alone and spent the tedious night in wishes for your safety and return. E'en now, though ignorant of the cause, your sorrow wounds me to the heart. (2.2.17–22; 30–35)[45]

The eroticism here is subtle but unmistakable. Trueman speaks with an intimacy that is reminiscent of the heroic tragedy of a generation earlier. In his lonely night of anxious worry, moreover, he anticipates the melancholy man of feeling who is only just emerging in sentimental literature. What is interesting in this context, however, is the very different use to which Lillo puts the trope of male-male desire. After all, Trueman's love for Barnwell is the one thing that could save him from the maelstrom of female vindictiveness in which he is caught. The play constantly holds up Trueman's love as the only true love, the love upon which an entire cultural system can be based.

William H. McBurney, Lillo's twentieth-century editor, finds these implications almost beyond comprehension: "the extravagant friendship of the two apprentices can hardly be explained except in terms of the heroic play. Trueman is the friend whom Barnwell loves 'above all,' and the breach of friendship is his 'first' offense."[46] McBurney goes on to connect this affection to that shared by Antony and Dolabella in *All For Love* or Jaffeir and Pierre in Otway's *Venice Preserved* (1682). But the heroic connection cannot explain away the erotic quality of this friendship, nor can the analogy to earlier plays be extended to any use of the friendship in the moral scheme of the play: though Trueman represents the friend for whom Barnwell *should* sacrifice the world, the reverse is by no means true.

The full power of this friendship, and its use within a patriarchal system, emerges most clearly later in the play, when Barnwell is in prison waiting to be executed. Trueman bursts into the cell:

TRUEMAN: We have not yet embraced, and may be interrupted. Come to my arms!

BARNWELL: Never, never will I taste such joys on earth; never will I so soothe my just remorse. Are those honest arms and faithful bosom fit to embrace and to support a murderer? These iron fetters only shall clasp, and flinty pavements bear me. (*Throwing himself on the ground*) Even these too good for such a bloody monster!

TRUEMAN: Shall fortune sever those whom friendship joined? Thy miseries cannot lay thee so low but love will find thee. (*Lies down by him*) Upon this rugged couch then let us lie, for well it suits our most deplorable condition. Here will we offer to stern calamity, this earth the altar and ourselves the sacrifice. Our mutual groans shall echo to each other through the dreary vault. Our sighs shall number the moments as they pass, and mingling tears communicate such anguish as words were never made to express.

BARNWELL: Then be it so! (*Rising*) Since you propose an intercourse of woe, pour all your griefs into my breast, and in exchange take mine. (*Embracing*) . . . Oh, take, some of the joy that overflows my breast!

TRUEMAN: I do, I do! Almighty Power, how you have made us capable to bear, at once, the extremes of pleasure and pain. (5.7.29–56)

It might seem at first that this could only be a parody of the scenes in the heroic tragedies I have just discussed. On the contrary, Lillo is absolutely serious in his attempt to translate that sexualized heroic friendship into his lower-class jail cell. He makes his two heroes perform an elaborate scene of love-making, moreover, on the floor of the cell, groaning as they do in the "intercourse" of misery, in order to evoke the greatest possible tragedy from the situation. In some ways this is the most powerful scene of the play, mingling tears, pouring griefs, and shouting in the ecstasy of painful pleasure. This is the erotic center of *The London Merchant*, to be sure, but I would argue that it is play's moral center as well.[47] The sexualization of the Barnwell-Trueman relationship almost overshadows that of Barnwell and the wicked Millwood.

I am not trying to argue that *The London Merchant* is a "gay affirmative" play, or that the desire that is represented here is in any way "homosexual." Lillo is forced to sexualize the relationship between males because his culture has made this the only option. As Sedgwick says in *Between Men*, "among the things that have changed radically in Western culture over the centuries, and vary across cultures, about men's genital activity with men are its frequency, its exclusivity, its class associations, its relation to the dominant culture . . . and perhaps most radically its association with femininity or masculinity in societies where gender is a profound determinant of power."[48] What Lillo does in this play is to take the heroic ideal of erotic male friendship and rewrite it for the purposes of middle-class morality. The "work ethic" after all would function more smoothly if all the men in

the workplace would only love one another. Barnwell would not have vio-
lated the terms of economic trust that the play celebrates if he had fixed his
desires in their "natural" homosocial path. Male-male desire is in this case
in the service, that is, of a capitalist economy. The bonding is sexualized,
just as the relationship to money itself is sexualized in the play, as a way of
making it attractive as an object of desire. Of course, once he has accom-
plished this dramatically, Lillo has also represented a middle-class version
of "heroic friendship" for men, a male version of the "romantic friendship"
that became the basis of female-female relations throughout the century.
And although it is articulated as a fully interpellated version of capitalist
friendship, it also represents the possibility of resistance: resistance in the
form of a recognition of the implicit sexuality of the homosocial bonds of
the lower classes. This recognition does not transpire unequivocally, of
course, until Whitman; but in the eighteenth century such friendships
occur with increasing frequency. The trajectory of male friendship, then,
does seem to be heading in the direction of the kind of male-bonding that
is familiar enough to us in contemporary business settings. It can be domesticated, that is, in accordance with the demands of a cultural system that
despises the idea of sex as much as our own. What is interesting for my purposes is to consider how thoroughly the culture of heroic friendship has
been betrayed by history. Rewritten as male-bonding, it tells only half its
intriguing story.

CHAPTER TWO

Gay Fops / Straight Fops

Gay Fops

The relation between effeminacy and sexuality is never unproblematic. No matter how thoroughly read as homoerotic, the fop or the effeminate man of any class as often as not defies an automatic sexuality designation, and no amount of cultural coding makes it possible to read effeminacy as an absolute marker of sexual object choice. Nor do popular attitudes about effeminate men make it any more or less likely that a man who dresses, walks, or talks in a manner that is coded as effeminate will be otherwise given to activities that challenge legal or social limits. If this is true in the late twentieth century, as I would argue that it is, how much truer in the eighteenth century, an age in which sexual codification was in a state of flux. When masculinity itself is the issue, all attempts to mark particular behaviors as identificatory are at best misleading. At the same time, to understand how a particular culture codes the effeminate man, how he is interpreted as a cultural icon, can tell us much about its attitudes toward gender and sexuality. The minoritizing procedure that marks some men out as different from others, that codes them as monstrous, and that manages to portray them as a threat to masculinity itself is surely of interest to students of cultural studies and the history of sexuality. In this chapter I concentrate on a figure who has always received a great deal of attention. By looking at the codification of the fop in the eighteenth century, I hope to show how sexuality became a feature of Enlightenment subjectivity and why gender codification became the central marker for difference, the central dichotomonic legacy of early modern culture.

By the middle of the eighteenth century the erotic valence of the fop is fairly clear. In order to understand representations of the fop at mid-century, it is necessary to look at a few early eighteenth-century examples of the type. From the time of Restoration comedy, the hint of erotic confusion has accompanied the fop on all his various outings. Randolph Trumbach argues that "the fop is often misinterpreted by twentieth-century readers of Restoration plays to be a 'homosexual.' " He goes on to cite Susan Staves, who "has pointed out that fops, while effeminate in manner from their contemporaries' point of view, were also presumed to be sexually interested in women."[1] I think that there is reason to challenge this *pre*sumption and at the same time to ask whether twentieth-century *as*sumptions haven't informed the way the question is posed in the first place. Sexual interest in both men and women is part of the libertine ethos, after all. And there is no reason to assume that the fop would operate on a dichotomized sexuality either. In most plays the fop would himself like to be a libertine, and he often plays up to the sexual aggressors with whom he is paired. His foppishness makes this a comic relation, however, and in key examples the comedy results from a confusion of sexual objects. I intend to look at a couple of examples of Restoration fops, but before I do, I want to assert a simple claim. Fops are always portrayed as sexually confused gender misfits. It is simply the reading of the misfit status that changes as the century proceeds. Another way of putting this is to say that Restoration fops are comically monstrous and later fops are morally monstrous. It will be the challenge of this essay to explain this difference historically.

Useful to this discussion is a chapter that is often overlooked in Ned Ward's 1709 account of the London clubs. In his description of "The Beau's Club," which immediately precedes his discussion of "The Mollies' Club," which I discuss below, he describes the following scene:

> At the upper end of their Club Room stands a Side-Board Table, which is constantly furnished with a Dozen of Flannel Muckinders, folded up for rubbing the dust off their Upper-Leathers, or an unfortunate speck off their Scabbords of their Swords. Next to these cleanly necessaries, stands an Olive-Box, full of the best perfum'd Powder, crown'd with three or four mighty Combs, that their Wigs may be

continually new scented, and every straggling Hair that has been
rufled by a Storm of their Mistresses Breath, may be carefully put into
Orders. Round the edges of the Table lies strew'd by the way of
Garnish, Scissors, Tooth-pickers, & Tweezers, Patches, Essences,
Pomatums, Pastes, & Washes, with all the artful implements Woman
can invent to turn Men into Monkeys: so that the Sir Foplings are no
sooner met, but they are as busie as so many Stage-Players before a
Comedy. . . . Then down they sit to their *Champaigne, Burgundy, &*
Hermitage, pull out their gilt Snush-Boxes, with *Orangeree, Brazil*,
and plain *Spanish* that each may fill his Elephant Trunk with
Odiferous Dust, & make his Breath as sweet as an *Arabian* breeze to
the Nostrils of a Seaman; & when they are thus scented, down goes a
delicious Health to some celebrated Harlot, Play-House Punk, or
Court Courtezan.[2]

A lot of careful argument has gone into the discussion of the veracity of
Ward's account.[3] But it does not seem to me important whether he is dealing in fact or fiction. Let us assume the "worst," that the account is entirely
fictional. Does it then tell us nothing about attitudes toward fops in the
early eighteenth century? Quite the contrary, I would claim: it begins to
show a great deal about how fops could be used in a culture that is going
about the business of constructing gender as well as sexuality. Ward, that is,
is tapping popular attitudes at the same time that he codifies public opinion. These images are not accidental. They are based on observed or imagined details of personal behavior that are being used to describe a sexually
inflected gender misfit.

Gender confusion begins with the many implements designed for
female ornamentation. The implicit irony of the list of items on the "Side-
Board Table" depends on a virulent assertion of gender division, which is
necessary in order to make the confusion meaningful. I would claim that
the assertion of gender division is so shrill because there is a lack of clarity
specifically around the question of personal adornment. The constant
emphasis on undue attention to personal appearance—the worry about
shoe dust, unpleasant odors, and straggling hair—all contribute to this
effect. Surely one element in this mockery is purely class-based: nasty
habits, such as taking wine and snuff, are hardly limited to men with effeminate traits. Indeed, I would claim that the feminization of the aristocracy is

already implicit in this description. These effete and overly self-conscious individuals, more concerned with outward adornment than inner substance, are identified with excess, and any list of the accoutrements of dress becomes a form of mockery in its very detail. They are ridiculous because they contaminate masculinity with the materials of a lady's dressing room. But anyone who has read Swift must understand how quickly the simple features of costume or "paint" can metonymize disease, particularly venereal disease. Implicit in the detailed description is a similar disgust, and Ward borrows from the misogynistic tradition to label his beaus symptomatic of decaying culture.

The mock adoration of prostitutes, with which Ward brings his account to a close, suggests that although the energy of this occasion goes toward entertaining one another, that does not stop these fops from pursuing females in their turn. In fact, when they arrive at the playhouse, they meet "their Matches" and "one of the Fraternity of sham Heroes makes an humble Bow to the Box-Ladies, and the rest follow him according to their custom to Drinking, W[horin]g, and Gaming till next Morning."[4] Again this grotesque behavior is not essentially different from contemporary libertine behavior. These "sham" figures, sham men, we might say, adopt the forms of libertine behavior—drinking, whoring, gaming—but this is merely a performance of masculinity. Transformed to monkeys, these men perform their class and gender as the culture demands. If the women like toys and monkeys, then men who mimic them are likely to be more successful in gaining their favors. But this success must always elude the fop. As various Restoration comedies also suggest, the fop is often at the right place at the right time, it is just *he* who is wrong.

The implications of these impersonations are spelled out more directly in the rhyme that brings Ward's account to a close:

To be a modish Fop, a Beau compleat,
Is to pretend to, but be void of wit,
'Tis to be Squeamish, Critical, and nice
In all things, & Fantastic to a Vice.
'Tis to seem knowing, tho' he nothing nowse
& vainly lewd to please his Brother Beau's,
'Tis in his dress to be profusely gay,
& to affect gay-like a wanton way.[5]

The fop is wrong, I would argue, in his gay profusion. Excess marks him sexually in ways that are directly analogous to the contemporary coding of the prostitute. Moreover, these beaus are "vainly lewd" for the sake of one another: never successful in his pursuit of the "play-house punk," the fop can only hope to please his brother beaus. If the fop is "gay-like in a wanton way," then that means that his extravagance is coded as somehow in itself monstrous. When this monstrosity becomes more specifically coded as sexual profusion, when "gay-like" and "wanton" become synonymous, as they are here, then the stage is set for the minoritization of effeminacy as an aberrant gender, threatening in the sexual profusion that it implies. In other words, unlike the libertine, who remains in control of his sexual activity, the fop becomes the victim of his own excess.

If we look closely at examples of foppish effeminacy, even in the Restoration, we see that the lines of demarcation can never be established with absolute clarity. There is so much emphasis on gender confusion, in fact, that misunderstood intention becomes as much the point as any simple object choice. Take, for instance, Sir Fopling Flutter, from Etherege's *The Man of Mode* (1676). Sir Fopling, we hear early in the play, has come "piping hot from Paris, . . . with a pair of gloves up to his elbows and a periwig more exactly curled than a lady's head newly dressed for a ball" (1.340, 346–348), with a "pretty lisp" and "looks more languishingly than a lady's when she leans at stretch in a coach" (1.349–354). At first, Sir Fopling fits Trumbach's unproblematic description of the Restoration fop rather nicely. He spends his time with the ladies, and he makes a genial fool of himself throughout his few appearances.[6]

Even at his third-act entrance it is difficult to take at face value some of his "witty" remarks. He begins by praising Dorimant's style and suggesting intimacy: "There is no living without making some good man the confidant of our pleasures" (3.2.148–149). Dorimant begs off, but in a few lines, in the middle of a conversation with the ladies about lace, Fopling turns his attention to Dorimant's friend Medley: "Forgive me, sir; in this *embarras* of civilities I could not come to have you in my arms sooner" (3.2.173–174). Then when the conversation turns, as it must, to his own French finery, there is the following interchange:

LADY TOWNLEY: He's very fine.

EMILIA: Extreme Proper!

SIR FOPLING:	A slight suit I made to appear in at my first arrival—not worthy of your consideration, ladies.
DORIMANT:	The pantaloon is very well mounted.
SIR FOPLING:	The tassels are new and pretty.
MEDLEY:	I never saw a coat better cut.
SIR FOPLING:	It makes me show long-waisted, and I think slender.
DORIMANT:	That's the shape our ladies dote on.
MEDLEY:	Your breech, though, is a handful too high, in my eye, Sir Fopling.
SIR FOPLING:	Peace, Medley, I have wished it lower a thousand times; but a pox on't, 'twill not be! (3.2.188–200)

Sir Fopling's attention to his dress creates a moment of arch comedy, and the "effeminacy" of his attentions is obvious, even if female behavior was by no means as clearly coded as "feminine" as it was later in the century. Sir Fopling gives the play a lot of its comic flair, and a scene like this makes it clear why.

Questions of same-sex desire are never far from the surface here. Note, for instance, that although Emilia starts the sequence, it is Dorimant and Medley who carry it on, playing with Sir Fopling and teasing him roundly. The "boys" taunt him because he would pretend to being a ladies' man, but they know better. When they turn to the shape of his pantaloon, however, and the height of his breech, it seems to me that they are addressing questions of gender confusion, albeit indirectly. For they are suggesting that Sir Fopling is a gelding. "A handful too high"; "I have wished it lower"; "a pox on't." A pox, indeed. Trumbach may be right to say that characters like Sir Fopling are innocuous, but they are also marked as sexual creatures who are as confused about who they are as they are confused about what (or whom) they desire. Sir Fopling may not be predatory, as later fops tend to be, but he is certainly not one of the boys, either. He just wants to play with the boys.

In the course of the play Sir Fopling attempts to become involved in a variety of intrigues, but they all fail because he misreads the codes of Restoration male bonding: he is left in a foolish solitary stance that keeps him from participating in the comic resolution of the play. After he has been duped by male and female characters like, Sir Fopling must attend only to his own "creative" endeavor:

MEDLEY:	Methinks the lady had not made you those advances today she did last night, Sir Fopling.
SIR FOPLING:	Prithee, do not talk of her.
MEDLEY:	She would be a *bonne fortune*.
SIR FOPLING:	Not to me at present.
MEDLEY:	How so?
SIR FOPLING:	An intrigue now would be but a temptation to me to throw away that vigor on one which I mean shall shortly make my court to the whole sex in a ballet.
MEDLEY:	Wisely considered, Sir Fopling.
SIR FOPLING:	No one woman is worth the loss of a cut in a caper. (5.2.333–343)

Sir Fopling backs away from interaction with the opposite sex and articulates a position analogous to the homosociality of the libertine, if less politically and more narcissistically motivated. What is clear, however, is that Etherege is suggesting that the Sir Foplings of the world do not fit easily into a gendered economy and roam dissatisfied in an area outside of comedy. Of course it is all in "good fun," but fun I would suggest, at Sir Fopling's expense. Foppish effeminacy is already coded as a gender all its own, or perhaps it would be more to the point to call it a non-gender. Sir Fopling pretends to understand the role of the male in a gendered society, but it simply doesn't understand him: he really only has eyes for the rakes who mock him.

The same is true of countless other Restoration fops. Eve Sedgwick has discussed the homosocial implications of Sparkish in Wycherley's *The Country Wife* (1675): "To misunderstand the kind of property women are," she says,

> or the kind of transaction in which alone their value is realizable means, for a man, to endanger his own position as a subject in the relationship of exchange: to be permanently feminized or objectified in relation to other men. . . . Sparkish's behavior when he introduces his friend Harcourt to his fiancée Alithea makes clear that his

strongest motive is really not even to use Harcourt as a sweetener for the marriage, but to use his wife, and Harcourt's approval of her, as an intensifier of his homosocial bond with Harcourt and the wits.7

The scene from the play is familiar, and Sparkish is perhaps the most recognizable fop of them all. His "false wit" leads him into several embarrassing situations, in each one of which he misunderstands jokes that are being played on him and, in trying to be one of the boys, becomes their victim, as in the scene Sedgwick discusses.

Kristina Straub suggests that this gender confusion continues through early eighteenth-century portrayals of the fop. Colly Cibber, for instance, was famous for his role as Sir Novelty Fashion in his play *Love's Last Shift* (1696). Straub talks about Cibber's "masculine masquerade" in the full-bottomed periwig that by the end of the seventeenth century was considered "ridiculous."[8] The wig in question became larger and larger as Cibber repeated the role, creating a figure, like the contemporary domino figure of the masquerade, who makes gender itself the feature of identity that most needs to be masked. Cibber strutting as Sir Novelty is a sign of gender ambiguity, to be sure. The play also suggests that a fop is not fit for female companionship. What that means becomes less endearingly comic and more morally offensive as the century proceeds.

In Vanbrugh's *The Relapse* (1696), in which Cibber again played Sir Novelty, newly created Lord Foppington, Straub suggests that another character is introduced to assure us that fops and sodomites are carefully distinguished from each other.[9] Coupler, the sodomitical pander, comes on to the central character at the same time that he aids him in his pursuit of a fortune. Although I think that Straub's reading is in many ways persuasive, I also think that we could shift the emphasis to say that the presence of a sodomite in the first scene of a comedy, a sodomite who is both integral to the comedy and included at its close, both defies readings of the sodomite as monstrous and colors the mood of the play. By making same-sex desire a central feature of the action, Vanbrugh creates an ethos that places all sexual relations under question. Later in the play Lord Foppington is expelled from a marriage because it does not suit him and is willing to hand over his wife with relatively little fuss to his more sexually attractive brother. These almost casual plot developments suggest that his own interests are surely as confused and confusing as those of other members of his foppish brotherhood:

LORD FOPPINGTON [*ASIDE*]:

> Now for my part, I think the wisest thing a man can do
> with an aching heart is to put on a serene countenance,
> for a philosophical air is the most becoming thing in the
> world to the face of a person of quality. I will therefore
> bear my disgrace like a great man, and let the people see
> I am above an affront. [*to young Fashion*] Dear Tam,
> since things are thus fallen aut, prithee give me leave to
> wish thee jay; I do it *de bon coeur*, strike me dumb! You
> have married a woman beautiful in her person, charm-
> ing in her airs, prudent in her canduct, canstant in her
> inclinations, and of a nice marality, split my windpipe!
> (5.5.246–261; misspellings intentional)[10]

Foppington's elaborate face-saving, his male-directed determination, and his affected pronouncements all mark him as an unsuitable husband and a character without a center. Happy marriage is not his prerogative, however much he may understand that a culture puts a high value on this norma-tive construction. Lord Foppington may have more in common, then, with the dirty old sodomite than at first it might have seemed. After all, they both appear to be relegated to an extramarital position: Coupler because he chooses to exercise his desires in a different direction and Lord Foppington because he has no other choice.

Straub makes the important point that "the fop's self-conscious exhibi-tionism, merely a ridiculous idiosyncrasy during most of Cibber's acting career, became associated with the effeminacy and sexual ambiguity of the 'macaroni' after midcentury."[11] In her chapter on fops, Straub notes a "grow-ing rigidification of the polarity between 'deviate' homosexual and 'normal' heterosexual masculinity."[12] She goes on to say that fops "are not, as Staves correctly points out, to be confused with homosexuals; rather they muddy the distinction between sexual object and sexual subject, spectacle and spectator, commodity and consumer."[13] Scholars who have seen a polariza-tion between hetero- and homosexual identity taking place in mid-century have understandably placed the fop at the center of this great divide.[14] In the standard argument cited by Straub, "the fop gradually becomes associ-ated with male homosexual identity in the period between 1660 and 1750."[15] While I would not disagree with various observations concerning the coding of effeminate behavior and its connection to male-male sexual desire, I am tempted to question the role of the fop in making homo/hetero distinctions. In the eighteenth century these distinctions have little meaning for any libertine or other upper-class gentleman. That does not mean that any connection between the fop and same-sex desire is misplaced. It simply means that the distinctions need to be more subtle than a simple homo/hetero reading suggests. The social behavior of these men surely includes the possibility of same-sex object choice as often as not, but no homo/hetero dichotomy results. The sexual imaginary of the eighteenth century does not match our own, and in this respect the difference is profound. Even when fops are accused of "run[ning] into unnatural Vices," as if they had taken up gambling or drinking, they are not accused of *being* unnatural. This is the distinction that I would like to keep alive.

At the other end of the social spectrum, the locus classicus for connecting effeminacy with a particular sexuality is Ned Ward's account of molly house activity in the early eighteenth century. Of course, various accounts of early eighteenth-century molly houses turn on the question of effeminate behavior, and even the "tabloid" nature of the sodomy trial reports of the 1720s should not blind us to the increasingly comfortable bond between an effeminate dress and manner and sexual transgression. Mollies are not fops, of course, and I doubt that anyone on the streets of early eighteenth-century London would confuse the lower-class cross-dresser and his showy aristocratic counterpart. Sodomy trials and molly house accounts are not concerned with fops, except insofar as the men in the molly houses ape their social superiors. And although the molly has been a rich resource for historians of sexuality, his class-based identity can never be ignored. In his revealing essay "The Birth of the Queen," Randolph Trumbach argues that male-male desire takes on a specific personality when the molly became a recognizable type.[16] The case is rarely made, however, that the mollies, or at least the ones who were brought to trial and executed, occupy a social status that is distinct from that of the aristocratic fops with whom they are sometimes confused. Both Ned Ward's account and the sodomy trials make this distinction clear.

Recent discussions of these accounts by Cameron McFarlane and Craig Patterson have challenged Ward's and other molly house accounts and placed their reliability in question, to say the least. For Patterson, for instance, such accounts reveal an "undiluted vitriol that figures the mollies as monstrous aberrations, threats to the proper hierarchies of gender." Moreover, Patterson argues that "[r]ather than yielding secrets about the establishment of a new social identity, [molly house accounts] encode the language of sexuality within a familiar trope of disorder: the world of gender turned upside down. Indeed, each of the four accounts we have of the molly houses is a shifting, unreliable text whose uncertainties render difficult any confident pronouncements about the existence of new identities"[17] Both these writers and others remind us that factual accounts do not exist. As culturally revealing as we might find Ward's account of the mollies—"When they are met, together, their usual Practice is to mimic female Gossiping & fall into all the impertinent Tittle-Tattle that a merry Society of good Wives can be subject to"—these writers claim that we are unable to base any reading of sexual identity into these problematic and unreliable accounts.[18]

As I suggested earlier, whether this is history or fiction does not really matter if we are talking about the cultural coding of certain kinds of behavior. For the historian of sexuality, what is said about what is done is often more important than any independent "fact," even if such a thing could be imagined. The account is, after all, the product of the cultural imagination in which any kind of identity is given shape. The account, then, not any actual event, is the fact that interests me. To have Ward's account, and to have the accounts of the secret agents in the sodomy trials—whether fact or fiction—tells us everything about the codification of certain forms of behavior. As Trumbach notes:

> Occasionally a group of mollies went dancing, with many of them dressed as women. Wild recalled that Hitchen, the sodomitical Under-Marshal, had arrested (in revenge for being ignored by some young men) a group of mollies as they returned home from a ball in Holborn. Some had gowns, petticoats, headcloths, fine laced shoes, furbelow scarves, masks and complete dresses for women; others had riding hoods; some were dressed like shepherdesses; others like milkmaids with fine green hats, waistcoats, and petticoats; and others had their faces painted and patched and very extensive whoop petticoats which were then very lately introduced.[19]

What this tells us about sexual identity is surely that it is never static and that no relation between social behavior and sexual identity is ever fixed. That mollies are arrested as sodomites because of private pique only emphasizes the malleability of such determinates. Hitchin arrests the mollies because the cultural moment allows this identification. Often Italians and Catholics were also seen as "sodomites" in the public imagination. It is surely not just the tireless campaigns of the Societies for the Reformation of Manners that rendered the mollies identifiable and monstrous. The increased social mobility and urbanization of the early years of the eighteenth century made masculinity itself the center of heightened cultural concern. Young men had better turn to industry and sober apprenticeship than to the lewd partying and sexual excess of the mollies. If this is never put into so many words, it is the implicit warning of many antisodomy tracts: the molly is everywhere.[20]

In 1726 there was a raid on a private house owned by one Margaret Clap in Field Lane. Several dozen men were arrested for "sodomitical behaviour" and several of these received the maximum sentence of death by hanging. Alan Bray describes the case in detail and talks about the systematic activities of the Societies for the Reformation of Manners, a crusading religious organization that organized the raids and saw to it that the maximum sentences were imposed. Furthermore Bray argues that the molly houses, together with other pubs and meeting places, formed a "coherent social milieu" and that "clothes, gestures, language, particular buildings and particular public places—all could be identified as having specifically homosexual connotations."[21] This is a controversial claim, and I would question Bray's use of *homosexual* in this context. What I want to consider instead, however, is the behavior that is described as sodomitical and what kind of male-male interaction was described when sodomy was the accusation.

Consider the trial of forty-three year-old Gabriel Lawrence, "indicted for committing, with *Thomas Newton*, aged thirty Years, the heinous and detestable Sin of Sodomy, not to be named among Christians," as reported in *Select Trials*. Bray has argued that these accounts should be read more as tabloid journalism than actual court records. Imagine, then, the provocative tone in which readers would "hear" Samuel Stevens, the informing agent, describe the following activity:

> Mother *Clap*'s House was in *Field Lane*, in *Holbourn*, it was next to
> the *Bunch of Grapes* on one Side, and joined to an Arch on the other
> Side. It was notorious for being a *Molly-house*. I have been several
> Times, in order to detect those who frequented it: I have seen 20 or
> 30 of them together, kissing and hugging, and making Love (as they
> called it) in a very indecent Manner. Then they used to go out by
> Couples into another Room, and, when they came back, they would
> tell what they had been doing, which, in their Dialect, they called
> *Marrying*.

Other documentary evidence suggests that the room into which the couples went and that contained little more than a bed was often called a
"Chapel" and that "Marrying" was the act of sexual intercourse.[22]
Furthermore, other accounts make it more apparent that the behavior of
these men was more than simply effeminate. In the trial of Thomas Wright,
for instance, who was tried and hanged at the same time as Gabriel
Lawrence, Joseph Sellers, an informant, states that

> I went to the Prisoner's House in *Beech-Lane*, and there I found a
> Company of Men fiddling, and dancing, and singing bawdy Songs,
> kissing, and using their Hands in a very unseemly Manner. I was
> introdc'd by P— who was one of their Members; but it seems they
> were jealous that he had some Discovery; for they call'd him a
> *Treacherous, blowing-up mollying Bitch*, and swore they'd massacre
> any Body that should betray them.[23]

Whether or not we are reading a factual account or titillating pseudo-
journalistic fiction, the details are still telling. In the first place this is more
like a club than a brothel, for there is no mention in any of the trial records
of money changing hands. It also seems that these men identify to some
degree as a persecuted minority. But the kissing and hugging, the fondling,
the marrying, and the dancing all take place between what we would call
consenting adults. There is no sense of libertine swagger, as in Rochester's
nostalgic reverie to his penis (in "The Imperfect Enjoyment"): "where'ere
it pierced a cunt it found or made"; there is no insistence on penetration.
Penetration is not even an issue in these particular trials. In other words,
this behavior is not like libertine behavior. It is not about power relations in

the way that every libertine sexual gesture might be. What these men have done that earns them public execution is to express their attraction for one another openly and in contempt of law and custom that labels them an aberration. If "marrying" is a euphemism for sexual congress, it is a telling euphemism. For, by marrying, these men mock the social forms of sexual relation and claim for male-male sexual activity the forms of codified human interaction from which they are marginalized and, as a result, subject to condemnation. Of course it would be useful to know how the men involved in these activities might have characterized themselves, as we know, for instance, what various eighteenth-century figures said in letters to their friends, as I discuss later. Such accounts would also be liable to the cultural conditioning of the time, however, and if one molly himself called another a *"Treacherous, blowing-up mollying Bitch,"* it would be less than transparent in its personal implications.

The by now familiar account of the molly house that Ned Ward offers in *The London Clubs*, although totally discounted as historical representation, still offers an interesting and telling "observation": "Not long since they had cushioned up one of their Brethren, or rather Sisters, according to Female Dialect, disguising him in a Night-Gown, Sarsanter Hood, & Night-rail who when the Company were me[t], was to mimick a woman, produce a jointed Baby they had provided, which wooden Offspring was to be afterwards Christened."[24] I am sympathetic with claims that this account may represent more or less total fabrication.[25] It is a telling fabrication, however, and as fiction it is equally useful to historians of sexuality. For what this account tells us includes both the fear that mollies want to parody the family and the threat that in parodying the family and claiming a prototype of "rights" for themselves, they will undermine the very institution that they mock. What might be comic in a Restoration comedy, that is, begins here to threaten society itself. Ward does not only want to amuse his readers, he also wants to frighten them. Ward is just learning how to code innocent and silly behavior as seriously threatening. He is codifying the terms according to which a culture can panic at the idea of the molly. What we have learned to call homosexual panic, in other words, has its origins in documents such as these.

What is the difference between these mollies and the heroic friends that they mimic? As I have already noted, the difference is a difference of class, and it would be wrong to ignore it. Gabriel Lawrence was a "Milk-Man"

and Thomas Wright a "Wool-Comber": neither of these men was in a position from which to violate the rigors of patriarchal law with impunity. In
chapter 1 I discussed heroic friendship and the meaning of male-male love
in the context of Restoration tragedy. What is different here is that these
men cannot be viewed in heroic terms. And were it not for the hideous
reversal of poetic justice that the sodomy trials represent, it might be possible to imagine that eighteenth-century readers were being asked to laugh at
these figures. Surely we can see in this molly house activity the beginnings
of the kind of subcultural identification that Bray describes.[26] What is
upsetting about the trial accounts is the clear fact that what among members of a higher class would be read simply as friendship must in this different social context be seen as monstrous. Randolph Trumbach, who is in
other ways so illuminating about the shift from libertine love of boys to
expressions of desire among adult males after 1700, seems to me to neglect
the issue of class, which is surely central to the distinctive love between
men that is described in these trials and the executions that took place as a
result of that love. Throughout the early years of the eighteenth century, in
rape as well as sodomy cases, the accused was usually acquitted if he could
prove himself to be an upstanding citizen (as it were).

   While it is true that what we are talking about here is sexual activity and
not identity—Gabriel Lawrence was, for instance, married twice, and the
fathers of both his wives testified on his behalf at the trial—what does seem
to be emerging here is a sexual position that is as far from that of Rochester
as it would be possible to imagine. Maybe these men are shown to "marry"
one another because marriage represents the very social respectability, the
bourgeois model itself, which they are being denied. The rituals of marrying and Christening begin to offer a different kind of relation than that
offered to same-sex partners in earlier accounts. The men in the molly
house accounts and even in the trial records are only rarely shown in sexual congress with one another. Such scenes are usually used to display sexual voracity and brute sexual aggression—as in the keyhole testimony in the
case from the Sessions at the Old Bailey, in which John Dicks is seen forc-
ing his "yard" into the "fundament" of the young John Meeson—or to mul-
tiply the range of social settings and public circumstances in which a
sodomitical seduction might occur, as in another case from the same
source in which George Duffus repeatedly (and with only partial success)
tries to force himself on men that he meets at meeting-house services and

engages by discussing the beauties of the sermon.[27] As brutal as these scenes are, however, they are less threatening than the scenes of men dancing together, using female names, and mocking Christian ritual. What molly house scenes display is finally more threatening because it attacks the fiction of heteronormative culture at its very foundations. Part of this attack is of course the simple social one: for two men to marry is a mockery of the very basis of social stability. I want to propose another perhaps even more dangerous threat, the threat that the men dancing, marrying, christening, and playing with gender in various ways might actually be motivated by affection. If they were to love one another, as Ward's and the trial accounts suggest, they would defy the hideousness with which male-male relations have been represented. Maybe this love is finally what is threatening about molly house behavior. Love, after all, poses a greater threat than that posed by secret sexual behavior. For bourgeois culture there is no love outside of marriage and the heteronormative relations leading to marriage or (at worst) adulterating it. The mollies appropriate love for other purposes, and this is when they pose the greatest threat.

Straight Fops

In *Satan's Harvest Home* (1749) sodomy and effeminacy seem to be interchangeable. The writer begins his discussion of "Reasons for the Growth of Sodomy, &c." by considering "the modern Modish way of bringing up young Gentlemen":

> Little Master is kept in the Nursery 'till he is five or six years old, at least, after which he is sent to a Girl's School, to learn Dancing and Reading, . . . and the Child is of a tender Constitution: well may it be so, when the Tone of his Stomach has been spoil'd with Tea, when his Blood is curdled with now and then a Dram, to keep the Mother in Countenance; when the Boy's Constitution is half torn to pieces with Apothecary's *slip slops*. . . .
>
> Besides, his whole Animal Fabrick is enervated for want of due Exercise; and he is grown so chilly by over nursing, that he gets Cold with the least Breath of Wind. . . . For at the Mistress's *School*, he was brought up in all respects like a *Girl*, . . . for his Mamma had charged him not to play with rude Boys, for fear of spoiling his *Cloathes*; so

that hitherto our young Gentleman has amused himself with Dolls, assisted at mock Christenings, Visits, and other girlish Employments, inviting and being invited to drink Tea with this or that School-fellow.[28]

This attempt to pathologize the aristocracy by means of a diagnosis of effeminacy is more interesting than earlier studies have suggested. "Mock Christenings" hints at scenes with which we are already familiar, and such language suggests the context of these observations might be nothing more than a close reading of Ward and other molly house accounts. Still, whether or not these comments suggest an analogy to the twentieth-century concept of "sexuality," they do tell us a lot about gender coding and the uses of diet and exercise as part of the mid- eighteenth-century construction of masculinity itself. The reference to the gentleman's "Animal Fabrick" suggests a line of medical thinking most readily represented by George Cheyne, whose ideas remained current throughout the middle and later years of the century.

Cheyne says, for instance, that "the original *Stamina*, the whole *System* of the Solids, the Firmness, Force, and Strength of the Muscles, of the Viscera, and great Organs, are they not owing to the *Male*? And does the *Female* contribute any more but a convenient Habitation, proper Nourishment, and an *Incubation* to the seminal Animalcul for a Time, to enable the *organised* living Creature to bear the *Air, Sun,* and *Day* the sooner?" Cheyne also says that "Soft and yielding, loose and flabby Flesh and Muscles, are sure Symptoms of weak and relaxed Nerves or Fibres, as hard, firm, prominent and brawny Muscles and Flesh are constant signs of firm Fibres"[29] Obviously the gendering of body type and the hierarchization of firm and loose tissue means that a man becomes "like a girl" to the extent that his fibres are not firm and his tissue soft. These observations begin to suggest a personality type that is defined by class. The embodiment of class and gender distinctions is not exactly new in the middle of the eighteenth century, as studies by Londa Schiebinger and Thomas Laquer have made clear.[30] Still, comments such as these suggest that a new energy is going into class and gender distinctions and the significance of an effete aristocratic class is being given new and more complex substance.

The author of *Satan's Harvest Home* makes this substance clear as his argument develops. He no sooner has diagnosed the causes of effeminacy than he discusses its consequences:

When our young Gentleman arrives to Marriage; I wish I could say fit for it, what can be expected from such an enervated effeminate Animal? What satisfaction can a Woman have in the Embraces of this Figure of a Man? Should she at last bring him a Child, what can we hope from so crazy a *Constitution*? But a feeble, unhealthy Infant, scarce worth the rearing; whilst the Father, instead of being the Head of the Family, makes it seem as if it were governed by two Women: For he has suck'd the Spirit of *Cotqueanism* from his Infancy. . . . Thus, unfit to serve his King, his Country, or his Family, this Man of *Clouts* dwindles into nothing, and leaves his race as effeminate as himself; who, unable to please the Women, chuse rather to run into unnatural Vices one with another, than to attempt what they are but too sensible they cannot perform.[31]

Sodomitical behavior is chosen by default. When an effeminate man realizes that he cannot serve, he turns to others like himself. So from a coddled nursery, to drinking tea, to girlish interests, to sodomy: this is a mystifying progression, but it is one that at the middle of the eighteenth century was already gaining considerable currency. As Eve Sedgwick says in *Between Men*, "an important, recurrent wishful gesture of [the] ideological construction [of the English class system] was the feminization of the aristocracy as a whole, by which . . . the abstract image of an entire class came to be seen as ethereal, decorative, and otiose in relation to the vigorous and productive values of the middle class."[32] *Satan's Harvest* represents an articulate account of the very gesture that Sedgwick describes. Vigorous and productive value is lost, precisely to the degree that effeminacy and "unnatural Vices" take their place. If class and gender work hand in hand this way, then effeminacy becomes the key to understanding how sexual behavior became codified and what its links to personality, if not identity, originally were. The figure who makes this connection inevitable, of course, is the figure of the fop. Not quite a man, and not by any means a "true" aristocrat, the fop is constructed as the parody of both masculinity and aristocracy that exposes their own contingency.

William Hogarth offers an occasional view of the connection between effeminacy and sexuality. Fops abound in his work, in the early scenes of *The Rake's Progress* (1733–1734), in the background in *A Taste of the Town* (1724), and in and about almost any large "conversation," revealed either by a style of dress or a particularly mannered wig. In at least one well-known case, however, Hogarth comments on sexual proclivities as an extension of appearance. This occurs in scene 4 of *Marriage-a-la-mode* ("The Countess's Morning Levée," 1743). Here a group of musicians and a dancing master gather under the sign of Ganymede (see below). They are not simple fops. The large figure stretching his limbs and singing in the foreground is obviously a castrato, who were always long-limbed because of hormonal imbalance, and therefore Italian by definition; the simpering figure to his right, who has his hair pinned up in papers and who is sipping tea, is the dancing master, almost surely French or, at least Frenchified; and the hook-nosed flautist might very well be typified as German, or at least "demonstrably foreign" in dress and manners.[33] In addition to their pernicious continental associations, these figures are grotesque in other ways. The huge, pig-faced castrato, wears a richly embroidered brocade coat and has rings at various joints

FIGURE 2.1   *Detail*: William Hogarth, scene 4 of *Marriage-a-la-mode* ("The Countess's Morning Levée," 1743). Reproduced by permission of The National Gallery, London.

of his distorted fingers; the figure next to him looks bug-eyed and affected, and while his costume suggests an elegant air, his crossed legs and delicate fingers serve to undermine his masculinity and his vacant stare could be read as harboring illicit desires. What interests me about this picture, however, is the association between appearance and sexual desire. Ganymede does not survey this grouping accidentally, and Hogarth is saying as much as any of his contemporaries about how to read effeminate dress and behavior. David Bindman claims that a figure like the dancing master is meant to be read as sodomitical and that part of the pleasure of Hogarth's image is the narrative of sexual transgression it implies.[34] Hogarth's image narrates a kind of sexual subjectivity, and the details of dress and comportment combine to make that subjectivity outwardly visible.

Similar in effect is Hogarth's familiar contrast in *The Analysis of Beauty*, plate 1 (1753), between a dancing master and the classical statue of

FIGURE 2.2   *Detail:* William Hogarth, *The Analysis of Beauty*, plate 1 (1753). Reproduced by permission of The British Museum, London.

Antinous. Here (at the back, left of center) the overly "straight" fop is con-
trasted to the curvilinear classical figure. True beauty exists in the easy
curve, Hogarth's "line of beauty," and there is nothing but grotesquerie in
the self-conscious figure of the dancing master.[35] Angularity for Hogarth is
foppish, and it contrasts with the easy grace of the figure at peace with itself.
Details that the twentieth century might read as effeminate—bent wrists,
angled pelvis, and so on—are here read as classically beautiful; what the
twentieth century might see as "straight" and uncompromised is clearly the
foppish fool. In his discussion of this image, Ronald Paulsen makes two
important points. First, quoting from Hogarth's text of *The Analysis of
Beauty*, he argues that "Hogarth uses *Antinous* to illustrate the 'utmost
beauty of proportion'; this statue 'is allowed to be the most perfect . . . of any
of the antique statues' "; and second, he reminds us that "something not
mentioned in the art treatises but evident in the history books, Antinous was
the minion of the Emperor Hadrian, deified and celebrated throughout the
ancient world in versions of this statue erected by the emperor in memory
of his drowned lover. . . . In the context of Hogarth's composition, the
effeminate dancing master activates these memories, suggesting that he
may be indecently propositioning Antinous."[36] If this is a seduction or an
attempt at indecency, then the image still suggests a contrast between the
easy self-possession of the classical boy-lover and the pert inappropriateness
of the powdered and overly self-conscious dancing master. The difference
lies in the "self-consciousness" of the two figures. The ridiculous dancing
master can never get it right, while the easy classical pose is beautifully correct. Distinctions between straight and gay, distinctions about which we
feel secure even as we historicize, simply do not apply. If the fop is too
straight, that is, then how "gay" is the true aristocrat? Or, we might say, the
fop is straight precisely because he does not know the right way to bend. His
rigidity shocks and disgusts because it is so clearly put on. His straightness
is false, as straightness often is.

Lord Chesterfield has memorialized this distinction in his advice to his
son concerning dress: "so far from being a disparagement to any man's
understanding, that it is rather proof of it, to be as well dressed as those
whom he lives with: the difference in this case between a man of sense and
a fop, is, that the fop values himself upon his dress, and the man of sense
laughs at it, at the same time that he knows he must not neglect it."[37]
Desmond Shaw-Taylor offers a useful visual rendition of this distinction by

contrasting Reynold's *John Campbell, 1st Baron Cawdor* (1778) and
Gainsborough's *Captain William Wade* (1771). Wade is stiff, self-conscious,
foppish, while Cawdor is easy, gracious, and well-fed. Cawdor's gestures are
spacious, his dress almost negligent, and his face open and clear-eyed.
Wade is tight, narrow, too sharply turned-out, and although his coat is
thrown open, it can only be seen as a pose. His eyes are close and heavy-lid-
ded, his mouth set in a near-sneer. Who would need to be told which one
was a country gentleman and which one the Master of Ceremonies at
Bath.[38] Foppish as he seems, however, and as clear a descendent of
Hogarth's Dancing Master as he is, it would be unreasonable to claim that
a comment about the sexual activities of Wade is being made here. Or
would it? Wade was in fact infamous for sexual intrigues, and a few years
after this portrait he was "named as the co-respondent in a messy society
divorce suit."[39] The figure, then, reads as sexual excess of a more general
kind than Hogarth's dancing master. But it is sexual excess nonetheless, and
as much writing at the time implies, foppishness at mid-century is always
available for a reading of that excess as monstrous.

One more image might help us to see how these two roles might be confused. Pompeo Batoni's portrait of *Thomas Dundas, Later 1st Baron Dundas*
(1764) was one of the most striking paintings in the 1996 exhibition at the
Tate Gallery in London, *Grand Tour: The Lure of Italy in the Eighteenth
Century*. Dundas is portrayed with all the openness of Cawdor, all the
assured grace of an aristocrat in training, but something is clearly overdone.
If not a "dancing master" figure, he is almost dancing his appreciation of
the classical beauties around him, which include the Apollo Belvedere, the
Laocoön, the Belvedere Antinous, and the Vatican Ariadne, all suggesting
something rather more lascivious than grand. His swagger mixes a lordly
leer with more than a little self-satisfaction. It could hardly be a mistake to
read erotic exploits into that image. A critic in the *New York Times* said that
"the milordi are models of aristocratic indolence in the paintings of themselves they commissioned" and Hogarth's parody still applies, but what
Batoni has done, perhaps unwittingly, is to read British aristocracy with a
flair that is unmistakably Italian.[40] The result is that the fop is invested with
a kind of Italian excess, and an eighteenth-century viewer would know that
Italian sexual exploits were both exciting and, by definition, transgressive.

"*Italy* [is] the *Mother* and *Nurse* of *Sodomy*," as the author of *Satan's
Harvest Home* announces, "where the *Master* is oftener *Intriguing* with

FIGURE 2.3   Joshua Reynolds, *John Campbell, 1st Baron Cawdor* (1778). Cawdor
Castle, Scotland.

FIGURE 2.4   *Thomas Gainsborough, Captain William Wade* (1771). Reproduced by permission of Victoria Art Gallery, Bath City Council, Bath, England.

FIGURE 2.5   Pompeo Batoni, *Thomas Dundas, later 1st Baron Dundas* (1764).
Reproduced by permission of the Marquess of Zetland.

his *Page*, than a *fair Lady*."[41] Batoni's portrait offers an insight into the Italianization of the fop: by getting too close to the art of Italy, this figure seems to swagger out of control. The catalogue of the *Grand Tour* exhibition tells us that Batoni's "boldness of colouring, precise draughtsmanship and overall polish resulted in an overwhelmingly sensuous image."[42] The tightness of the dancing master gives way to the gay profusion that Italy promised. The figure that emerges is just that much more dangerous and that much more powerful than Ward's beaus and Hogarth's fops. He steps into history with a world behind him. He is a man who takes his effeminacy in his stride, a radical fairy, we might call him, who seems ready to take off.

This "history" of the fop and his relation to early construction of (homo)sexuality has already to a certain extent been told.[43] Randolph Trumbach explains how, for instance, the innocuous and gentle fop of the later years of the seventeenth century—he cites the character Maiden in Thomas Baker's *Tunbridge Walks* (1703), who lisps that "I never keep company with lewd rakes that go to nasty taverns, talk smuttily, and get fuddl'd; but visit the ladies, and drink tea, and chocolate"—gives way to a sexually marked figure of contempt by the mid-eighteenth century—Trumbach cites the notorious Captain Whiffle from Smollett's *Roderick Random* (1748), who is accused of "maintaining a correspondence with his surgeon, not fit to be named."[44] Trumbach argues further that the "beau" appeared in the late seventeenth century as a role that mediated between fop and rake, allowing the fop to become more exclusively associated with adult male-male desire (as opposed to the man-boy desire common to rakes).[45] For Trumbach, then, the relationship between foppish effeminacy and particular forms of sexual behavior becomes more explicit as the century proceeds. Whether or not we are prepared to accept the programmatic claims he is making—the fob/beau dichotomy is never really tenable—it is possible to see in mid-century figures a more pronounced comment on sexual practice in descriptions of fops. The familiar examples are Beau Didapper in Henry Fielding's *Joseph Andrews* (1742) and Smollett's Captain Whiffle.

Fielding's "Beau" strikes an amusing pose. He is described as "a young gentleman of about four foot five inches in height." His physical weakness is emphasized: "His face was thin and pale: the shape of his body and legs none of the best; for he had very narrow shoulders, and no calf; and his gait might more properly called hopping than walking." Fielding grants him a smattering of French and Italian, and profusion without generosity. But Fielding's most subtle irony enters the description with the mention of gender: "No hater of women; for he always dangled after them; yet so little subject to lust, that he had, among those who knew him best, the character of great moderation in his pleasures. No drinker of wine; nor so addicted to passion, but that a word or two from an adversity made him immediately cool." A weak and uninterested lover, he seems more committed to a homosocial system of sycophancy and abuse, with the implication that obedience includes the granting of sexual favors: " 'Tho' he was born to an immense fortune, he chose, for the pitiful and dirty consideration of the place of little consequence, to depend entirely on the will of a fellow, whom they call a great man; who treated him with the utmost disrespect, and exacted of him a plenary obedience to his commands; which he explicitly submitted to, at the expense of his conscience, his honour, and of his country; in which he had himself so very large a share." The description concludes: "Such was the little person or rather thing that hopped after Lady Booby into Mr. Adams's kitchin."[46]

Martin C. Battestin explains that John, Lord Hervey was "the original of Beau Didapper," suggesting that Hervey is also memorialized in Pope's "Epistle to Arbuthnot" as "Sporus, that "mere-white Curd of Ass's milk . . . This painted Child of Dirt that stinks and stings" (ll. 305–333).[47] Pope's portrait suggests a confusion of gender—"His Wit was all see-saw between *that* and *this*, / Now high, now low, now master up now Miss, / And he himself one vile antithesis"—and the terms suggest the ways in which outward behavior could be used to mark a kind of sexual monstrosity. Hervey was attacked elsewhere in similar terms: in one political satire, for which he challenged the author to a duel, he is charged with "a certain, unnatural, reigning Vice (indecent and almost shocking to mention)." Robert Halsband tells us that "satirists lifted from [this] pamphlet the caricature of an effeminate courtier, and the scandalous innuendo of homosexuality, to create a *persona*."[48] The substance of these attacks may be more political and literary than sexual, but it is nonetheless clear that effeminacy (and aristocracy) are readily available for the sodomitical label to be invoked and, in this case infamously, to stick.

In his biography of Hervey, however, Halsband tells of a life of constant political involvement and deep personal friendships. These friendships, especially those with Stephen Fox and Francisco Algarotti, are intensely erotic, and every indication suggests that in spite of his marriage (although "in spite of" already suggests a twentieth-century perspective), Hervey's only love affairs were with other men. At one point Halsband considers whether or not the "sentimental sodomite" label might not be the most appropriate one to use for a man of Hervey's sexual temperament. I would resist this label for various reasons. The love that is articulated in the letters to Stephen Fox is more than sentimental and less than sodomitical. In other words, it is, simply, love as it has been defined in heteronormative culture: emotionally extreme and physically expressive. Like Walpole and Gray, whom I discuss below, Hervey loves his friends and is happy to celebrate that love in letters that are steamy and suggestive. "You have left some such remembrances behind you," he writes to Fox, "that I assure you . . . you are not in the least Danger of being forgotten. The favours I have received at Your Honour's *Hands* are of such a nature that tho' the impression might wear out of my Mind, yet they are written in such lasting characters upon every Limb, that 'tis impossible for me to look on a Leg or an Arm without having my Memory refresh'd." Or: "I have often thought, if any very idle Body had Curiosity enough to intercept & examine my Letters, they would certainly conclude they came from a Mistress than a Friend." And: "I love you & love you more than I thought I could love any thing."[49]

Effeminacy and sodomy are labels that disguise these intense personal relations and render them available for public scrutiny and censure. There is no other way to talk about the figure who "Now trips a Lady, now struts a Lord." As Sedgwick points out in the passage I quoted earlier, in the mid-eighteenth century, "the abstract image of an entire class came to be seen as ethereal, decorative, and otiose in relation to the vigorous and productive values of the middle class."[50] In other words, Hervey's social position is as important as anything else in establishing the labels with which he is mocked. It is interesting to me that at the center of this public scandal are these intense loving relations that form the basis of a male-male intimacy and defy the sodomitical label. I would go so far as to claim that out of such circles of male intimacy a new kind of self-awareness gradually merges. This spirit of eroticized male friendship is memorialized in the "conversation" by Hogarth, known as the Holland Group or "Lord Hervey and his Friends" (c. 1738), which still hangs in the dining room at Ickworth, Hervey's family home. Hervey is the diminutive man in the center, pointing at the plans for his friend's house. He hardly looks like the outrageous fop whom Fielding describes or Pope ridicules, but note the sharply bent wrist, the suggestively hooded lids, the pointed toes, the stiff angularity of the figure. His overly straight "prettiness" marks him as a fop, and the intimate male relations narrated here suggest a circle of affectionate but transgressive friends. Stephen Fox and his brother Edward flank Hervey, along with their friends Thomas Winnington, M.P. and Charles Spencer, 3d Duke of Marlborough, a political crony. The parson, Dr. Middleton, who had been seeking favors from Hervey for some time, looks over the prospect, but in doing so, he *overlooks* the affectation around him. More to the point, by looking so high he has upset the balance of his position, and like many a figure in Hogarth's works, he is poised on the brink. In her discussion of this painting, Jill Campbell argues that these men provide "their own parody of themselves, destabilizing both domestic structure and artistic genre." But she also feels that these male-male relations might in some

FIGURE 2.6   William Hogarth, *The Holland Group or "Lord Hervey and his Friends"* (c. 1738). Reproduced by permission of The National Trust, London.

way function as "challenges" to "normative domestic models" as well.[51] The challenge of this conversation group resides in the playful irony that Stephen Fox's arch look suggests. These men share a secret that the viewer is invited to share. Other images of Hervey, other views of fops in general, attempt to codify sex and gender in ways that have become all too familiar. In this painting the codification falters before the love that these men share, and their straightness begins to cohere in a way that might strike the late-twentieth and early twenty-first-century viewer as "gay."

In her study of *Hellenism and Homosexuality in Victorian Oxford*, Linda Dowling outlines a conflict between the language of Greek ideality, in which male love is celebrated and honored, and the language of classical republican thought "that had come to dominate civic discourse in England through the seventeenth and eighteenth centuries."[52] For Dowling, the conflict between the language of purified male devotion and "corruption," "effeminacy," and "virtue" is most vividly registered in the trial of Oscar Wilde, in which Wilde gives his famous speech defending male affection and the prosecutor uses the language of moral disgust. I would argue that this distinction animates much of the language of male friendship that emerges throughout the eighteenth century. I would claim that the inherent conflict in depictions of sodomy can be seen even in these homophobic attacks on fops like Lord Hervey. If love animates private discourse, and effeminacy the public, it is easy to see how fear—a kind of protohomophobia—functions in a culture that is just learning how to gender masculinity.

Fielding's Beau Didapper is "profuse" in his expenses, but not in his affection for women; he is dependent on the will of a great man, to the "expence of his conscience, his honour, and his country." He is a small man, with a tiny mind, suited more to what the eighteenth century thought of as the image of a "dancing master" than that of a gentleman. He attempts to rape Fanny, more as a sexual grotesque than a traditional aggressor, stepping out of character to fulfill his role as a figure defined primarily in sexual terms. Didapper's sexual energy and his refusal to contain desire are problematic, and try as he might to give these features identificatory power, Fielding's portrait is more confusing than it is defining. It illustrates Fielding's panic around the figure of Hervey, and the contradictions themselves reveal how potent such characters had become. In his brilliantly succinct phobic presentation, Fielding offers a convenient short-hand for social and political disgust.

Similarly, in discussing Smollett's foppish sea-captain, George Rousseau says that the "portrait of Whiffle-the-sodomite, powdered, perfumed, and dressed in clothing so stereotypic that it must have been archetypal in the 1740s, is well worth deciphering since it may represent the first authentic description of the enduring male homosexual stereotype in modern culture."[53] Whiffle's dress is described in detail, and his "sensibility" is mocked. When Random enters his chamber to "bleed" him, he finds him "lolling on the couch with a languishing air, his head supported by his *valet de chambre*, who from time to time applied a smelling-bottle to his nose."[54] Later, his regular surgeon Simper enters: "a young man, gayly dressed, of a very delicate complexion, with a kind of languid smile on his face, which seemed to have been rendered habitual, by a long course of affectation" (198). Smollett is of course satirizing Whiffle for "maintaining a correspondence with his surgeon, not fit to be named" (199). Without this articulation, however, it would by no means be obvious that the connection between effeminacy and sexual irregularity was as vividly connected as it is here. Rousseau may be right to claim that this is the first "homosexual" couple—male-male couple, I would say—in English literature: for the "long course of affectation" in which these men are involved can also be read as a long course of affection. This may not be the kind of physic of which Smollett approved, but it is memorialized here for posterity nonetheless. The affectation that links these two characters, although histrionic and at times ridiculous, is an intimacy that is rendered almost sympathetic just in the care with which Smollett describes it. For whatever these two men do in private, what we see is their affectional relation. In spite of dress, manners, speech, affectation, I would claim, we are looking at men in love.

Later, when Roderick meets Lord Strutwell, the peer attempts to catechize him on the question of sodomy, calling it a passion that is "a more fashionable vice than simple fornication" (310). Lord Strutwell begins a partly facetious defense of the practice, arguing that there will be fewer bastards in the world, that the debauchery of young maidens will be prevented, and "the consideration of health, which is much less liable to be impaired in the gratification of this appetite, than in the exercise of common venery" (310). What becomes more and more obvious here is that Strutwell is describing more than a simple issue of behavior. The "passion" he describes and that Whiffle exhibits is much more than simple sexual behavior; for it involves an affectional and circumstantial system of relations that renders it an entity in its own right. We are not talking about sexual identity here, we are talking about an affectional system that creates a space out of which the concept of sexuality itself may emerge. Cameron McFarlane argues that this episode "undermines the certainties about the self and the 'other' which structured the Whiffle scene. . . . First Roderick simply fails to recognize Strutwell as 'other.' Second, . . . Roderick cannot be certain that he does not appear as 'other' himself."[55] This fear is of course the key to homosexual panic, and Smollett emphasizes the "danger" of this situation in order to give homophobia a rationale.

Smollett did not abandon such characters after his first novel, and later works are peopled with an assortment of "pretty gentleman" who seem to fall into a similar category. At one point in *The Adventures of Peregrine Pickle* (1751), for instance, Pickle's cynic friend Crabtree talks about the hero's exploits with the ladies at Bath, comparing his actions to the "foppery and folly" around him: "this dog was not on the footing of those hermaphroditical animals, who may be numbered among the number of waiting-women, who air your shifts, comb your lap-dogs, examine your noses with magnifying glasses, in order to squeeze out the worms, clean your teeth-brushes, sweeten your handkerchiefs, and soften waste paper for your occasions."[56] Crabtree is himself a misanthrope, and this extreme description tells us as much about him as it does about his subjects. These fops are grotesque in the degree to which they make themselves servile, and they are scatologically defiled as a way of making their "unnatural" position clear.

At another point in this novel, however, after a disastrous "classical" dinner given by Pickle's friend the Doctor, an Italian Marquis and German Baron, whom Pickle has invited to the dinner "to enhance the joy of the entertainment" (234), are publicly disgraced. After the meal, when the Baron has collapsed in the corner and everyone else is bored by the painter's monologue, the Italian introduces the element of same-sex desire into this otherwise ludicrous occasion:

the [Italian] count, tired with the eternal babble of the painter, reeled towards the sleeping [German] baron, whom he viewed with rapture, repeating from the *Il Pastor Fido* of Guarnari:

Come assetato infermo
Che bramò lungamenté
Il vietato licor—
Tal' Io! Gran tempo infermo
E d'amorosa sete arso, e consunto. (242)

[Act 3, scene 3 mirtillo: Like the thirsty sick man, who long desired forbidden liquor, such am I, a long-time ill, burning and consumed with amorous thirst (trans. J. Mazzeo, in notes to *Peregrine Pickle*, p. 789)]

Of course, the pastoral poetry is meant to mock the Italian, but at the same time, it expresses a deeply felt emotion that other poets at the time also expressed. Early letters between Thomas Gray and Horace Walpole employ identical language and analogous tropes of thirst and long-delayed satisfactions.[57] The beauty of the lines works as ridicule, but at the same time it gives the love that these men share a legitimacy that mere mockery of dress or action would not. Like any mock-heroic, it must celebrate what it mocks.[58] Cameron McFarlane says that "this short scene is representative of the instabilities of sodomitical practices as they operate in *Peregrine Pickle* and *Roderick Random*. . . . Demonizing rhetoric aside, however, the actual encounter with the sodomite and his transgressive passion effects a destabilization of the certainties by which the self is distinguished from the 'other.' "[59] I would argue that this destabilization is the basis of homophobia in the text. The actual sexual encounter between these men is oddly presented:

Then [he] boldly ravished a kiss, and began to tickle him under the ribs, with such expressions of tenderness, as scandalized the virtuous painter, who, conscious of his own attractions, was alarmed for his person, and staggered in great hurry and discomposure into the next room, where he put himself under the protection of our hero, to whom he imparted his suspicions of the count's morals, by describing the indecency of his deportment.

Peregrine, who entertained a just detestation for all such abominable practices, was incensed at this information; and stepping to the door of the dining-room where the two strangers were left together, saw with his own eyes enough to convince him that Pallet's complaint was not without foundation. (242)

As in the passages from *Roderick Random*, the key feature of the presentation is the personal fear felt by a putative attractive observer, "who, conscious of his own attractions, was alarmed for his person." Although the count and the baron seem to have no eyes for anyone but each other, this phobic response has meaning because of the excess sexuality that is being described. Peregrine, "who entertained a just detestation for all such abominable practices," resorts to ocular proof, as if unable to resist the spectacle of male-male desire. But Peregrine also is paralyzed and unable to act, and it remains for the landlady to break up the happy couple. It seems to me remarkable that in Smollett a dinner party in London can result in a confrontation such as this: we are not on the high seas now. But of course, London offers other remarkable options as well. In the scene immediately after this, Peregrine and the painter decide to attend a masquerade, but the painter "expressed his apprehension of losing [Peregrine] at the ball; an accident which could not fail to be very disagreeable."

> To obviate this objection, the landlady, who was of their council, advised him to appear in a woman's dress, which would lay his companion under the necessity of attending him with more care, as he could not with decency detach himself from a lady whom he should introduce; besides, such a supposed connexion would hinder the ladies of pleasure from accosting, and employing their seducing arts upon a person already engaged. (243)

Astonishing that in fleeing the abominable practices of the sodomites, Peregrine and the painter should decide that masquerading as a pair of lovers should both reassure the painter that he will be protected and shield them both from the "seducing arts" of the women at a masquerade. Lee Edelman says that "as if to signal that the landlady's transformation into an animated 'virago' . . . has not put an end to the logical disturbances produced by the sodomitical scene, Peregrine and Pallet celebrate the punishment of the amorous 'offenders' by attending a masquerade that night, with Pallet in full female drag." For McFarlane, "the thwarted desire of the sodomitical scene seems to linger in the text, deflected though into the type of homosocial activity that Smollett celebrates."[60] But I would say that the homosocial is precisely intended to cancel the force of the homoerotic, in the ways that Sedgwick explains in *Between Men*.[61] Smollett in fact insists on this relation by putting Pallet in drag and sending the happy couple off to the masquerade. We would call this relation homophobia, and this is one of its richest articulations in the century.

Notice that the landlady's advice includes a few offhand and seemingly unimportant remarks about the "ladies of pleasure." I would claim that far from unimportant, these remarks help to give homophobia its crucial structural link to misogyny. Homophobia and misogyny work as the glue of patriarchy, as it were. Men bond in order to ward off predatory women and infectious sodomites. So of course homophobia and misogyny do not prevent two men from masquerading as a male-female couple. Or rather, homophobia and misogyny, if clearly enough articulated, actually make it possible for two men to masquerade as a male-female couple with impunity.

At the same time, the cultural implications of this sodomophobia suggest that deep within the dark recesses of culture this kernel of erotic male relations exists in order to give meaning to Smollett's homosocial relations. Peregrine's fear and disgust are not for something outside culture and foreign to it, no matter how the participants are coded as "foreign." If this scene shocks the male viewers into a playful mimicry of male-female relations, then the "real" sexual energy of the scene remains with the sodomitical couple, and the heteronormative couple functions only as masquerade.[62] Smollett seems to have internalized the lesson of the other accounts I have cited. The sodomitical dinner party places same-sex desire at the heart of culture. The dark secret of trial records and pornography emerges into the candle-lit London interior with its suggestion that all men are part of the circle of desire known as patriarchy. When Peregrine and the painter go out arm in arm, moreover, the terms of this negotiation are clear. Relations between the sexes are, finally, imaginary. It is same-sex desire that the eighteenth-century understands as "real."

In *The Adventures of Ferdinand Count Fathom* (1753) Smollett does not set aside such characters, but the storm of reaction to *Peregrine Pickle* makes him more circumspect. Here he talks vaguely from time to time about Fathom's "effeminate amusements," by which he seems to mean nothing more than time spent with women; and a "petit-maitre," who is a foppish money lender, and various "pretty gentlemen" appear in coffee houses and gaming rooms. What strikes a twentieth-century reader most forcefully, however, is Smollett's description of the "gay" world. Because for him *gay* means sexually transgressive as well as foppish, and it is used in situations that finally clarify how the fop is viewed. The first time the narrator uses the expression, he is talking about the "gay dishabille," of a group of prostitutes (142); soon he mentions the "gay expectations" (156) that Fathom anticipated before a sudden reversal; and later, when Fathom is setting up appearances in the hope of securing a rich wife, he starts with "a very gay chariot, adorned with painting, gilding and a coat of arms according to his own fancy" (201). But most important of all, the various of implications of this "gay" world come forward vividly when he notes that in Tunbridge Wells "in spite of the arrows that were levelled against his reputation from every tea-table at Tunbridge, He made his party good among almost all the gay young company that frequented the place; far from avoiding his company, they began to court his conversation" (315). Who are the "gay young company" but the "pretty gentleman of London" and their female friends; the "Bath Beaus" and other men of compromised masculinity who frequent places of amusement and prey on their betters.

In a mid-century attack on the "softness of manners," the "Fraternity of PRETTY GENTLEMEN" is attacked in the following terms:

> As no associated Body can possibly subsist, unless they are cemented by an Union of hearts, the grand principle of this Fellowship is mutual LOVE, which, it must be confessed, they carry to the highest Pitch. . . . Such an Harmony of Temper is preserved amongst them, such a Sameness is there in all their Words and Actions, that the Spirit of *One* seems to have passed into the *Other*; or rather, they *all* breathe the *same* Soul. This is the secret Charm, that the *Platonists* talk of, the intellectual Faculty, which connects one Man with another and ties the Knot of virtuous Friendship.[63]

This is an elaborate and subtle mockery, but it is suggestive enough to bring my discussion to a close. Everything that this author cites in order to mock the pretty gentlemen could also be used in their defense. I have written at length about the ways in which love has been written out of discussions of sodomitical practice in the eighteenth century. Here, love is recognized and celebrated as a way of damning the mutual affection of the group. Indeed, it becomes the basis of the irony of the passage, which plays at expressing the physical in terms of the spiritual. The climax of the passing of spirits and the sharing of souls is the "secret Charm the Platonists talk of." This mocking celebration of Platonic affection offers a glimpse of what in the later nineteenth century will become a subcultural commonplace, as Oscar Wilde's defense oration suggests.[64] What it also does in this context, unwittingly, is to suggest a way of understanding the phenomenon of the fop: the mutual love of a foppish circle is precisely what is feared. The ability of the fops to "tie the Knot of virtuous Friendship" with one another defies attempts to codify masculinity in terms of rivalry and opposition. It suggests, moreover, that love as much as sex, or sex expressed in terms of love, animates these relations and gives them personal meaning. Such an alternative has of course at all times been available for heteronormative relations. What the author of this passage does, however, is to extend the rationale of "love" to the sodomitical fops themselves. In so doing, he offers them a way to withstand public censure and articulate relations both justifiable and worthy of public applause.

CHAPTER THREE

Sensibility and Its Symptoms

Dear sensibility! source inexhausted of all that's precious in our joys, or costly in our sorrows! thou chainest thy martyr down upon his bed of straw—and 'tis thou who lifts him up to HEAVEN—eternal fountain of our feelings!—'tis here I trace thee—and this is thy divinity which stirs within me—not, that in some sad sickening moments, *"my soul shrinks back upon herself, and startles at destruction"*—mere pomp of words!—but that I feel some generous joys and generous cares beyond myself—all comes from thee, great—great SENSORIUM of the world! which vibrates, if a hair of our heads but falls upon the ground, in the remotest desert of thy creation.[1]

Sensibility and Sexuality

With this sentimental apostrophe, Sterne's Yorick, in A *Sentimental Journey* (1768), puts his finger on the pulse, as it were, of mid to late eighteenth-century thinking concerning the individual's relation both to his or her own experience and to the discourse surrounding the body and its responses to the world. John A. Dussinger suggests the philosophical context which gives Yorick's outburst precise significance and demonstrates that to dismiss the passage as mere ironic infatuation is to misconstrue the paramount preoccupations of an entire age. Dussinger quotes Chambers' *Cyclopaedia* (1728) as defining *sensorium* as "that part of the brain wherein the nerves, from all the organs of sense, terminate," or "that part of place where the sensible soul is supposed more immediately to reside."[2] In *Tristram Shandy* (1759–1767) Sterne himself calls the sensorium the "head-quarters of the soul."[3] Sterne's claim that sensibility is the source of all that is generous and good in the world, that it is the soul which unites all creation in active emotional interdependence, reverberates throughout the last half of the eighteenth century.

As the "fountain of our feelings," sensibility is what places a person—in this case a "bourgeois" male person—in direct physical relation to the world and allows him, Sterne is saying, to reach beyond the privacy of his own feelings into "some generous cares and generous joys beyond [himself]."[4]

Sensibility is by no means a unitary concept or a simple mode of interpreting experience. As various critics have suggested, sensibility could be different things to different writers, from a source of benevolence and good will on the one hand to the cause of madness and death on the other.[5] It is a mistake, however, not to recognize the full range of sentimental response as "political." By considering the workings of desire within the concept of sensibility, it will be possible to suggest a great deal about the dynamics of power distribution in an age of social flux. It seems to me that the culture of sensibility itself, moreover, suggests the outlines of what Foucault calls "a completely new technology of sex."[6] In this chapter I hope to show that there is an intimate connection between the discourse of sensibility on the one hand and the exploration and control of bodily functions on the other. The functions I am most concerned with are those connected with sexual response, but in the later eighteenth century these functions are by no means limited to mere genital activity. Rather, the body becomes an agent of sexual response in its very emotional organization. For the man or, in a very different way, the woman of feeling a sigh, a tear, the touch of a pulse, or the distribution of a charitable coin can carry with it an unmistakably erotic charge, and each of them becomes, in various circumstances, the carefully articulated substitute for sexual activity. By considering the language in which physical and emotional problems are expressed and by relating that "expression" to the larger concern of ideological appropriation, by which language is marked, gestures are coded, and feelings are mediated, I will show how sensibility shifted from a liberating and potentially radical social force to a threateningly repressed and repressive system of control.

Slavoj Žižek argues that "With the establishment of bourgeois society, the relations between domination and servitude are *repressed*: formally, we are apparently concerned with free subjects whose interpersonal relations are discharged of all fetishism; the repressed truth—that of the persistence of domination and servitude—emerges in a symptom which subverts the ideological appearance of equality, freedom, and so on."[7] Sensibility is just such a symptom, but the range of what it represses includes not just relations between domination and servitude but also the fetishization of those rela-tions in the erotics of benevolence and emotional mutuality. As Žižek uses the notion of a symptom, any ideology necessarily contains a fissure that exposes its hidden agenda and at the same time gives the ideology its sub-stance. Sensibility is the fissure in the bourgeois ideology that emerges in the late eighteenth century. As sensibility's influence became more pervasive, "sensibility" itself became a "symptom" of nervous disorders of various kinds. That medicalization of emotional pleasure, however, disguises the ideologi-cal symptom with which it is identical. Far from only allowing us to diagnose individual psychological complaints, that is, sensibility offers a means of diagnosing a culture's refusal to acknowledge the repression inherent to its hegemonic realization.

For Žižek , "it is precisely the symptom which is conceived as . . . a real kernel of enjoyment, which persists as surplus and returns through all attempts to domesticate it, to gentrify it (if we may be permitted to use this term adapted to designate strategies to domesticate the slums as 'symptoms' of our cities), to dissolve it by means of explication, of putting-into-words its meaning."[8] What is sensibility but the eighteenth-century attempt at gen-trification that fails because of the rock of the "real" of desire that breaks through all attempts at "generosity" and subverts goodness with pleasure?

The sexual-political "meaning" of the novel of sensibility has everything to do not just with concerns of class and gender but also, and importantly, with the ideology of desire that takes the man of feeling as its subject. In her discussion of A Sentimental Journey Eve Kosofsky Sedgwick talks about the ways in which Yorick manages to create "instant, supportive, apparently egalitarian 'families' around himself by his deftness in playing gender and class attribution off against one another. . . . Not the least deft of his strate-gies . . . is the casting of a veil of nostalgic pathos, linked to the traffic in women within an idealized 'classless' nuclear family, over his power negoti-ations with men."[9] These pseudofamilies are almost by definition the pro-jections of male ego: the man of feeling needs to feel that he is the support of any number of dependents. In Yorick's case the dependency begins with the servants, women, and other indigent members of the lower class for whom his tears have an inevitable financial valence. Desire in Yorick's case, the desire for an idealized male-defined family, is so diffused as to have no object but the man of feeling's own sense of his importance to this structure. The scene in the "desobligeant" is the key to understanding the self-directed trajectory of Yorick's desire: there the man of feeling shuts himself off from the world and writes about his experience in an oddly masturbatory gesture—the stationary coach rocks with the jerky activity of writing—suggesting that the pen becomes the tool of narcissistic realization.[10] "Rather than read Yorick psychoanalytically," Sedgwick says, "I would like to read him as pioneering in the ideological use of male 'androgyny' and of ostensibly universal psychoanalytic perceptions to express and assuage the specific homosocial anxieties of the middle-class intellectual."[11] Mackenzie's Harley and other men of feeling are "androgynous" in certain ways as well, but it is also important to see these figures as codifying a particular form of middle-class male behavior: this behavior takes the form of benevolence and works to idealize the relations of "others" to oneself; but in the end it only takes oneself as the object of desire and exposes sensibility as inherently narcissistic. Finally it sees within desire an ideology of male ascendancy that precludes objects outside the self in any but transitory positions as the occasion for self-appreciation and self-satisfaction.

A *Sentimental Journey* makes clear, however, that Yorick's "generosity" is deeply imbued with eroticism and that the blood that flows through the arteries of fine feeling can also enlarge the organs of sexual response. In the case, for instance, of the Grisset of whom Yorick asks directions in a Parisian shop, simple communication gives way to throbbing intercourse without so much as skipping a beat: "She repeated her instructions three times over to me with the same good natur'd patience the third time as the first;—and if *tones and manners* have a meaning, which certainly they have, unless to hearts which shut them out—she seem'd really interested, that I should not lose myself."[12] "*Tones and manners*" have a meaning for Yorick because his heart is open. A delicate sensibility can translate inarticulate impressions into significant speech and action, speech acts, because it closes off no avenues of meaning. The heart understands experience in a way that the intellect does not, because it does not have to deal with the interposition of language. Here it is clear that Yorick hears something very different from what is being said and that the language uttered, not even articulated for the reader, is beside the point. The body becomes articulate, and emotional reflection creates significance in the simplest gestures. Yorick's soul is in touch with his body, as it were, and it is the body that prompts his response. Where the experience comes most alive, however, is in its writing. Yorick must "lose [him]self" to find himself again in writing, as he does here. This experience is not merely sexual; nor is Yorick's response as transparent as it seems. For were Yorick to listen *to* the language of the Grisset rather then beyond it, he would be trapped in the literal. Instead, he reads the body. His flattery, which follows, suggests the terms of his heightened understanding:

> Any one may do a casual act of good nature, but a continuation of them shews it is a part of the temperature; and certainly, added I, if it is the same blood which comes from the heart, which descends to the extremes (touching her wrist) I am sure you have one of the best pulses of any woman in the world—Feel it, said she, holding out her arm. So laying down my hat, I took hold of her fingers in one hand, and applied the two fore-fingers of my other to the artery—

The potential for innuendo in such a scene is unlimited, and the descent of blood to the extremes could certainly be understood to animate the moment with erotic intensity. At the same time that the dilation of the arteries, the flowing of the blood, the free flow of spirits are all connected in the ethos of sensibility with the goodness of a responsive nature, the pulse of desire, the simply pleasurable physical sensation, breaks through the symbolization of feeling with unmistakable force. The scene creates a symptomatic relation—Yorick is after all taking the woman's pulse—that exposes sensibility in all its complexity. Of course there may be a benevolent motivation here, and it is not mere bravado that causes Yorick to claim that "I care not if all the world saw me feel it." Yorick attempts to defy the compartmentalization that insists that the physical is private and inevitably sexual. Yet what Yorick's grand gesture of sensibility and sentimental response really shows is the self-deception inherent to the pose.

As Judith Frank says, "A *Sentimental Journey* . . . disavows its own authority and self-consciously rehearses its own marginalization." One might add that it posits a marginalization of its central figure as a differently defined male whose relation to the world is primarily emotional and whose attitude to male power is decidedly indifferent. For Frank, "Sterne dissociates his own project from the apparatus of social control, displacing the implied disciplinary capacity of literature onto other kinds of narrative. Consequently, his novel seems free from motives of power. . . . But we know that . . . the novel does fantasize a literature that does have power."[13] Yorick's "power," in a scene such as the one just quoted, is the power of gender, class, and race; but it is also the power of sensibility itself, the power to appropriate physical response and attempt to write it large in the realm of the symbolic. That Yorick even partly succeeds is a measure of the legacy of sensibility, what Foucault (and others) would call the medicalization of pleasure.

Harley, the title character in *The Man of Feeling* (1771), is also attempting to reach beyond the privacy of his own feeling, but in his case the project simply fails. Issues of gender and class are so vividly depicted in this novel that it becomes almost an allegory of the capitalist crisis of middle-class experience. Here the alienated protobourgeois subject wanders in search of engagement with the world that will somehow liberate him from himself. He feeds on others, consumes them as it were, as a way of giving substance to his own responses. He is passive and self-involved for all his "interest" in others, and his "action" is a kind of unwitting aggression that emotionally "commodifies" whomever he encounters. Out of this "self" of pseudosuffering subjectivity emerges the "Man of Feeling," who sighs, at times sheds a tear or two, and dispenses "goodness" in a patronizing and even a victimizing—ultimately a self-victimizing—way. To witness the experience of the man of feeling, however, is like watching someone make his way through a hall of mirrors: everything he thinks he sees, everything he tries to react to, everything that causes him to feel—all these things are merely reflections of himself. If readers do not immediately recognize the position of the man of feeling as narcissistic that is perhaps because the mirrors in question do an awfully good job of distorting the subject, which is never anything else but the hero himself.

As the "fountain" of feeling, sensibility makes physical response the source of the self which has become identified with that feeling. Feeling, or sensation, is, in other words, the foundation of selfhood (*je sens, donc je suis*), and the act of feeling itself becomes tantamount to self-knowledge.[14] The "organs of sense," in Chambers' terms, therefore have a crucial function in the activity of self-definition. The problem inevitably arises, however, that the body, separate from and potentially a brute exposure of the lie of the language of sentimental response, undermines the process of ideological mystification that Yorick describes.[15] Although language is essential to any attempt to give feeling form, it always threatens to appropriate that feeling for the purposes of ideological reconstruction. Hysteria, hypochondria, melancholy, and other eighteenth-century illnesses are symptomatic of this dysfunction and the resulting confusion of discourse and desire. The language of sensibility offers the terms for physical response, that is, at the same time that it diagnoses physicality itself as a kind of illness. Writers of sensibility are aware of this tension, as Yorick's apostrophe suggests, but they are not always successful in breaking it. Their characters rarely do. If Sterne and other writers of the Age of Sensibility are opposed to the mind-body duality that paralyzed the previous age in a ritual of self-negation, they repeatedly express their concern in terms of the difficulty with which language can be used to represent private experience.[16] Another way to look at this crisis, however, is to say that they must find their bodies in language in order to be able to feel. They must discover their sexual selves in the language of sensibility in order to know pleasure. Discourse precedes desire in a way that the literature of the later eighteenth century repeatedly laments. The crisis of the thinking, feeling bourgeois male is already in place before the turn of the nineteenth century.

The obtrusion of the real within sensibility as the symptom of what it must repress is dramatized most vividly in *The Expedition of Humphry Clinker* (1771). Smollett's novel dissects sensibility in order to expose its inner workings, the flow of spirits is stopped by the contamination of the world, and the man of feeling, "Smelfungus" as Sterne called him, keels over in a swoon. The putrefaction that this novel purveys is the secret behind sensibility, the corrupt world that it hides, the real of which it is the symptom. Here is how Matthew Bramble describes his collapse at a ball in Bath, where he accompanies his niece Liddy:

> I sat a couple of long hours, half-stifled, in the midst of a noisome crowd; . . . The continual swimming of these dull figures before my eyes, gave me a swimming of the head; which was also affected by the fouled air, circulating through such a number of rotten human bellows. . . . Then, all of a sudden, came rushing upon me the Egyptian gale, so impregnated with pestilential vapours, that my nerves were overpowered, and I dropt senseless to the floor.[17]

At another point, while visiting the King's Bath, Bramble's senses again cut through the veneer of sensibility and see into its putrid core:

> Two days ago, I went into the King's Bath, by the advice of our friend Ch[arleton], in order to clear the strainer of the skin, for the benefit

of a free perspiration; and the first object that saluted my eye, was a child full of scrophulous ulcers, carried in the arms of one of the guides, under the very noses of the bathers. I was so shocked at the sight, that I retired immediately in indignation and disgust—Suppose the matter of those ulcers, floating on the water, comes in contact with my skin, when the pores all open, I would ask you what would be the consequence?—Good Heaven, the very thought makes my blood run cold![18]

The physical limitations of the receptive dynamics of sensibility are here exposed, as are the political implications of the sanctity of the physical dimensions of the (bourgeois) individual. What is particularly striking for the purposes of this study, however, is the way in which the flow of blood becomes the marker of class panic. Like Yorick, that is, who is constitutionally so different from him, Bramble finds himself in a passive relation to the sensations that overwhelm him in moments such as these. That Bramble finds pestilential gales and scrophulous ulcers playing upon his feelings, and Sterne a Grisset, or a Maria, should not disguise the fact that both these men portray themselves to a certain extent as victims of feelings that they cannot control. The response is in each case particularly the character's own, but at the same time there is a formal similarity in these and the responses of other men of feeling that suggests a position as victim in a world that seems instinctively to understand where the man of feeling is most vulnerable. In each case, moreover, the rush of feeling comes as a result of a slippage in class ascendancy: blood flows or does not flow in response to a person or a situation "lower" than the one in which the man of feeling knows himself to be placed. Feeling, after all, is a response more than it is an activity. The activity of feeling is constantly articulated as a passivity, a seeming victimization, a middle-class panic.

Out of this panic, however, Mackenzie fashions a potentially radical sentimentalism. This radicalism is founded in Harley's seeming carelessness concerning gender and class distinctions. Harley is in other words feminized and déclassé. He uses the dynamics of emotional response to challenge the control of language, and, far from inscribing patriarchal values, he asserts them as a means of undermining their force. *The Man of Feeling* thus uses a radicalized form that at once resists the order and progression of patriarchal narrative and substitutes a passive and vulnerable narrative development that seems always on the verge of collapse. This alternative to patriarchal narrative offers Mackenzie the chance to express emotions in a manner outside language. Formal class- and gender-transgression, in other words, enables the man of feeling to cross boundaries that are otherwise sacred. "If sensibility tends to be a feminine prerogative," Mullan says, "— and even in Mackenzie's stories of lachrymose males the virtuous virgin has an important place—then it exists to be assailed."[19] I do not think that it is so easy to distinguish masculine and feminine behavior in novels such as *The Man of Feeling*. The "lachrymose male" himself mimics "virginity," in a way that could finally undermine male supremacy and effect an equality between the sexes through feeling.

When, for instance, Harley follows Miss Atkins, a prostitute, to her "obsequious tavern," he tries to reconstruct the role that the culture has provided for him:

> [Harley] had walked some time along the strand, amidst a croud of those wretches who wait the uncertain wages of prostitution, with ideas of pity suitable to the scene around him, and the feelings he possessed, and had got as far as Somerset-house, when one of them laid hold of his arm, and, with a voice tremulous and faint, asked him for a pint of wine, in a manner more supplicatory than is usual with those of whom the infamy of their profession has deprived of shame: he turned round at the demand, and looked steadfastly on the person who made it.[20]

In this sentence, Mackenzie uses syntax to recreate the process described. From pity to confrontation, from self-involvement to awareness of another, from complacency to panic, the sentence balances those clauses of which Harley has control (walking, feeling) with those in which the prostitute asserts her presence (laying hold, asking, supplicating) until he is forced to turn. There is an almost ritualized balance of action and reaction at play here. In turning and looking, of course, whether out of curiosity or pity or desire, Harley seems destined to play the role established for the male. He seems destined, that is, to use his position as a man of feeling to subject this woman to his pleasure—even if that is simply the pleasure of benevolence. When this woman notes Harley's hesitation, she "endeavour[s] to force a leer of invitation into her countenance" (48), at which he takes her arm and walks off with her. It is difficult to determine what Harley's response means in this context. Is he to be censured for lasciviousness or praised for his generosity? At the moment there is no way of knowing. Harley's "benevolence" is an ambiguous position that has yet to be inscribed with meaning.

On the question of meaning, the narrator professes ignorance: "From what impulse he did this, we do not mean to inquire; as it has ever been against our nature to search for motives where bad ones are to be found. — They entered [the tavern], and a waiter shewed them a room, and placed a bottle of claret on the table" (49). There is still a broad range of possibilities. Among them of course is the possibility that Harley will encounter himself in this tavern more profoundly than he encounters anyone else. Still, the narrator's coyness suggests that he has knowledge, the knowledge of desire, an intention hidden perhaps from Harley himself, which captures him in its hold and deceives him with the rhetoric of benevolence. But there is a reconfiguration of desire here as well. In only the most naive response, it seems to me, would a reader attribute to Harley mere lust. The narrator's refusal to probe Harley's motives can only serve, however, to raise this possibility and indeed forcibly to suggest it. The narrator thereby underlines the paradoxical nature of Harley's stance. Readers are confronted, that is, with the alternative of a sexually corrupt "man of feeling" or a strangely passive and desexualized hero (why *does* he walk off with this woman if not to engage her sexually?); while what the novel of sensibility articulates is a position between these two, a position more akin to eighteenth-century notions of sensibility as eroticized benevolence. For by raising the possibility of sexual attraction at the same time that he emphasizes Harley's passivity, Mackenzie sexualizes what has seemed an alternative to sexuality and hints that Harley's very passivity is charged with sexual energy. Why is it assumed that benevolence itself lacks the charge of sexual energy that a scene like this one insists on? In becoming the victim of this woman's misery, Harley substitutes his own response for any active engagement with her. His seemingly "desexualized" stance is full of the erotics of benevolence: his pleasure arises from his resistance to her "leer of invitation" and from his ability to go with her to a tavern and not abuse her physically. But at the same time he emerges as the sentimental hero, who can reorder her life and reunite her with her father. In so doing, Harley assures his position in the social hierarchy as well as in the hierarchy of feeling. His desire is merely self-directed after all. This narcissistic mode of interaction with the prostitute is not very different from the role of the late capitalist subject in similar circumstances: rarely is desire for the other more powerful or more satisfying than the narcissistic satisfaction of having given pleasure or, what is in some ways worse, done good.

Sterne's Yorick manipulates his sexual identity as a way of establishing his position within a social hierarchy that valorizes neurasthenia and prefers its sexual aggression veiled in vague sentimental apostrophe. Mackenzie's Harley, however, is more a victim of ambiguity than its manipulator. The difference between the two novels is subtle, but no one who has read them both could mistake the delicate and precise positioning of Yorick for the clumsy erotic posturings of Harley. Mackenzie attempts to understand what the man of feeling might be able to accomplish within a social configuration that is quickly conventionalizing male feeling and rendering remote the possibility of valid sympathetic response. In addition to noting the ways in which the "ideological use of male 'androgyny'" can "express and assuage the specific homosocial anxieties of the male middle-class intellectual," Sedgwick also points to a "newly emerging 'universal' literary consensus based on the normative figure of the pseudo-androgynous, sexually highly valent male intellectual within the content of an increasingly eroticized and family-dominated public discourse."[21] Harley represents Mackenzie's attempt to examine for himself the "anxieties of the middle-class intellectual" and to discover whether the man of feeling offers an alternative to the ideological imperatives of late eighteenth-century society.

For Sterne and those contemporaries who shared this belief in the body, the refusal to prize mental over physical process results in a kind of linguistic ambiguity similar to that described by Foucault in *The Order of Things*: "to make use of signs (in the eighteenth century) is not, as it was in preceding centuries, to attempt to rediscover beneath them the primitive text of a discourse sustained, and retained, forever; it is an attempt to discover arbitrary language that will authorize the deployment of nature within its space, the final terms of its analysis and the laws of its composition."[22] Writers of the Age of Sensibility are searching for both the "deployment of nature" and the "arbitrary language" with which to represent it. In some ways language opens the space within which nature can function. For in addressing themselves to the question of how language can be made to represent the workings of nature, these writers suggest a relation that belies the simple model of "language as a representation of feeling." For writers of sensibility there is more at stake than "representation." They are attempting to "deploy" a sensitive, sexual self in a world that language has created for them. There is no question about the frustration of this project or the harrowing results of the failure of such attempts. The middle and late years of the eighteenth century are the record of the quest for physical experience that could embody the increasingly complex subjectivity represented in the discourse of sensibility.

John Mullan argues that "With the publication of Mackenzie's *Man of Feeling* in 1771, the sentimental novel has evolved into a terminal formula precisely because, with all its talk of virtue, it cannot reflect at all on the problems of conduct, the practices of any existing society."[23] Such an argument is anticipated in the conservative self-analysis of Mackenzie himself: Mackenzie's own fear that sentimentalism places nature before law suggests its power to undo social classification entirely and revolutionize society.[24] The implications of the code of sentimentalism are potentially far more radical than recent critics have suggested. Like other "men of feeling," Mackenzie in this novel postulates a world in which feelings are paramount and that gives absolute value to personal emotion. By implication, political relations are structured to reflect communal value and personal identity remains unfixed by class or even gender restrictions. Feeling liberates individuals into a communism of sympathy and a nonhierarchical system of relations based on benevolence and good will. But Mackenzie draws back from his radical project because he learns that to give way to feeling is to open an abyss of narcissistic self-appreciation that threatens to undermine the integrity of society itself. He fears that dissolution even more than he desires emotional liberation. Mackenzie is caught, that is, between a radical reformulation of male subjectivity as the locus of feeling and a desire not to threaten hierarchical social arrangements or even lose the power of male prerogative in an age of social flux. Mackenzie sees how high the stakes of narcissistic identification really are, and his character Harley dies because of an inherent anxiety about where this project might lead.

The urge to put feelings into words was both a reaction against the anxiety that the Lockean model of perception made inevitable and an attempt to resolve the resulting discontinuity of experience.[25] As Ernest Tuveson has argued, Locke's version of the self as an accumulation of impressions undoes the notion of a static ego and opens the way for the analysis of personal response and the gradual shift of interest from objective to subjective states of being.[26] By dismissing the distinction between matter and spirit (on the one hand) and equating consciousness to sensibility of pleasure and pain (on the other), Locke was further confounding attempts to place the soul anywhere but in the apparatus of perception. Locke, and more intensely Berkeley and Hume emphasize the difficulty in interpreting sensual data and therefore placing the self in relation to the world. For Hume, self-consciousness is the mental recreation of a physical impression:

> An impression first strikes upon the senses, and makes us perceive heat or cold, thirst or hunger, pleasure or pain, of some kind or other. Of this impression there is a copy taken by the mind, which remains after the impression ceases; and this we call an idea. This idea of pleasure or pain, when it returns upon the soul, produces new impressions of desire and aversion, hope and fear, which may properly be called impressions of reflexion, because derived from it. These again are copied . . . and become ideas; which perhaps in turn give rise to other impressions and ideas.[27]

This process of copying and recopying also casts the certainty of sensual experience into question. Hume suggests that knowledge cannot be guaranteed on the basis of impression, and that all such relations—of idea to impression and impression to world—lie beyond the realm of certainty. Self-consciousness becomes suspended in its own uncertain universe.

Such observations suggest an uneasy and indeed anxious relation to the world itself. Together these features suggest an age of isolated and self-involved beings, unsure of anything but their own bodily responses and even uneasy about the authenticity of those. Thomas Weiskel suggests that Locke's concept of the self led him to a theory of "uneasiness," in which "anxiety replaces the will as the principle of individuation" and "exceed[s] its occasion because the soul can never be entirely filled by the sensations and reflections which arise from an object 'out there'—an object whose essential absence is presupposed by perception."[28] Feeling, inarticulate and imprecise as it can seem, understandably becomes the only basis of "authentic" communication; it asserts a relation where reflection can only imagine one. The relation to experience in the world is most vivid, that is, to the extent that it is most deeply (and most literally) felt. But as successful as feeling might be in creating the relation, it relies on language to give it form. The challenge of sensibility, then, is to find the language that can give private impressions public significance and even value beyond the limits of self-consciousness.[29] As Foucault's discussion of the discourse of sexuality makes clear, however, this project is inevitably a self-defeating one. For as soon as the body recognizes itself in language, it loses itself as well.

Class, gender, and race create the hierarchical differences that make sensibility a possibility.[30] In Sterne, Smollett, and Mackenzie these differences are so vividly portrayed as to be unmistakable. It is almost as if sensibility is what enables them to establish the hierarchies so deeply in their own subjective systems as to make them seem inevitable. In this sense sensibility makes them the subjects of the emerging bourgeois ideology. Žižek argues that

> Ideology is not a dreamlike illusion that we build to escape insupportable reality; in its basic dimension it is a fantasy-construction which serves as a support for our "reality" itself: an "illusion" which structures our effective, real social relations and thereby masks some insupportable, real, impossible kernel (conceptualized by Ernesto Laclau and Chantal Mouffe as "antagonisms": a traumatic social division which cannot be symbolized). The function of ideology is not to offer us a point of escape from our reality but to offer us the social reality itself as an escape from some traumatic, real kernel.[31]

Sensibility is the name of the ideological fantasy-construction at work in these texts and in the culture of which they are a part. The "traumatic social division which cannot be symbolized" occasionally emerges as the very difference that defines sensibility itself: its own symptom.

For Markley, the "ideology of sentiment . . . explicitly promotes narrowly conservative and narrowly essentialist views of class relations, implicitly identifying the victims of social inequality—men, women, and children—with 'feminine' powerlessness."[32] I would argue, however, that the men of feeling were unaware of their own essentialism and that they imagined instead that they were opening a space for a revolution of social relations. It is easy for us to look at scenes of benevolence or generosity as ideologically charged, but that is only because sensibility is ideology itself. Their attempt at subverting a system of personal relations ends up only reinscribing them in a more pervasive system of bodily response. Each of these novels has a signal moment, image, or trope, however, by means of which the terms of its ideological fantasy becomes both vivid and unmistakable.

Other symptoms of sensibility abound in the literature and personal writings of the later eighteenth century. The passages I have quoted from *A Sentimental Journey*, *Humphry Clinker*, and *The Man of Feeling* could surely be discussed in these terms. Uncle Toby's "wound," the posteriors of Clinker and Lishmahago, Yorick's "desobligeant" could serve a similar function. The one "case" that I would like to pause over briefly, however, is a more elaborate and difficult one: the case of James Boswell.

Boswell's Symptoms: The Hypochondriack In and Out of Context

In *The English Malady* (1733), George Cheyne attempts to *"[explain] the Nature and Causes of* Nervous Distempers . . . *from Principles easy, natural and intelligible, deduc'd from the best and soundest* Natural Philosophy." Chief among these disorders are "[t]hose Nervous Distempers that are attended with *Spasms*, Cramps, Convulsions, or violent Contractions of the Muscles. Of this kind," he says, "are all of the *Convulsive* Tribe from *Hypochondriacal* and *Hysterical* Fits, or the Convulsions of the *Epileptick* Kind down to Yawning and Stretching." Throughout the study he groups together a set of diseases that he says can be "deduced from too thick and glewy or sharp Juices, some great Bowel spoil'd, or strong Obstructions form'd, and the regorging Fluids thereby brought on, struggling and laboring under the *Animal Functions*, in relaxed feeble, and unelastick Solids." These are "the Spleen, Vapours, Lowness of Spirits, Hysterical or Hypochondriackal Disorders," and Cheyne lists as "Symptoms" of these disorders:

> Wind, Belching, Yawning, heart-burning, Croaking of the Bowels, (like the Noise of *Frogs*) a *Pain* in the *Pit of the Stomach* . . . and sometimes there is an *Inflation*, an actual visible Swelling, to a very considerable Bigness, in the Stomach to be seen, especially in the *Sex*; a *Coldness* or *Chilliness* upon the Extremities, and sometimes Flushing (especially after a full Meal) and Burning in the Hands and Feet, *Cold damp Sweats*, *Faintings*, and Sickness (especially before a Solution of the Bowels) the Stools being sometimes very *costive*, sometimes *loose* and slimy, a *Feeling* like that of *cold Water* poured over several Parts of the Body, *Head-Aches* either behind or over the Eyes, like a *Puncturation*, *Flies* and *Atoms* dancing before the Eyes, a

Noise like the *dying* Sound of Bells, or a Fall of Water, in the Ears; *Yawning*, and *Stretching* and sometimes a Drowsiness or *Lethargy*, at other times *Watching* and Restlessness, and several other *Symptoms*, which it is impossible to enumerate.[33]

As usual, Cheyne leaves little to the imagination. Himself a sufferer of hypochondria, he understands this illness in its physical manifestations, and he lists even the most unpleasant consequences of these nervous complaints in utterly physical terms.[34] His enumeration of the senses is precise because the very illness he is describing is thought to be related to the physical sensibility of the subject concerned. In his analysis of "the Author's Case," with which he concludes his treatise, Cheyne lists an astounding array of physical symptoms and modes of treating them. Throughout his study the physical detail makes his account compelling, but it also suggests the degree to which Cheyne's bodily fascination might mask a more deeply rooted complaint, a complaint that is beyond his powers of diagnosis and treatment.

This is confirmed by the description of a further stage of the condition, in which Cheyne's terms of analysis shift:

The *Second* Stage of this Distemper is attended with all these Symptoms, in much higher and more eminent Degree, and some new ones, which were not felt, and consequently not described under the *first* Stage: such are instead of Lowness of Spirits: a deep and fixed *Melancholy, wandering* and *delusory Images* on the Brain, and *Instability* and *Unsettledness* in all the intellectual Operations, *Loss of memory, Despondency, Horror* and *Despair*, a *Vertigo, Giddiness* or *Staggering, Vomitings* of *Yellow, Green*, or *Black Choler*: sometimes unaccountable Fits of *Laughing*, apparent *Joy*, Leaping and *dancing*; at other Times, of *Crying, Grief* and *Anguish*; and these generally terminate in *Hypochondriacal* or *Hysterical Fits* (I mean *Convulsive* ones) and *Faintings*, which leave a Drowsiness, *Lethargy*, and extreme Lowness of Spirits for some time afterward.[35]

In this passage, Cheyne talks with analytical clarity about symptoms that are only for the first time being understood as the manifestation of a single illness. Here states of severe mental distress and violent mood swings are classed with a range of gastrointestinal disorders to constitute an increasingly vivid picture of the eighteenth-century understanding of hypochon-

driacal affliction. By bringing the brain into this dangerous phase of the illness, Cheyne makes it clear that intellectual operations are as seriously
affected as physical ones. With very little fanfare, Cheyne outlines a physical process that his contemporaries would implicitly understand: this progression from physical distress to mental disorder, this gradual breakdown
of the logic of physical and emotional response, and this abject lethargy, all
these careful descriptions lead to a realm that hovers on madness, abject
and absolute. The danger of this air of transgressive self-projection that
hypochondria always implies, I will argue, is precisely what makes it attractive to figures such as James Boswell, who found in hypochondriacal self-
indulgence a fullness of identity that a late twentieth-century reader might
see as excess.

Cheyne's method, however, is to relate even this seemingly mad behavior to diet, nutrition, and the proper function of internal organs. At one
point in his discussion of nervous distempers, for instance, he attends to the
function of the liver:

> A vitious *Liver* seem to be one of the primary and immediate Causes of
> *Nervous* Distempers. I never once in my Life saw an *Hysteric* or
> *Hypochon-driac* Case, of a deep Nature, or extreme Degree, in strong
> Persons especially, where the *Liver*, and its Appendages were not emi-
> nently faulty, either by a praeternatural *Size, Tumefaction, Obstruction,*
> or *Schirrosity*; and when by *ponderous*, alternative, active Medicines,
> join'd with a cool thin Diet, the Obstructions have been opened, the
> *Gall Bladder* and *Porous Bilarious* pervious, then, either *green, yellow,*
> or *black Choler* has poured out abundantly in to the Stomach.[36]

Cheyne's search for a physical cause of the nervous complaints he
describes might seem almost quaint, and one wonders whether his "cool
thin diet" could help if the liver really were compromised in some way or
how this diet could cure nervous disorders if the liver were not involved.
But Cheyne always turns to his own case and explains, in *The English
Malady* and in his letters, how he himself used diet to counteract the effect
of a hypochondriacal disposition. These remarks, and others like them in
The English Malady, are still being studied from the perspective of medical
history.[37] From the point of view of the "history of madness," however, as
Foucault and others have argued, such analyses of the mental functioning
of the human frame signal nothing less than a profound shift in the notion

of what it is to be human. Foucault says, for instance, in *Madness and Civilization* that "it was during the eighteenth century . . . that the theme was suddenly modified, changed direction—that a dynamics of corporeal space was replaced by a morality of sensibility. It was then and only then, that the ideas of hysteria and hypochondria were to *veer*, and definitely enter the world of madness."[38]

Boswell's *The Hypochondriack* participates in this shift of direction in a particularly active way. *The Hypochondriack* is a monthly series of periodical essays that Boswell published in *The London Magazine* from October 1777 until August 1783.[39] Throughout the series he addresses his own affliction with the "disease" of hypochondria, and he goes to some length to explain the degree of his own infection and the terms of his treatment. Anyone familiar with the Boswell's journals knows that his physical and mental health are a constant preoccupation. But *The Hypochondriack* essays systematically and publicly theorize the illness and its manifestations in ways that the *Journal* does not. By signing himself "the hypochondriack," moreover, Boswell posits an identity that can be read into even the most casual observations about human nature. This is a pose, to be sure, but in adopting it Boswell mines a rich lode of personal as well as cultural information about this remarkable eighteenth-century affliction.

In *The Hypochondriack*, no. 5, for instance, Boswell reveals a fascination with the disease that can only be understood in personal terms:

Melancholy, or Hypochondria, like the fever or gout, or any other disease, is incident to all sorts of men, from the wisest to the most foolish. . . . For I do not dispute that men are miserable in a greater or lesser degree in proportion to their understanding and sensibility. It is not every man who can be exquisitely miserable, any more than exquisitely happy. But the distemper indubitably operates, though in different degrees, upon every species or constitution, as fire produces its effects, though in different degrees, upon every species of matter, however much or however little of a combustible nature.

Fire having been mentioned in the way of comparison with Hypochondria in one particular, I shall carry on the allusion somewhat further, and observe, that as no wise man remains in supine negligence when he sees a fire break out and threaten destruction to his house, neither should he allow Hypochondria to gather strength, but should exert himself with all possible speed and activity to crush it in its beginning. As the first smoke from burning rouses activity to extinguish it; such should be the consequence upon the first rise of gloomy vapour in the mind. There is not the least doubt that Hypochondria, as well as fire, may be checked, if diligence, sufficiently early and sufficiently vigorous, be used. Indeed, in some very particular instances, the smoke and the melancholy are of such force as to incapacitate.[40]

Boswell's discussion of the distemper suggests a physical cause and a material analysis, and his "fire and smoke" analogy makes it seem as if his focus will be on practical physical evidence and a search, like Cheyne's, for causes in the material realm. Boswell's use of this analogy indicates the degree to which he views this distemper as dangerous to the whole fabric of the person affected, and it suggests that emergency treatments are not only available but necessary. Like Cheyne, Boswell might be thought to favor a "cool thin diet" to calm the "gloomy vapour" in his mind, quenching the fire before it spreads. His analogy suggests that however severe the danger from a hypochondriacal condition, care, vigilance, and quick action can quell the threat and render it innocuous. This is a heartening, if a somewhat false impression of the ease with which hypochondria can be contained. But something else comes through here as well. In spite of Boswell's attempt to argue the nondiscriminating quality of the illness, his emphasis on the "exquisite" misery of those with greater "understanding and sensibility" only highlights the elitism with which he approaches the subject. It may be difficult at first to see how such hierarchical language applies to the case at hand.

When Boswell goes on to outline the terms of the illness as he sees it, however, the source of this implicit superiority emerges. Later in the same issue, for instance, he remarks that: "Hypochondria affects us in an infinite variety of ways; for, a disordered imagination teems with a boundless multiplicity of evils; and the disorders of the body, which I believe always attend the direful disease, make such diversities of combination, that it is scarcely possible to specify all the sufferings of a Hypochondriack" (1:138). Suddenly the distemper seems like a disease *of the imagination* as much as a disease of the body. The greater the imagination involved, Boswell suggests, the greater the misery that results. The imagination takes precedence in Boswell's account not only because of the "boundless multiplicity of evils" with which it "teems" but also because it lies beyond the reach of accepted medical practice. If the imagination is not responsible for the physical effects in Boswell's account, then it does hover in the background of illness in some way that Cheyne has not outlined and Boswell himself seems unable to specify. Anyone familiar with the gloomy ruminations of Boswell's journals will recognize the role that imagination plays in the etiology of hypochondria. Here, for instance, is a signal moment of self-induced hypochondria: "I got up somewhat gloomy. Knowing that I would be immediately relieved when I got to town, I indulged hypochondria, which I had not felt of a long time. I called up to my fancy ideas of being confined all winter to an old house in the north of Scotland, and being burthened with tedium and gnawed with fretfulness." At other times, Boswell is the victim of more a negative imaginative power than a positive creator of moods, but the effect is similar: "so ill was I from a disorder in my stomach, partly from scurvy in my blood and partly from some inexplicable cause, that I was wretchedly despondent; nay my mind could not perceive the distinction between what was excellent and what not, at least with any clearness; and what is most strange, I again felt what recovery has not been able to correct: a dismal apprehension that I should never again be well or have any relish of anything."[41] Such moments are present from the first in the journals, but they are especially intense in later volumes, when hypochondria becomes a chronic complaint. In transforming a simple bad mood or even wild intoxication into a case of paralyzing and self-destructive hypochondria, Boswell depends on something more than a merely physical condition. In Boswell's descriptions, hypochondria becomes a *nervous* disorder, to be sure, but it also becomes a disorder that is centered in the imagination.

In making this subtle shift from bodily disorder to imaginative or nervous disorder, Boswell is reflecting a general pathologization of sensibility that Foucault and others have remarked. John Mullan, in *Sentiment and Sociability*, for instance, outlines the growth of interest in "nervous fibres" as the eighteenth century proceeds and connects that interest to an increasing fear of a kind of morbid sensibility that could "haunt" those predisposed to hypochondria, "the grave and studious, those of a sedate temper and enlarged understanding, the learned and wise, the virtuous and the valiant," as one eighteenth-century text on the disease puts it.[42] "By the time of William Smith's *A Dissertation upon the Nerves*" Mullan tells us, "the emphasis is upon a system of 'nervous fibres' as an exemplary model, but the truism remains to be repeated in another form: 'People of weak nerves are generally quick thinkers, from the delicacy of their sensitive organ.' "[43] As Foucault says, "if the notion of the 'irritated fiber' certainly plays this role of concerted confusion, it also permits a decisive distinction in pathology. On one hand, nervous sufferers are the most irritable, that is, have the most sensibility: tenuousness of fiber, delicacy of organism; but they also have an easily impressionable soul, an unquiet heart, too strong a sympathy for what happens around them."[44]

Boswell puts the irritability of the hypochondriac in dramatic form in one of the essays that he says he wrote in "a state of very dismal depression":

> His distempered fancy darts sudden livid glaring views athwart time and space. He cannot fix his attention upon any one thing, but has transient ideas of a thousand things; as one sees objects in the short intervals when the wind blows aside flame and smoke. . . .
>
> An extreme degree of irritability makes him liable to be hurt by every thing that approaches him in any respect. He is perpetually upon the fret; and though he is sensible that this renders him unmanly and pitiful he cannot help shewing it; and his consciousness that it is observed, exasperates him so, that there is great danger of his being harsh in his behavior to all around him.
>
> He is either so weakly timid as to be afraid of every thing in which there is a possibility of danger, or he starts into the extremes of rashness and desperation. He ruminates upon all the evils that can happen to a man, and wonders that he has ever had a moment's tranquillity, as he never was nor ever can be secure. (2: 42–44)

The bout of hypochondria begins with a "disordered fancy," becomes intensified because of an "extreme degree of irritability," and culminates in a kind of desperate and self-destructive "rumination." What Boswell outlines here are the very qualities that are celebrated as the foundation of sensibility, and in describing his illness he is doing little more than diagnosing a case of sensibility gone awry. As Mullan argues at length, the features that are prized as sources of sensibility bring with them the danger of the misery of hypochondria.[45] Boswell was not alone in articulating the dangers of sensibility, nor was he the only member of his class to feel the debilitating effects of an overactive imagination. Several critics of sensibility have pointed out that because they indicate a more finely tuned sensibility and a richer source of feeling, there is something attractive about the diseases of the imagination.

Because of the implicit elitism it suggests and because of the "deeper understanding" it presupposes, susceptibility to emotional distress—vapors, the spleen, hypochondria, and hysteria—becomes the defining quality of the bourgeois individual. As Klaus Doerner says in *Madmen and the Bourgeoisie*, "With the establishment of this thesis of hysteria [and, by extension, hypochondria] one element of sequestered unreason—specifically the passions—became accepted as a vital component of bourgeois society, not simply as a dangerous evil crying out for rational control, but as a recognizable, physical, autonomous social, and moral force."[46] In a later entry, Boswell makes this connection explicit:

> It was once proposed to me as a difficult problem, by an elegant lady of good understanding, but subject to Hypochondria, how to account for that complaint, being sometimes most uneasy when one is to all appearance in the best health. My solution of this problem, is, that often when there are no visible symptoms of bodily disorder, the finer parts, the nerves, or the nervous fluid, or whatever is the exquisite seat of sensation and sensibility, may be hurt and fretted, of the effects of which, in variety of degrees, every person of any delicacy of feeling has had experience: or the mind may be sick, it may be "full of scorpions," or have "a pale cast of thought" altogether unconnected with the state of the body.[47] (2:238)

Boswell here claims a connection with "an elegant lady of good understanding," which is not by any means beside the point in his analysis of a nervous disorder. The elegance is a feature that explains the "delicacy of feeling" that in turn gives rise to the "hurt and fretted" state itself. The interest in the "exquisite seat of sensation and sensibility" exposes the elitism at the heart of "sensibility," which this passage hardly bothers to disguise. Sterne's "Sensorium of the world" is not far from this, nor are the bitter complaints about offended sensibility in Smollett or Burney. What is surprising here is the abrupt alternative that Boswell offers at the end of the passage: "the mind may be sick, it may . . . have a 'pale cast of thought' altogether unconnected with the body." This possibility that hypochondria has nothing at all to do with the body—this attempt to diagnose a "sick mind"— is what Boswell offers his own and succeeding generations. His is an illness that can only ever exist in the mind.

Boswell's hypochondria is a symptom of more than personal conflict. His private misery must take a public form because he is diagnosing more than himself. Boswell is in fact diagnosing the culture that makes his complaint the fashionable one. Hypochondria could be seen as the symptom of a culture somehow at odds with itself. After all, if the very sensibility that is making benevolence possible is also turning imaginative gentlemen like Boswell against themselves, then it must measure more than the ability to respond to experience in the world. Sensibility so quickly becomes irritability and irritability so quickly becomes madness that fine feeling can only be understood as a serious social liability. What sensibility does measure, it appears from these accounts, is the degree to which the bourgeois individual is inadequate to the demands that the culture is making upon him. I would claim, in other words, that Boswell's hypochondria is the symptom that exposes sensibility as a false relation and an inadequate response to the growing inequities of social "progress."

If, as I have argued, sensibility can be seen as a fissure in the bourgeois ideology that emerges in the late eighteenth century, then Boswell's hypochondria is one of the symptoms of a corrupt and corrupting social system that turns a man's attention to the permutations of his own responses and makes them an adequate forum for the development of his ideas. Boswell was an intelligent and an educated man, to be sure, but his literary legacy includes one of the most extensive documentations of extremes of private feeling on record. *The Hypochondriack* itself could be understood as the attempt to give private distress a kind of public significance that it would otherwise lack. As such, it becomes a series of attempts to come to cultural terms with the diseased imagination that hypochondria represents. The diseased imagination thereby becomes the symptom of bourgeois ideology in its first hegemonic assertion.

Boswell thinks that his introspective speculations will release him from the torment of his diseased imagination, but in fact they pull him toward the "traumatic real kernel" of self-unimportance that makes bourgeois ideology possible. The horror of meaninglessness, to which Boswell again and again returns, gives solid force to the antagonism he feels toward those around him, and it is out of this horror that Boswell's own bourgeois self-importance emerges. If such discussions as Cheyne's and Boswell's own can be seen as part of the eighteenth-century origins of psychoanalytic discourse, as Foucault and others have argued, then it might not be entirely inappropriate to consider the language of twentieth-century post-Freudian thinking as a way of reimagining the cultural function of these diagnostics.[48] According to Žižek , the symptom is foundational to the way that the social and the private bourgeois individual is constituted. As he notes in his reading of Lacan on the symptom:

> The symptom arises where the world failed, where the circuit of the symbolic communication was broken: it is a kind of "prolongation of the communication by other means"; the failed, repressed word articulates itself in a coded, cyphered form. The implication of this is that the symptom can not only be interpreted but is, so to speak, already formed with an eye to its interpretation: it is addressed to the big Other presumed to contain its meaning. . . . [But] why, in spite of its interpretation, does the symptom not dissolve itself; why does it persist? The Lacanian answer is, of course, *enjoyment*. The symptom is not only a cyphered message, it is at the same time a way for the subject to organize his enjoyment—that is why, even after the completed interpretation, the subject is not prepared to renounce his symptom; that is why he "loves his symptom more than himself."[49]

Boswell enjoys his hypochondria. He almost preens at times with satisfaction at the distress his sensibility causes him to suffer. His symptoms are the badges of his bourgeois respectability. The most devastating physical paralysis becomes a symptom of social ascendancy. As John Mullan suggests, there are many reasons why a man of feeling might be tempted to indulge his darker moods: "the refined or studious hypochondriac is a necessarily exceptional figure, deriving both his status and his 'Distemper' from preoccupations and proclivities which remove him from 'the common People' or 'the ordinary state of human nature.' " Mullan cites Robert James's *Medicinal Dictionary* in this regard, where the definition of hypochondria includes the stipulation that "Those are . . . in a peculiar manner, subject to this Disorder, who lead a sedentary Life, and indulge themselves too much in Study, continual Meditations, and Lucubrations. Hence the Disorder is very common among the *Literati*."[50]

Boswell, however, worries that there might be a kind of madness that is beyond his control. As Mullan notes, "One step from a privileged affliction, however, is something more dangerous—'Mania' and 'Madness.' It is the proximity of such excesses which complicates perceptions of learned melancholy."[51] This is the concern that must lie behind such discussions as the following, which Boswell composed rather late in the series:

> Of the epistles of Hypocratus there is one entitled περί μχνιης λόγος, "A Discourse concerning Madness", from which I have taken the motto of this paper. He tells us that the brain is disturbed either by phlegm or by bile.[52] That the first produces dull madness, the latter produces furious madness, and he recommends different medical treatment accordingly. But there is doubtless a madness seated much deeper, a disorder in the mind itself, which neither the most potent medicines nor the most violent exercise can remove. That man is composed of two distinct principles, body or matter, and mind, I firmly believe; and that these mutually act upon one another, is I think, very certain. That the body influences the mind is commonly admitted; and it is equally certain that the mind influences the body; . . . Dr. *Battie*, in his Treatise on Madness, a book sufficiently corporeal, allows *original* madness to be incurable, or that which is owing to a fault in the first formation of the organs, while he maintains that *consequential* madness, owing to some accidental hurt or disorder, may be cured. But it will be found, upon a fair enquiry, that many cases of supervenient madness, both dull and furious, have baffled all the art and power of physick. The unfortunate incurables in St. Luke's Hospital, which I have visited out of sad curiosity, are not all the victims of native insanity. (2:236–238)

Here Boswell feels the connection between his own mental disorder and that of "the unfortunate incurables in St. Luke's hospital." The implication here and in his discussion of Dr. Battie, whose own theories of madness and its treatment were in many ways ahead of his time, is Boswell's deep-seated fear that his hypochondria may not be as culturally reassuring as he would like to believe.[53] One wonders what passed through his mind as he wandered among the madmen of St. Luke's: is this the "traumatic, real kernel" that hovers at the borders of Boswell's hypochondria and that gives rise to the fantastic structures of sensibility as a way of making social reality seem inescapably real? Is Boswell horrified at the sight of the wretches who suffer the opprobrium of insanity, or does he enjoy the thought that his own social position is simply a construction that could easily be overturned by the "supervenient madness" that he feels threatens him constantly? For Žižek, "When we are confronted with the patient's symptoms, . . . we must accomplish the crucial step of going through the fantasy, of obtaining distance from it, of experiencing how the fantasy-formation just masks, fills out a certain void, lack, empty place in the Other."[54]

Boswell's hypochondria, the dark melancholy that seems so often akin to madness, masks the emptiness that would otherwise make him the partner of the incurables in St. Luke's. But it also marks him *as* their partner. This is Boswell's *jouissance*. The symptoms of his class superiority also allow him to transgress class boundaries and feel at one with the wretches in chains at public hospitals. It gives him, that is, a kind of class mobility that mere sanity could never allow. Boswell knows that sensibility gives him this power, just as, in other circumstance, it threatens to take power away. Boswell knows, in other words, that he is merely a construct that sensibility makes possible and that he has the power, in the fantasy of madness, to unmake himself in the image of the incurables. Žižek's analysis of the Lacanian *sinthome* suggests a response to Boswell in this context: "Symptom as *sinthome* is a certain signifying formation penetrated with enjoyment: it is a signifier as a bearer of *jouis-sense*, enjoyment-in-sense."[55] Boswell's hypochondria is a *sinthome* of sensibility: it is the signifier of sensibility's ruse, of its ability to abstract the body as a cultural product and to isolate the bourgeois subject from himself. Boswell's hypochondria represents the fissure, at it were, in the system of cultural organization that takes the bourgeois individual as its only possible subject. This symptom-fantasy becomes the only source of meaning in an meaningless system of social relations.

Žižek takes us one step further in coming to terms with the symptom as a condition of ideology:

What we must bear in mind here is the radical ontological status of symptom: symptom . . . is literally our only substance, the only positive support of our being, the only point that gives consistency to the subject. In other words, symptom is the way we—the subjects— "avoid madness," the way we "choose something (the symptom-formation) instead of nothing (radical psychotic autism, the destruction of the symbolic universe)." . . . That is why the final Lacanian definition of the end of the psychoanalytic process is *identification with the symptom*. The analysis achieves its end when the patient is able to recognize, in the Real of his symptom, the only support of his being.[56]

Of course, Boswell does recognize this, and when he decides to publish essays that explore the disorder in luxuriant detail and when, encouraged by Johnson, he even thinks that his hypochondriacal musings merit publication as a book, he is surely admitting that his pathology makes him who he is. For Žižek, "This, then, is a symptom: a particular, 'pathological', signifying formation, a binding of enjoyment, an inert stain resisting communication and interpretation, a stain which cannot be included in the circuit of discourse, of social bond network, but is at the same time a positive condition of it."[57]

Boswell knows that his symptoms are more than a private matter. He knows too that the self is a construct of which his own elaborate self-probings are the proof. They represent the vain attempt to produce a self that is not a chimera, to answer with an unequivocal "yes" the question that haunts him. But that "yes" must always and everywhere elude his grasp: in the *Journals*, in the *Life of Johnson*, in his *Letters*, but most of all in the essays he calls *The Hypochondriack*, there is no answer but his own hypochondriacal subjectivity. Žižek puts it this way:

> The subject is constituted through his own division, splitting, as to the object in him; this object, this traumatic kernel, is the dimension that we have already named as that of a "death drive," of a traumatic imbalance, a rooting out. Man as such is "nature sick unto death," derailed, run off the rails through a fascination with a lethal Thing.
>
> The process of interpellation-subjectiviation is precisely an attempt to elude, to avoid this traumatic kernel through identification: in assuming a symbolic mandate, in recognizing himself in the interpellation, the subject evades the dimension of the Thing.[58]

Boswell recognizes himself in the symptoms of a culturally induced form of madness that would be known by later generations as "the bourgeoisie." In his description of the malady he suffers, he comes close to diagnosing the class that he as much as any other writer of the later eighteenth century helps to bring into existence:

> Hypochondria sometimes brings on such an extreme degree of languor, that the patient has a reluctance to every species of exertion. The uneasiness occasioned by this state, is owing to a vivacity of imagination, presenting, at the same time, the ideas of activity; so that a comparison is made between what is, and what should be. Languor, simply considered, is not uneasy; nor is any being unhappy by the privation of powers of which it has no notion. The snail nor the oyster is never dissatisfied for want of animation — but a being that has experienced activity is dejected in a quiescent state, after it has continued long enough to fill up the full measure of repose. To be therefore overpowered with languor, must make a man very unhappy; he is tantalized with a thousand ineffectual wishes which he cannot realize. For as Tantalus is fabled to have been tormented by the objects of his desire being ever in his near view, yet ever receding from his touch as he endeavored to approach them, the languid Hypochondriack has the sad mortification of being disappointed of realising any wish, by the wretched defect of his own activity. While in this situation, time passes over him, only to be loaded with regrets. The important duties of his life, the benevolent offices of friendship are neglected, though he is sensible that he shall upbraid himself for that neglect till he is glad to take shelter under the cover of disease. (1:144–145)

Part of the process whereby sensibility attempts to overcome the anxiety that Boswell's hypochondria represents is by insisting on the very absence that Weiskel describes. The eighteenth century's increasingly elaborate moral and ethical resistance to any explanation of response but an impressionistic one suggests a fear of knowledge. If Locke's "uneasiness" seems increasingly to undermine eighteenth-century complacency, assertions of providentiality and natural goodness attempt to prop it back up again. George Cheyne, for instance, articulates the hope of the age when he says that "in all the Works of God there is a *ne plus ultra*; . . . that Nature and its

Author, to distinguish itself from finite *Mechanism*, always operates by *Systems* and *Organs* in Number even infinite . . . and thus he leaves *Images* and *Signatures* of himself on all his Works."[59] By placing God infinitely beyond the power of human knowledge, Cheyne and other practical thinkers of the age placed him beyond the reductive and objectifying power of language, except in a system of "Images and Signatures" that suggest his infinite presence by insisting on his infinite absence.[60] God, in other words, is like Boswell's despair. He is the lack around which the ideology of sensibility is constructed: he is its symptom.

The literature of sensibility is about the relation between language and the body—a relation Shoshana Felman calls a "theoretical, empirical, and historical" scandal—and about ways in which language can expose itself in its scandalous relation to the body and never quite give up the attempt to normalize relations.[61] The language of feeling ideally transforms the body with its rush of sensation and its urgency of desire into an ideological construct that can experience the world at the same time that it remains aloof and self-absorbed. This "ideal" project, however, founders on both the insufficiency of language and the intractability of desire, as the works of sensibility so regularly demonstrate.

The radical reconsideration of the emotions that takes place in the eighteenth century, then, has political as well as linguistic implications. Unchecked sensibility is a threat to order in the later eighteenth century. The emphasis on emotion and the body is a radical rejection of the tenets of rationality and the assertion of public power. But sensibility turns out to be an ineffectual revolutionary force, in England at least, because it betrays itself though its very success at finding the language of emotion. For that language corrupts syntax and becomes finally only self-referential, in the madness of private metaphor. The language of emotion becomes the language of diagnosis. As the discourse about sensibility flourishes throughout the century, the possibility of a genuine expression of feeling diminishes. As discourse about the self proliferates, as a new impulse to inscribe the facts of private experience in authentic language expands, the culture uses this discourse as a means of deploying its own power by extending, by institutionalizing and formalizing the meaning of individual as opposed to public power. Sterne's paean to sensibility is in this sense a cry of desperation. Žižek says that "the only way to break the power of our ideological dream is to confront the real of our desire which announces itself in this dream."[62]

In Sterne's paean to sensibility, the real of desire is that embodied presence that everywhere eludes the man of feeling. He can never effect change or even recognize the degree to which he is ideologically determined precisely because he has lost his body in the discourse of sensibility.

In the literature of sensibility, the discursive exploration of feelings, the objectification of privacy, became possible only in a process that negated the self at the same time that it gave it form. As Foucault says in *The Birth of the Clinic*, "Western man could constitute himself in his own eyes as an object of science, he grasped himself within his language, and gave himself, in himself and by himself, a discursive existence, only in the opening created by his own elimination: . . . from the integration of death into medical thought is born a medicine that is given as a science of the individual."[63] That is why so potentially liberating a project as that of the publication of feeling becomes by means of its own processes a repressive force, asserting limits at the same time that it tries to break through them. Men of Feeling are looking for a form that can embody the force of experience; a truth that is in touch with present substance. The discourse of the self that emerges in this period defuses the potentially radical implications of a new kind of self-awareness. At the same time the tension between the ideological imperatives of the age and the local pockets, as it were, of resistance, expressed in terms of bodily reality and sexual urgency, seem at times to promise an avenue of subversion or liberatory politics. The drama constituted by the emergence at one and the same moment of a sexuality and the appropriation of private feeling, the tension surrounding the sacrifice of privacy and the codification of sexual response, the tragedy of domesticity—all of these issues suggest that heterosexual privilege is built on a shaky and unstable foundation that is symptomatic of deep internal conflict. Straight masculinity collapses into itself.

PART TWO

Sexualities

➤ ←

CHAPTER FOUR

Gray's Tears

Large was his bounty and his soul sincere,
Heaven did a recompense as largely send:
He gave to Misery all he had, a tear,
He gained from Heaven ('twas all he wished) a friend.

—THOMAS GRAY, *Elegy Written in a Country Church-Yard*

"*O lachrymarum fons*"[1]

Any discussion of Thomas Gray's "sexuality" faces insurmountable problems. Although a wide range of biographers and critics have long assumed
that Gray's attraction to friends such as Horace Walpole and Richard West
and his later infatuation with other young men were erotically charged,
there is no keyhole testimony to "prove" that Gray participated in any transgressive sexual activity.[2] Recent arguments concerning Gray's homosexuality often use "readings" of his work to prove the repression of his sexual
desire and turn on the question of whether or not his anger and frustration
are revealed in his writing.[3] Even though such readings may be irresistibly
persuasive, they also raise serious doubts about how the notion of homosexuality is being used and what is being assumed about sexual identities in
the eighteenth century. Late twentieth-century assumptions about "sexuality"—that it defines an individual, that it can or should be hidden, that its
repression breeds anger, that it creates a subculture—hinder the clarity of
many attempts to talk about eighteenth-century figures and their emotions
and desires. If same-sex desire is palpable in Gray's writing, as I will argue
that it is, what needs to be explained is not how this reclusive eighteenth-
century figure kept his sexuality hidden, but rather how he could write it so
large as to make it indistinguishable from values that were celebrated in the
dominant culture.[4]

"He gained from Heaven ('twas all he wished) a friend": the melancholy pose that the poet adopts at the close of the "Elegy," the answer to the poetic dilemma that had baffled earlier attempts to finish the poem, completes the cultural transaction that Gray begins much earlier in his poems and his letters to his friends. This elegiac solution, as it were, is to constitute identity at the moment of loss and to articulate desire in the very terms of its utter inaccesssiblity, which in this case is represented as the poet's own gravestone. I will return to a discussion of the "Elegy" later in this chapter. First I would like to look at the personal context for this amazing poem.

If, as I have discussed at length, the term *sexuality* itself had no currency in the eighteenth century, nevertheless a certain sexual sensibility emerges that begins to have recognizable contours.[5] When Charles-Victor de Bonstettin, whom Gray loved with an almost reckless passion in the 1760s, described Gray many years after Gray's death, he spoke of a man with a peculiar "sensibilité."[6] This term did have currency in the eighteenth century, of course, and, as the previous chapter shows, the characteristics of sensibility included the earliest conceptualization of the notion of sexuality.

If the culture of sensibility suggests the outlines of what Foucault calls "a completely new technology of sex," then to say that Gray is a "man of feeling" must be only the beginning of an exploration of his position as a desiring subject in the age of sensibility.[7] Recent cultural examinations of sensibility have largely neglected the question of sexuality, perhaps for the very reason that feeling seems to be an end in itself. What I hope to show in this chapter is how feeling can function culturally to constitute the subject of male-male desire within a melancholic framework of prohibition and loss. If I go so far as to argue that male-male desire is the open secret of sensibility, that is only to correct what I see as the heterosexist assumptions behind most of the work done in this field.[8] In other words, it seems to me that my attempts to "queer" sensibility, here and elsewhere, must be placed in this context, in which all attention to same-sex desire is at best marginalized.

I have argued that the man of feeling begins to redefine masculinity in the middle years of the eighteenth century. The seeming feminization of the man of feeling has been seen by some cultural historians to have resulted in the domestication of the male and a harnessing of male aggression and male libido for the good of family life and middle-class morality.[9] An important and usually neglected counterpart of this domestication of male-female relations is an equally pervasive and culturally significant

emotionalizing of male-male desire. The melancholy cast to male friendship, familiar in a range of mid-century examples but most apparent in the
writings of Gray, was a crucial restraint on the freedoms of earlier codifi-
cations of masculinity and masculine prerogative.[10] Gray and other men of
feeling reject the libertine model of masculine license in favor of a more
inward-looking expression of sexual sensibility. The difference between
these two models of masculinity is more than a mere reflection of class distinction or of the rise of middle-class morality. It hints at a cultural shift
that reorders the models for masculinity, rejecting libertine license in favor
of a model of friendship that the classical tradition had already richly articulated. What Gray does, however, by working the gestures of classical literature into his private friendships is to articulate a kind of male love that
challenges the culturally determined notion of "friends." Or does he? After
all, Gray dramatizes emotion to give substance to his love, but he also uses
that emotion to insist that his desire is (always) already frustrated. He
expresses male-male desire, in other words, in terms that the culture not
only allows but also requires. The erotics of friendship tie the bonds of cultural organization all the tighter.[11] Far from transgressing cultural norms or
confronting an "antisodomitcal culture," I wish to argue, Gray's world of
male-male desire is a central element in the dominant fiction of the age.[12]
What Gray alludes to in his poems and his letters is transgressive, to be
sure. And the love he felt for his friends, if physically expressed and publicly exposed, could have been the cause for hanging. But the physical
expression and the public exposure are written into Gray's poetry of feeling, where they tremble with the frustration that they must already imply.
Gray's is the love that does dare speak its name, publicly and profusely, at
the expense, as Gray's poems make clear, of the love itself. If Gray's poetry
is a poetry of loss, then what he loses is the love he everywhere expresses.
What is left of course is the feeling.

Gray and his Eton College friends were timid, intellectual boys who
avoided sports and were "poetical and romantic in temperament."[13] They
took pride in their mutual intellectual abilities, challenging one another in
verse and prose, walking in the fields or sitting for hours reading Horace or
Tacitus. The years at Eton must also have been full of fun and various forms
of mischief: the letters that appear just after the boys leave Eton are ecstat-
ically inventive and giddily intellectual. These early letters glow with the

privilege that their Eton experience imbued, and the very language in which they express their love for one another depends for its depth and its resonances upon the shared experience of an elitist education. The "secret society" that these boys formed, their "Quadruple Alliance," has been likened to the " 'intelligence communities' of the mid twentieth-century Oxbridge moles," similarly emerging from the intellectual enthusiasms of eroticized male relations within a classical tradition.[14] But the secrets that Gray and Walpole and West shared are the open secrets of the age of sensibility: their letters do not so much expose as realize the rich complexity of their experience as men of feeling. In this experience (providing the differences are not rejected) we may trace the origins of late-twentieth-century gay sensibility, with its open secrets, its spectacles of confession, its giddy masquerades, and its moments of deep and painful loss.

Gray's letters to West and Walpole, it is important to remember, were subjected to the editorial abuse of both Mason and Walpole, who combined letters, rewrote passages, and excised entire sections that were "infantine," according to Walpole, and "hardly fit for schoolboys."[15] Even in the letters that do survive, however, certain passages might cause more than an eyebrow to be raised. When Gray addresses Walpole as "mie Nuss [nurse] att London," for instance, speaks of "your kind promise of coming to tend me yourself," and signs himself Walpole's "ever-dutifull & most obedient & most affectionate, loving God-daughter, PRU"; or when he chides Walpole, "perhaps its policy in you to stay away so long, that you may increase my Desire of seeing you," it only confirms the educated speculation that these friendships are rich in the dynamics of eroticism.[16] "Miss Gray," as his fellow pensioners called him, wrote exhilarating letters that are effusively poetic and aggressively emotional.[17] To Walpole, he is zany and irresistible; to West, he is thoughtful and sublime; but to both he can be an amazingly attentive and loving friend. In his letters and in his poetry he celebrates them both as objects of desire and as objects, inevitably, of loss.[18]

In the terms of the Quadruple Alliance, Gray is Orozmades, the Zoroastrian divinity, who is mentioned in Lee's The Rival Queens as a "dreadful god" who from his cave issues groans and shrieks to predict the fall of Babylon.[19] Walpole is usually addressed as Celadon, the amorous shepherd in Durfé's Astrée. In one early letter Gray plays with these roles:

> From purling Streams & the Elysian Scene,
> From Groves, that smile with never fading Green
> I reascend; in Atropos' despight
> Restored to Celadon, & upper light:
> Ye gods, that sway the Regions under ground,
> Reveal to mortal View your Realms profound;
> At his command admit the eye of Day;
> When Celadon commands, what God can disobey? (ll. 1–8)[20]

One of Gray's earliest poems, this fantasy on the power of friendship, this vision of transcendence by means of his devotion to another suggests the terms of Gray's private fantasy: here are the Edenic groves that return in the "Eton College" ode and the "upper light" of poetic imagination. But, importantly for Gray, that light is shared with a friend and is in fact impossible without the friend as an inspiration. Walpole is the light that will reveal the underground realms of the brooding Orozmades and transform the gloomy genius into a bird in flight:

> That little, naked, melancholy thing
> My Soul, when first she tried her flight to wing;
> Began with speed new Regions to explore,
> And blundered thro' a narrow Postern door; (ll. 12–16)

Could Gray be alluding to a sodomitical sexual awakening here? Could his "little, naked, melancholy thing" refer to the adolescent penis that Walpole may have taught to "reascend" within the intimacy of friendship? Could the exploration of "Realms profound" that Celadon commands be a journey into the physical? It may seem speculative or even a mere insinuation to answer "yes" to these interpretive possibilities, but later the poem takes a turn that makes them much more likely, as the terms of the relation between the poet and his muse becomes explicit:

> Believe, that never was so faithful found
> Queen Proserpine to Pluto under ground,
> Or Cleopatra to her Marc-Antony
> As Orozmades to his Celadony. (ll. 38–41)

At another moment, after reading *The Turkish Spy*, Gray utters effusively,

When the Dew of the morning is upon me, thy Image is before mine
eyes; nor when the night overshadoweth me, dost thou depart from
me. . . . I have beheld thee in my Slumbers, I have attempted to seize
on thee, I sought for thee & behold! thou wert not there! . . . thou art
sweet in my thoughts as the Pine-apples of Damascus to the tast; &
more refreshing, than the fragrant breezes of Idumea. . . . Be thou
unto me, as Mohammed to Ajesha [his wife]; as the Bowers of
Admoim to those the Sun hath overtaken; or as the costly Sherbets of
Stamboul to the thirsty.[21]

The extent of the physical exuberance of this letter is unmatched and its
emphasis on the promptings of desire is unmistakable. If this is not a love
letter to Walpole, it is difficult to imagine what it is. Of course, no one can
assign a specific meaning to these verbal antics, as far-flung and parodic as
they are. In Gray's work they represent the tantalizing possibility of fulfillment, the giddy hope that his feelings are returned, the physical assurance
that desire can be realized through the senses and not just nurtured in the
imagination.

After Gray's much discussed quarrel with Walpole on their tour of
Europe, this celebratory mood of friendship takes a melancholy cast. Gray's
attention turns to Richard West, the Favonius (West wind, and sometimes
Zephyrille) of Eton, who may be said to have inspired this mood. West was
an almost angelic presence in Gray's life, "tall and slender, thin-faced and
pale complexioned," brilliant but troubled; he was a sensitive and, as Gray
later calls him, a "loving" boy who inspired some of Gray's most moving
poetry.[22] In a letter Gray wrote to West in Latin (in 1738), which included
an ode on West's beginning the study of law, Gray appended a single stanza,
Lucretian in tone and form, that has been justly celebrated for its haunting
beauty:

O lachrymarum fons, tenero sacros
Ducentium ortus ex animo; quater
Felix! in imo qui scatentem
Pectore te, pia Nympha, sensit!

(O fount of tears, that draw their sacred sources from the tender mind; four
times happy is he who has felt you, holy Nymph, gushing forth from the
depth of his heart.)[23]

With a personification as bizarre as anything in William Collins, Gray articulates his attraction to his tearful friend in startling terms. The font of tears itself is sacred, springing as it does from the "tender mind," the seat of emotions of the man of feeling. This could be himself, of course, or the friend to whom he addresses the letter. The confusion of identities to a certain extent memorializes the love he is describing. The suggestion of physical intimacy in the feeling and in the happiness with which he experiences the bodily sensation of emotion is almost seductively blurred, so that the "holy Nymph"—"pia nympha"—who colors this moment of self-realization with a female presence could come to represent the emotional and physical bond between them. Happiness in a feeling that gushes forth from the heart cannot be fully divorced from the mechanics of sexual response, nor can this ecstatic address, both to himself and to his friend, suggest much less than an act of physical intimacy.[24] Desire here is constituted not only in West's poetic presence but also in the absence that a letter implies. Like other men of feeling, Gray eroticizes emotional distance as a way of understanding the melancholy with which he knows he has been marked, and he takes pleasure in the symptom (*sinthome?*), the tears that both commemorate and define this moment of intimacy.[25]

Another poem in Latin, "Ad C: Favonium Zephyrinum," sent to West from Rome, begins:

> Mater rosarum, cui teneræ vigent
> Auræ Favonî, cui Venus it comes
> Lasciva, Nympharum choreis
> Et volucrum celebrata cantu!

(Mother of roses, for whom the gentle breezes of Favonius rise, and whose companion is pleasure-loving Venus, honoured in the dances of the Nymphs and the songs of the birds!)[26]

If this is Gray's "Ode to the West-wind," it shimmers with the tactile emotions through which Gray has learned to express the complexities of his love. Roses, Venus, the dance of Nymphs, birdsong, and of course the gentle breezes of Favonius: this is Gray's erotic universe, as rich and enticing as anything in Keats or Shelley, and equally inaccessible. In the poem Gray talks about the distance between the two friends: this is now merely a physical distance, but he almost seems to understand that it will become the distance of time and memory as well. For it is finally time and memory that lock the poet in the pose that in these Latin poems he only begins to reveal: the pose of the isolated, melancholic poet of loss. When Gray finds the voice of love in this recognition of loss, his cultural transaction is complete.[27]

West's death in the late spring of 1742 affected Gray deeply. The poems he wrote that summer, both the "Ode on a Distant Prospect of Eton College" and the "Sonnet [on the Death of Richard West]," as well as the "Ode to Adversity," can all be considered testaments of his love for his friend. These poems establish Gray's position as the melancholy poet, the man isolated in his own desire at the same time that that desire is realized in melancholy itself. "Eton College," for instance, states:

> Ah, happy hills, ah, pleasing shade,
> Ah, fields beloved in vain,
> Where once my careless childhood strayed,
> A stranger yet to pain!
> I feel the gales, that from ye blow,
> A momentary bliss bestow,
> As waving fresh their gladsome wing,
> My weary soul they seem to soothe,
> And redolent of joy and youth,
> To breathe a second spring. (ll. 11–20)[28]

This poem that so uniquely celebrates the vulnerability of childhood and looks with forbidden desire on the world of personal memory manages, I would argue, with its single syllable "Ah" to change the course of English poetry.[29] The force of this monosyllable is to introduce private feeling of a very special kind into poetry. This is the "Ah" of fond reminiscence, the "Ah" of memory and loss, the "Ah" of friendship and youth, the "Ah" of pure and simple emotion. But to borrow a phrase from Oscar Wilde, emotion is never pure and rarely simple. For Gray, emotion and desire are at times indistinguishable. "Ah," after all, can represent fulfilled as well as frustrated desire.

If friendship and youth are, like the field of Eton, "beloved in vain," they call to mind the sonnet in which Gray laments the loss of his emotional companion, Richard West:

In vain to me the smiling mornings shine,
And reddening Phoebus lifts his golden fire:
The birds in vain their amorous descant join,
Or cheerful fields resume their green attire:
These ears, alas! for other notes repine,
A different object do these eyes require.
My lonely anguish melts no heart but mine;
And in my breast the imperfect joys expire.
Yet morning smiles the busy race to cheer,
And new-born pleasure brings to happier men:
The fields to all their wonted tribute bear;
To warm their little loves the birds complain.
I fruitless mourn to him that cannot hear,
And weep the more because I weep in vain.[30]

These lines allude to a tradition of elegiac verse that is rich in its ability to express loss. Loss of course is what is being expressed here: the blank and the frustrations of loss. As Lonsdale points out, "the poet is mourning the only friend that could have understood and shared such a grief."[31]

I have elsewhere offered a reading of this poem that suggests that its "homoplatonism"—the term is G. S. Rousseau's—works to refigure as elegiac loss what for Gray is actual physical longing and frustrated physical desire.[32] As I say there, it can hardly be an accident that Gray chose as his model a Petrarchan love sonnet or that many of his images can be traced to a range of love poetry from Virgil and Ovid to Thomson. The octave expresses a distinctly physical longing that is no longer available—"In vain to me the smiling mornings shine" (note that "me" is the object of loss here rather than its subject), and the sestet answers by developing this contrast. By mourning to West (rather than *for* him), Gray underlines the personal quality of the loss—just what it means to him—and explains the loop of grief that the last line expresses. With West finally out of reach, at the end of the poem Gray withdraws—as the man of feeling must—into the privacy of his own misery. "I . . . weep the more because I weep in vain": Gray must stop short of breaking through the language of grief to something (or someone) outside himself. "I" is the source of grief, that is, rather than "he" or "you."[33]

Grief becomes the substitute for the friend and offers protection against the implications of desire. But at the same time it commemorates that desire, and perhaps its fulfillment, in conventional imagery that hides its personal intensity. Every line reveals as much as it conceals, and poetry itself, decorous and allusive, becomes the vehicle for private longing. Gray's melancholy stems from the failure of the elegy to lead him to an encounter with anything more than his own private emotion. "Friendship" involves an internal contradiction and self-confrontation that West's death now make inevitable.

In "Mourning and Melancholia," Freud discusses the elaborate contours of grief and suggests that "it is really only because we know so well how to explain it that this attitude does not seem to us pathological." Gray's grief in this poem would seem pathological, as well, if we did not know that the man of feeling is constituted by loss. Freud says that "melancholia is in some way related to an unconscious loss of a love-object, in contradistinction to mourning, in which there is nothing unconscious about the loss."[34] Gray is conscious of the loss he mourns but unconscious (perhaps) that in losing West he has lost himself as well. This is the basis of his melancholy, and in the poems of 1742 he discovers his poetic voice in this dynamic of despair.

This dynamic has broader cultural implications than my discussion of Gray might suggest. Other critics have begun to see the outlines of the twentieth-century "closet" in the literature of sensibility and have suggested that a mode of secrecy is essential to the construction of bourgeois subjectivity in the later eighteenth century.[35] Gray's melancholic pose seems to me to offer another vantage point on the shimmering edifice of twentieth-century sexual secrecy. To commemorate desire as loss is to begin the construction of a more viable closet, the one into which culture can place the man-loving-man or woman-loving-woman, whether or not he or she chooses to stay there. Eve Sedgwick has theorized the closet most persuasively in terms of the later nineteenth and early twentieth centuries. The history of the closet that she describes must go back to this act of accommodation that Gray and other writers of sensibility make with their culture, this act of self-realization in the lonely pose of melancholy. Sedgwick says that "same-sex desire is still structured by its distinctive public/private status, at once marginal and central, as *the* open secret."[36] Gray understands implicitly how this mechanism works, and his attempts to articulate desire in loss create a closetlike structure from which he can utter his devastating pronouncements without the risk of public exposure. Sedgwick says that "[c]ognition itself, sexuality itself, and transgression have always been ready in Western culture to be magnetized into an unyielding though not unfissured alignment with one another." She points out that in some eighteenth-century texts, "the desire that represents sexuality per se, and hence sexual knowledge per se, is a same sex desire. This possibility, however, was repressed with increasing energy, and hence increasing visibility, as the nineteenth-century culture of the individual proceeded to elaborate a version of knowledge/sexuality structured with its pointed cognitive *refusal* of sexuality between women, between men."[37] What I am arguing here is not that there is an eighteenth-century freedom of expression later repressed by Victorian squeamishness at same-sex desire, but that the expression of same-sex desire—in Gray, in other writers of sensibility, in Gothic fiction, in the literature of female friendship—always constitutes desire within a closetlike framework that couches desire itself in terms—melancholy, madness, sensation, platonic love—that culture provides for the purposes of naturalization and accommodation. Even in the eighteenth century, that is, there is no same-sex desire without the public/private structure of the open secret—*the* open secret—that both celebrates the variety of same-sex desire and hides its meaning within the very language with which it is expressed.

One final poem from the summer of 1742 brings Gray's position into clearer focus. As expressive and moving as either the "Sonnet" or the "Ode" is the much less discussed Latin elegy that Gray appended to his "De Principiis Cogitandi," the first book of which was dedicated "AD FAVO-NIUM."[38] The thirty lines of book 2, which I quote in their entirety because I imagine they are unfamiliar to many readers, are as follows:

Hactenus haud segnis Naturae arcana retexi
Musarum interpres, primusque Britanna per arva
Romano liquidum deduxi flumine rivum.
Cum Tu opere in medio, spes tanti et causa laboris,
Linquis, et aeternam fati te condis in umbram!
Vidi egomet duro graviter concussa dolore
Pectora, in alterius non umquam lenta dolorem;
Et languere oculos vidi et pallescere amantem
Vultum, quo numquam Peitas nisi rara, Fidesque,

Altus amor Veri, et purum spirabat Honestum.
Visa tamen tardi demum inclementia morbi
Cessare est, reducemque iterum roseo ore Salutem
Speravi, atque une tecum, delecte Favoni!
Creduolus heu longos, ut quondam, fallere soles:
Heu spes nequicquam dulces, atque irrita vota!
Heu maestos soles, sine te quos dulcere flendo
Per desideria, et questus iam cogor inanes!
At Tu, sancta anima, et nostri non indigna luctus,
Stellanti templo, sincerique aetheris igne,
Unde orta es, fruere; atque oh si secura, nec ultra
Mortalis, notos olim miserata labores
Respectes, tenuesque vacet cognoscere curas;
Humanam si forte alta de sede procellam
Contemplere, metus stimulosque cupidinis acres,
Gaudiaque et gemitus, parvoque in corde tumultum
Irarum ingentem, et saevos sub pectore fluctus:
Respice, et has lacrimas, memori quas ictus amore
Fundo; quod possum, iuxta lugere sepulcrum
Dum iuvat, et mutae vana haec iactare favillae.

(So far had I, interpreter of the Muses, assiduously uncovered the secrets of Nature and first led a lucid stream from the Roman river through British fields. But now you [Tu], the inspiration and cause of so great a task, have departed in the midst of it and have hidden yourself in the eternal shadow of Death! I myself watched your breast cruelly racked by cruel suffering, a breast never slow to respond to another's pain; I watched your eyes grow dull and your loving face grow pale, a face in which only the most exalted affection, and loyalty, and deep love of truth, and unsullied integrity were alive. Still the harshness of your lingering sickness seemed to be abating, and I hoped for the return of Health, with rosy cheeks, and you yourself with it, my dear Favonius! foolishly trusting, alas, that we might while away the long, sunny days as before. Alas, the hopes, vainly sweet, and the futile prayers! Alas, the sunny days, now spent in mourning, which I am forced to pass without you, in weeping because you are not there, and in vain complaints.) [translation continued below]

It would be difficult to imagine a more poignant or a more pointed elegy. The eloquence of Gray's devotion to West—West the physical as well as the spiritual friend—and of his frustration and his desire makes even the "Sonnet" pale by comparison. The poet's desire is realized in this loss and made real in the language that echoes the "vain complaints" of the sonnet. Here, however, the poet more directly embraces his dead friend with the tears of grief and offers them in a gesture of love that is fulfilled in this moment of frustrated desire. "Alas," the term that colors so much of Gray's poetry with regret, here has a particular meaning in the loss of this friend. It is almost as if Gray finds himself in this moment of regret and realizes his own poetic capabilities in this moment of loss. Bentman says that the "picture that emerges of Gray from the letters is of a deeply passionate man who was powerfully constrained by his fear."[39] This is an attractive reading, to be sure, but it seems to me that regret is far more palpable than fear throughout Gray's work. I would argue that Gray eroticizes the regret itself in this poetry of loss, not because he is afraid of expressing his sodomitical desires but because he knows that his love has cultural meaning only in loss.

In the next section he turns to his dead friend, as he does in the sonnet, and admits, as clearly as he does anywhere, the torment of desire, not because West is a man but because he is Other—inaccessible, unrealizable, lost:

> But you, blessed spirit, who do not need my grief, rejoice in the starry circuit of the heavens and the fire of pure ether whence you sprang. But, if, released from cares as you are, and no longer mortal, you should look back with pity on the labors which you yourself once suffered and have the time to acknowledge my trivial anxieties; if, by chance, you should look down from your lofty seat on the storm of human passion, the fears, the fierce promptings of desire, the joys and sorrows and the tumult of rage so huge in my heart, the furious surges of the breast; then look back on these tears, also, which stricken with love, I pour out in memory of you; this is all I can do, while my only wish is to mourn at your tomb and address these empty words to your silent ashes.[40]

The tears that Gray pours out at the tomb of his friend are the tears of sensibility that identify love and loss in modern culture. They are the tears that open the possibility of a sexual identity that emerges from the "soul" (rather than from behavior). The historians of sexuality who place the codification of sexuality in the later nineteenth century ignore this prescient understanding of the relationship between same-sex desire and the culture that produces it. The tears that culture provides as consolation for the loss it demands are the fountain from which sexual identity can later spring. They are the tears of accommodation that culture provides to those who feel.

> O lachrymarum fons, tenero sacros
> Ducentium ortus ex animo; quater
> Felix! in imo qui scatentem
> Pectore te, pia Nympha, sensit!

"Four times happy is he who has felt you, holy Nymph, gushing forth from the depth of his heart": tears, poetry, and desire—for Gray the three are inextricable. Gray does not fear a system of cultural oppression that might expose him because he exposes himself as the melancholy figure of male-male desire. He does not have to create this position for himself, for culture is all too happy to provide it for him. Just as in the late twentieth century gay people have been recognized only in their mourning, so in the eighteenth century male love is recognized only in the tears of sensibility.

"The voice of Nature"

Gray turns these tears toward himself in one of the most celebrated poems in the English language. In the "Elegy Written in a Country Churchyard," Gray's sense of his sexual self shapes the poem and gives it the life that he could only realize by envisioning his own death.[41] If I approach the poem from the perspective of abjection, that is in part because theories of abjection help to make sense of the the unique combination of self-obsession, sex, and death that the "Elegy" articulates. In the "Sonnet," the poet has lost an object in the world but refashions it in his grief into nothing more than a heightened expression of subjectivity. Grief becomes the substitute for the friend and offers protection against the implications of desire. At the same time, however, it commemorates that desire—and perhaps its fulfillment—in conventional imagery that hides its personal intensity. Every line reveals as much as it conceals, and poetry itself, decorous and allusive, becomes the vehicle for private longing. Gray's abjection stems from the failure of the elegy to release him from the privacy of his emotion. For Julia Kristeva,

"There looms, within abjection, one of those violent, dark revolts of being, directed against a threat that seems to emanate from an exorbitant outside or inside, ejected beyond the scope of the possible, the tolerable, the thinkable. It lies there, quite close, but it cannot be assimilated."[42] In his "Elegy Written in a Country Churchyard," Gray acts out such a "revolt of being," easily mistaken for simple melancholy but filled with the sorts of ambiguities and anxieties that Kristeva describes.

Gray begins his "Elegy" with the oddly passive and objectified expression of his own presence in the poem. The "to me" with which the first quatrain ends is reminiscent of the opening of Gray's other poems, such as the "Sonnet," but it also dramatizes a more complicated relation between subjective and objective experience than that found in his earlier poems:

> The curfew tolls the knell of parting day,
> The lowing herd wind slowly o'er the lea,
> The plowman homeward plods his weary way,
> And leaves the world to darkness and to me. (ll. 1–4)

The opening stanza displays none of the inflated diction for which Gray is famous, but instead expresses the scene in simple, neatly parallel subject/predicate statements. The final line, however, insinuates the subject of the poem, the Poet, as indirect object of the sentence, thereby implying the passivity of reflection and the solitude necessary to his ruminations. By refusing to articulate his subjectivity directly, the poet places himself in the scene and stands remote from—beside—himself.[43] The poet must establish his passivity as a way of avoiding the moral implications of self-assertion. But he is also establishing a quality of isolation and anxiety.

As the poem proceeds, this anxiety is given concrete form in the sounds of the night and the graveyard itself, "where heaves the turf in many a mouldering heap" (l. 14). The poet has an even more shadowy, self-effacing presence here, for the reasoned and precise observations of the countryside in the evening and the exceptions to the growing tranquility all ultimately focus on the absent object of the owl's complaint, wandering near her sacred bower and molesting her with his private ruminations. That object is of course the subjective presence that exists everywhere but nowhere (yet) in the poem, the poet himself:

> Now fades the glimmering landscape on the sight,
> And all the air a solemn stillness holds,
> Save where the beetle wheels his droning flight,
> And drowsy tinklings lull the distant folds;
> Save that from yonder ivy-mantled tower
> The moping owl does to the moon complain
> Of such as, wandering near her bower,
> Molest her ancient solitary reign.
> Beneath those rugged elms, that yew-tree's shade,
> Where heaves the turf in many a mouldering heap,
> Each in his narrow cell for ever laid,
> The rude forefathers of the hamlet sleep. (ll. 5–16)

We take it for granted that a mid-century poet should depict himself wandering in a graveyard in the evening and that his stoicism will lead to pointed moralizing rather than to proto-Gothicism. But by confusing the division between subject and object, as he does here, Gray creates a mood different from what we might expect and emphasizes the impossibility of finding the object of his rambles even in these graves. The opening quatrains in fact repress the real desire behind this poem and postpone it in a delusion of identification and loss.

In the three stanzas that follow, the poet depicts what Lonsdale calls "the lives of the humble villagers."[44] It is their deaths, however, that oxymoronically suggest their lives to Gray, just as the neat regularity of the lines poeticizes what could only have been a far from poetic existence in the English countryside. Patricia Meyer Spacks says that "the psychic drama which unfolds through these scenes is surely more important than the scenes themselves."[45] The psychic drama involves creating a world that is unavailable to the poet and then negating it, as he does subtly in the sixth stanza:

> For them no more the blazing hearth shall burn,
> Or busy housewife ply her evening care:
> No children run to lisp their sire's return,
> Or climb his knees the envied kiss to share. (ll. 21–24)

This is not a depiction of experience but a negation of experience. The structure of parallelism heightens the sense that this is a description of what is not. "No . . . or" is the repeated substitution for neither . . . nor, because it qualifies the negativity of the presentation with the openness of possibility. This implicit conflict between affirmation and negation is reflected as well in the terms of the description itself: the very conventional nature of the lines renders them remote from experience. Perhaps the "doubtful" scribbled in Gray's manuscript next to "envied kiss" suggests his own discomfort with the idea as well as the image.[46] Gray narrates a tale the meaning of which lies in its impossibility. It is a narrative of suffering. He dramatizes loss as a way of experiencing the implications of his own abjection imaginatively. Kristeva says that "narrative is, all in all, the most elaborate attempt . . . to situate a speaking being between his desires and their prohibitions, in short, within the Oedipal triangle."[47] Gray enters the eerie geometric form of his unconscious by calling to mind his "rude forefathers" and depicting the scene of familial intimacy—an intimacy that he never knew—and then negating them both, subtly but surely.[48] His desires lead him elsewhere.

The poet hints at the nature of his desire first in admonitory and even accusatory terms. The poem proceeds from "Let not Ambition mock their useful toil / Their homely joys and destiny obscure" (l. 29–30) to "Nor you, ye Proud, impute to these the fault, / If Memory o'er their tomb no trophies raise," (ll. 37–38). Gray's tone shifts from the reflective to the judgmental, in part because he has articulated a familial ideal in which he does not believe, or at least never dramatizes as a possibility for himself. Though "homely joys" are present in the poem, they are present as a result of their inaccessibility, to the dead and to the poet. This section of the poem turns on the aphorism "The paths of glory lead but to the grave" (l. 36), a brutal reminder to those who are tempted to sneer but also a suggestion of the abjection the poet feels and the utter uselessness of the usual patriarchal terms of personal achievement.

The climactic stanza of this group directly articulates the object Death as a competing subject and seems for a moment to illumine the darker purpose of the poem:

Can storied urn or animated bust
Back to its mansion call the fleeting breath?
Can Honour's voice provoke the silent dust,
Or Flattery soothe the dull cold ear of Death? (ll. 41–44)

This subtle personification enables the poet to express his sense of the final-ity of Death against the world of language and seeming. In other contexts Honour could "provoke" or Flattery "soothe," but Gray seems to insist on the inability of the poetic personification of such abstractions to have any power in the real world of emotion and pain. Death, also personified, is not a false but a real subject and its "dull cold ear" is the most distinct physical feature yet observed in the poem. Personification, in other words, insists upon the force of Death to resist and to undermine the world of public value and the semblance of grandeur in favor of its own physical power.

Death has been hovering in the poem as a shadowy Other, but as he attains a physical presence here, it might seem that he is really the lover that the poet has been courting all along. The poet chooses Death as the only expression of a sexuality that terrifies him. The personified figure acts as the perfect agent of repression. Kristeva claims that "A certain sexuality . . . which does not even adorn itself with pleasure but with *sovereignty* and *knowledge*, is the equivalent of disease and death."[49] The "Elegy" begins with such a sexuality of Death. Gray defiles the country graveyard in a flirtation with Death and an attempt to establish his sovereignty and knowledge over it. He makes this choice because the repression of his own sexuality leaves him no other.

Gray expresses his own sexual frustration in terms that are both beautiful and haunting:

> Full many a gem of purest ray serene
> The dark unfathomed caves of ocean bear:
> Full many a flower is born to blush unseen
> And waste its sweetness on the desert air. (ll. 53–56)

We hardly need a Freud to suggest that the "dark unfathomed caves of ocean" suggest Gray's fear of his own sexuality, and the "waste [of] sweetness," echoing as it does Shakespeare's "waste of shame," hints at the death-like masturbatory implications of the poet's lonely stance. In any case, these famous lines surely point to a disturbed and disturbing privacy.

Gray's letter to West (May 27, 1742) offers a helpful gloss to passages such as this:

> Mine, you are to know, is a white Melancholy, or rather Leucocholy for the most part; which though it seldom laughs or dances, nor ever amounts to what one calls Joy or Pleasure, yet it is a good easy sort of

a state, and ça ne laisse que de s'amuser. The only fault of it is insipidity; which is apt now and then to give a sort of Ennui, which makes one form certain little wishes that signify nothing. But there is another sort, black indeed, which I have now and then felt, that has somewhat in it like Tertullian's rule of faith, Credo quia impossibile est; for it believes, nay, is sure of every thing that is unlikely, so it be but frightful; and on the other hand, excludes and shuts its eyes to the most possible hopes, and every thing that is pleasurable; from this the Lord deliver us![50]

Gray examines his own psychology as a way of answering ennui, fear, and desire. He personifies these humors as a way of giving them substance and understanding the most personal traits of his character. In the way Gray objectifies his emotion, he seems afraid to establish a boundary between internal and external, and he lapses into French and Latin as a way of avoiding the power of his own feeling. "Little wishes that signify nothing," "every thing that is unlikely": these phrases ring with the force of repression and the struggle to maintain it.

Gray's abjection has led him to this graveyard self-confrontation as a way of redirecting sexual desire and substituting an object—in this case death— for his own threatening melancholy. Of course, as his letter to West suggests, death is not the real object of Gray's desire, but at least it offers an alternative to his own self-involved sexuality. Death has the virtue as the ultimate Other of being in the grave indistinguishable from self.

Gray is trapped in a kind of a dance with death in the opening of the poem, and its first ending is abjection itself:

> No more with Reason & thyself at strife;
> Give anxious Cares & endless Wishes room
> But thro' the cool sequester'd Vale of Life
> Pursue the silent Tenour of thy Doom. (Eton manuscript)

The poet steps back from the grave with the distance that a moralistic stance allows and steps into "cool sequestered Vale" and "silent" "Doom." It is precisely this stance that the poet learns to move beyond in the course of revising the poem, a process that took several years and that was for Gray a kind of reopening of the issues on which the poem is based.[51]

In the final version, the tension surrounding the figure of Death is given

voice. Gray pulls himself out of his moralizing closet and into confrontation with his own tormented sensibility:

> For who to dumb Forgetfulness a prey,
> This pleasing anxious being e're resigned,
> Left the warm precincts of the cheerful day,
> Nor cast one longing lingering look behind? (ll. 85–88)

This stanza takes us from a flirtation with the "dumb Forgetfulness" of
death, that final repression, to a crucial assertion of Gray's own subjectivity.
"One longing lingering look" challenges the repression that has brought
the poet to the graveyard in the first place and begins to open up the possibility of a more honest recognition of his own desire in more powerful self-
confrontation or even self-acceptance:

> On some fond breast the parting soul relies,
> Some pious drops the closing eye requires;
> Ev'n from the tomb the voice of nature cries,
> Ev'n in our ashes live their wonted fires. (ll. 89–92)

Here at last the real subject of the poem forces itself into view: not death
but the "fond breast" of companionship; not the tomb, but the "voice of
nature"; not the "ashes," but the "fires." Kristeva says that abjection exists
"at the crossroads of phobia, obsession, and perversion" and that language
itself becomes a defense against desire.[52] Gray places himself at this turning
point between the forces of life and death in the poem as a way of confronting his own abjection and opening the language of the poem to the cry
of nature that he earlier silenced.

Gray breaks out of his isolation in a way that hints at the dangers of the
solitary stance that the poem at first celebrates. This process begins first
with that odd shift in person, which creates an alter ego through which the
poet can begin to talk about himself:

> For thee who, mindful of the unhonoured dead,
> Dost in these lines their artless tale relate;
> If chance, by lonely Contemplation led,
> Some kindred spirit shall inquire thy fate,
> Haply some hoary-headed swain may say, (93–97)

If the lonely poem now seems crowded with "spurious" egos, they at least lead the poet through abjection to an attitude of tentative but meaningful self-assertion. Narcissism, in other words, gives way to desire of a different kind.

"Thee" refers of course to the poet himself—an earlier draft reads, suggestively, "And thou, who mindful of the unhonour'd Dead / Dost in these Notes *thy* artless Tale relate" (my italics)—but it also suggests the presence of an idealized Other, a substitute for Death, a friend, perhaps lost in death. At the very least we can say that by addressing himself in terms of second-person intimacy, Gray posits a soulmate who participates in and even in a sense creates his poetry. Lest we think this merely the private experience of imagination, the "kindred spirit" suggests that there is a communion of such souls, bound together in the loneliness of contemplation and drawn to a common fate. At the heart of privacy in the poem is this unnamed other, more than kind but less than kin. A lover. Our model of subjectivity is subtly undermined, if not exploded.

The "hoary-headed swain" multiplies egos further, but this time the device offers an objective rather than a subjective view of the poet:

> Oft have we seen him at the peep of dawn
> Brushing with hasty steps the dews away
> To meet the sun upon the upland lawn.
>
> There at the foot of yonder nodding beech
> That wreathes its old fantastic roots so high,
> His listless length at noontide would he stretch,
> And pore upon the brook that babbles by.
>
> Hard by yon wood, now smiling as in scorn,
> Muttering his wayward fancies he would rove,
> Now drooping, woeful wan, like one forlorn,
> Or crazed with care, or crossed in hopeless love.
>
> One morn I missed him on the customed hill,
> Along the heath and near his favourite tree;
> Another came; nor yet beside the rill,
> Nor up the lawn, nor at the wood was he;
>
> The next with dirges due in sad array

> Slow through the church-way path we saw him borne.
> Approach and read (for thou canst read) the lay,
> Graved on the stone beneath yon aged thorn. (ll. 98–116)

Now we see the poet projected onto the scene of his wanderings, an object with supposed feelings, but feelings we can never really know. Surely Gray chooses this "decorum" in order to veil as much as he reveals.[53] For the "hoary-headed swain" cannot be expected to imagine the real cause of this poet's unhappiness, nor would he dare to speak the name of the "wayward fancies" if he could. The "woeful" poet is lost in the frustration of a fully conscious but unattainable desire. "Love" is "hopeless" because unexpressed or unexpressible. The suffering is more intense than earlier in the poem, but it is also more honest. The fear is perhaps most directly expressed in the poet's own corpse here produced.

The corpse itself carries the poem into a new range of possibility. For, as Kristeva says, "it is the corpse . . . that takes on the abjection of waste. . . . A decaying body, lifeless, completely turned into dejection, blurred between the inanimate and the inorganic, a transitional swarming, inseparable lining of a human nature whose life is undistinguishable from the symbolic — the corpse represents a fundamental pollution."[54] Gray drags his own corpse into the poem and violates this fundamental taboo as a way of liberating himself from the repressed death-in-life that the early sections of the poem express. By seeing himself through death he rejects its power over him. His funeral becomes an odd celebration of life, and his corpse becomes the symbol of his physical desire, "inseparable lining of a human nature," and a sign of his triumph over the forces of death that were threatening to engulf him. Death cannot be proud because the poet finally flaunts the irrepressible desire that a culture's logic about death would repress.

The clearest statement of this "coming out" resides in the epitaph:

> *Here rests his head upon the lap of earth*
> *A youth to fortune and to fame unknown.*
> *Fair Science frowned not at his humble birth,*
> *And Melancholy marked him for her own.*
>
> *Large was his bounty and his soul sincere,*
> *Heaven did a recompense as largely send:*
> *He gave to Misery all he had, a tear,*
> *He gained from Heaven ('twas all he wished) a friend.*

No farther seek his merits to disclose,
Or draw his frailties from their dread abode,
(There they alike in trembling hope repose)
The bosom of his Father and his God. (ll. 117–28)

The poem ends, as Hagstrum so eloquently suggests, in the anxiety of sexual fulfillment and "trembling" desire.[55] Whether the "friend" was West or Walpole, or them both, matters less than the fact that Gray recognizes the solace implicit in his unique wish. He expresses that solace in the "dread abode" with which the poem closes. "The bosom of his Father" both reverses the earlier negation of family and sexualizes the prospect of heavenly life. The abjection of this poem is a kind of death-in-life that threatens literally to bury the ego, but also leads it through the bottom of its corpselike isolation in the merely contemplating self to possible real (and possibly liberating) communion with the other, a "thee" of friendship and emotion. Beyond the power of death and repression, the poet comes alive to the possibility of intimacy in the world. He moves from the ignorance of abjection to at least the beginnings of self-knowledge. That knowledge liberates him to the other roles and other possibilities that are to come.

In memory of Bill Kinnucan

CHAPTER FIVE

Beckford's Pæderasty

What was the exact business, how, when,
& by whom, & with whom discovered?
Who passive & who active?

—Pembroke Papers (1780–1794), ed. Lord Herbert

Beckford is a Professor of Pæderasty.

— *THRALIANA*, ED. KATHERINE C. BALDERSTON

On November 27, 1784, the following notice appeared in the pages of the London *Morning Herald*:

> The rumour concerning a *Grammatical mistake of Mr. B—* and the *Hon. Mr. C—*, in regard to the genders, we hope for the honour of Nature originates in *Calumny!*—For, however depraved the being must be, who can propagate such reports without foundation, we must wish such a being exists, in preference to characters, who, regardless of Divine, Natural and Human Law, sink themselves below the lowest class of brutes in the most *preposterous* rites.[1]

Anyone reading this newspaper report, it seems, would have known that the unnamed gender transgressors were the enormously rich William Beckford and his aristocratic cousin William Courtenay.[2] The occasion for the remarks had come to be known as the Powderham Affair, and private accounts of it had been circulating for some time. Beckford and Courtenay had been caught in compromising circumstances of some kind, and Courtenay's uncle Lord Loughborough, Chief Justice of the Court of

Common Pleas, was determined to ruin Beckford.³ The appearance of this announcement, however, set the scandal on new, openly public terms. These remarks in the *Morning Herald*, which Brian Fothergill suggests were planted by Loughborough, plunged the twenty-five-year-old Beckford into a disgrace that was to haunt him until his death sixty years later. Coming as it does, however, mid-way between the molly-house raids and executions of the 1720s and the Vere Street arrests of 1810, the Beckford scandal exposes an overlooked feature of the history of sexuality and the codification of sexual identities.⁴

This first newspaper account already begins this process. It is surely significant that perceived irregularity in gender roles is labeled a "Grammatical Mistake." Grammar, in this reading, becomes the figure of hegemonic control, and it is control exercised most effectively at the level of language. Alain de Lille's twelfth-century *The Complaint of Nature* had made a similar claim: the "Man [who] is made woman . . . both predicate and subject, he becomes likewise of two declensions, he pushes the laws of grammar too far." Gregory W. Bredbeck claims that "De Lille's readers must 'read' sodomy, and hence sodomy becomes a part of who they are as readers. Obviously *The Complaint of Nature* . . . ascribe[s] a subjective potentiality to the rhetoric of homo-eroticism."⁵ By 1784 the naturalization of grammar is such that a "grammatical mistake" of this kind challenges the "honour of Nature." The passage from the *Morning Herald* also ascribes a subjective potentiality, but it does so by means of an inscription that renders subjectivity itself a grammatical impossibility. The "characters" who would be the subjects of this report, its "beings," are here rendered the object of a dependent prepositional phrase. Grammar works, in other words, to marginalize and control that which it finds threatening. But it needs that threat in order to justify, as it were, its exclusionary system. By inscribing gender as a grammatical system without a subject, moreover, the *Morning Herald* writer suggests ways in which sexuality itself is inscribed. In cultural terms, subjectivity is only possible when a sentence is already passed: this sentence posits a being that could not, should not exist, but that by the very articulation of this "rumour" can and does. Sexual identity, sexuality itself, then, emerges from this cultural attempt to inscribe subjectivity in its own likeness. Beckford's "Grammatical mistake" becomes the sign of sexual difference.

Significantly, the report fails to distinguish between the two "characters" involved. One would imagine that if Beckford alone were the object of the attack, it would emphasize his relation to the much younger William Courtenay (who had reached seventeen by the time of the scandal).[6] If it were not articulated as pæderasty as such, at least some mention of sexual victimization might be expected. But not here: Mr. B. and the Hon. Mr. C. are both involved in "*preposterous* rites": here the language of religion, devotions contrary to nature, gives their activity a status that can render it threatening to social order. For however sunk below the lowest class of brutes, these "*preposterous* rites" threaten, by their inversion of the natural order, the very terms by which a society constructs it own identity. Because "Law" determines what is "Natural," these characters are placed outside of nature. In practical terms, however, nature comes to mean merely polite society. As one writer from Italy asked "Is Beckford at Fonthill, and is he chassé or still received in company?"[7]

A week later, another popular strain is introduced, and the "scene" of transgression is reinterpreted: "If anything could heighten the detestable scene lately acted in *Wiltshire*, by a pair of fashionable *male lovers*, the ocular demonstration of their infamy, to the young and beautiful wife of one of the monsters, must certainly have effected it."[8] The laws of grammar work similarly here: not only are the "lovers" relegated again to a prepositional position, but the scene of their "infamy" is exactly what is not represented. The point of this piece, of course, is to evoke an image of male lovemaking and place it squarely in the public imagination. Margaret Beckford becomes a kind of conduit of voyeuristic pleasure for the reader of the *Morning Herald*, and the "ocular demonstration" that is described invites a range of fantastic recreations of the "detestable scene." More effective, perhaps, than grammar, the visual evocation of the "male lovers" fixes them in all their monstrosity in the imagination of anyone reading this passage. At the same time, however, "a pair of fashionable *male lovers*" is hardly the expression of monstrosity that contemporary accounts of sodomy would lead one to expect. In fact, it articulates the possibility of a male relation in a way that is rare in the eighteenth century, suggesting in its turn of phrase something more like our own configuration of relational possibilities. Of course, it may be possible that the writer, by coining this expression, was attempting to register horror, but what he or she does register is something like difference—the difference that the description of two men as lovers continues to make today.

Beckford met his cousin William Courtenay at Powderham Castle, the home of Beckford's aristocratic Courtenay relatives, when Beckford was on a tour of England in the summer of 1779. He was eighteen years old and Courtenay eleven. His attachment to the boy quickly became an intense romantic obsession that his closest friends seemed to know about and (perhaps) encourage. To Alexander Cozens, for instance, the drawing master who might himself have introduced young Beckford to exoticized desires, Beckford wrote at Christmas 1779 that he has been walking by moonlight: "I was so charmed with the novelty of the prospect that setting the cold at defiance, I walked to and fro on the platform for several minutes, fancying the fictions of romance realized, and almost imagining myself surrounded by some wondrous misty barrier no *prophane* could penetrate. How I wished for my dear Wm. to share with me this imaginary contentment."[9] All the elements of Beckford's sexual sensibility are implied in his few remarks to Cozens: the nervous anxiety, almost irritability, the romantic fictions, the imaginative isolation, the mist, the barrier between life and death, and, of course, William. These elements are so worked and reworked over the next five years—some throughout his entire life—that they begin to have an identificatory quality quite unlike that of any simple report of sodomitical behavior.

Just after Christmas 1779 he writes to Cozens again:

> My cares have been a little while suspended—for I have been listening these several Evenings to plaintive Sicilian Airs. You can hardly believe what a melancholy has of late possessed me. My ideas of Happiness are at length very simple, for they consist alone in a secure retirement with the one I love. . . . Never could I have believed myself so entirely subdued—by whom you solely are acquainted. I wonder at myself every instant and only wish you was here to be surprized at me—One moment I am for flying into . . . the next . . . my Cheeks glow and I determine to remain immured in my Cell. Is it possible that a few Weeks' absence can have produced such effects—can have rendered me so miserable—Am I not the strangest of Beings?[10]

The exuberance of youthful infatuation becomes more like misery when emotion gives way to desire. What seems at first a pose—the Sicilian Airs, the melancholy, the "retirement with the one I love"—becomes an almost hysterical torment of frustrated desire. Beckford uses the vocabulary of disease to emphasize the depth of his overheated emotion. The blood rushes to his cheeks in an anatomical redirection that calls to mind the reactions of "female" sensibility. This sensibility combines with the misery of the monkish "Cell" to color potentially "unnatural" desires with an exotic glow that resists the label of criminality. Beckford celebrates his own misery as a way of validating the feelings he has already been forced to question. In doing so, he attempts to defy the cultural conventions that would turn him against himself. This may be the gloomy sensibility of the exoticized man of feeling, but it begins to suggest the makings of a sexual "identity."

As a result of such careful probings of his own sexual make-up, Beckford became for his generation, in Byron's phrase, the "Apostle of Pæderasty," and his novel, *Vathek* (1786), a primer of man-boy love. Hesther Lynch Piozzi announced that she found Beckford's "favourite propensity" in the "luscious descriptions of [the young boy] Gulchenrouz" when she read *Vathek* a few years after publication. She returned to this idea some years later, when complaining of the "luscious fondness" with which Richard Cumberland describes the *"personal Charms"* of the heroes in his novel *Henry* (1795); "The same is to be observed in Vathek," she says, "but then Beckford is a Professor of Pæderasty."[11] Apostle of Pæderasty and Professor of Pæderasty are close enough—although the difference between a religious and an academic metaphor is hardly negligible; if Mrs. Piozzi's comment rings with the astuteness of a cultural critic, then Byron's shimmers with the excitement of a devotee—to suggest that a sexual role was being established for Beckford. This role seems to approximate our own notion of the pederast. It seems, in other words, that Beckford played a crucial role in the popular evocation of a sexual identity distinct from the various sodomitical labels that were current at the time. Beckford's unique blend of erotic desire and almost sickly sensibility makes pæderasty newly available as an explanatory label for male sexuality. Beckford creates his own sexuality in a series of letters that are astonishing in their directness and devastating in their implications. From this material and from the accounts of his life that were circulated in the popular press and in private accounts of his "scandalous" behavior, I hope to show how a sexual identity is articulated and why the public recognition of this articulation is both swift and unequivocal. For Beckford threatened to expose the very foundations of culture. His pæderasty sings out in a voice that had never been heard before.[12]

The OED defines "pæderasty" as "unnatural connexion with a boy; sodomy," and it defines "pæderast" as "sodomite." The elision between pæderasty and sodomy, which the OED reports and reproduces, is inherent in the translation of the Greek: boy-lover in the original becomes an "unnatural connexion" or even an activity. But unlike "sodomy" and "sodomite," pæderasty and pæderast imply no activity, natural or unnatural. The words speak of love. Boy-love, if you will. And while this love is often erotic and at times explicitly physical, the term *pæderast* is not necessarily associated with behavior. It represents a relation that is nonetheless powerful and, some would argue, pervasive in Western culture. Feminist and cultural critics have argued that pæderasty is the structural basis of Western civilization and that it goes a long way toward explaining the inherent misogyny of our culture.[13] David Halperin has taught us to understand Greek pæderasty, moreover, not as some cozy classical prelude to "domestic partnership" but rather as a carefully hierarchized system of male relations that both regulated desire and determined sexual positioning.[14] When Halperin says, for instance, that in Greek terms there is nothing problematical "about a desire on the part of males to obtain sexual pleasure from contact with males—so long as that desire respects the proper phallocentric protocols (which . . . identify 'masculinity' with an insertive sexual role)," the distance from late twentieth-century sexual assumptions is clear. There is little question of seeing classical pæderasty as anything even approximating our own notions of mutual, same-sex desire.

Greek love, however, has often been idealized or sentimentalized, and a sentimental reading of the Greeks was implicit in the first articulations of sexual liberation—particularly for male homosexuals—in the late nineteenth century.[15] This emotional understanding of pæderastic love was to a certain extent implicit in the Greek original: platonic love itself involves the idealization that leads to an extravagantly poetic expression of the beauties of the object of desire, the boy, to the extent that the boy himself becomes lost in the effusion of language articulating his attractions.[16] Alice Kuzniar notes that in eighteenth-century Germany, where Wincklemann's influence was of course most profound, "it is difficult to read mention of same-sex Greek friendship without noticing the homoeroticism that infuses them." She goes on to articulate "the possibility of homoeroticism grounding the concept of the beautiful."[17] During the later eighteenth century love and beauty both were made answerable to a Greek ideal, and as Kuzniar suggests, in Germany at least, that ideal was understood as homoerotic.

If this emotional pæderasty existed in early modern England, as a rich range of sources suggest that it did, then by the time of the Restoration, the tendency—at least in aristocratic circles—was either to condemn it as sodomitical or condone it as no different structurally from other exercises of male privilege, or both.[18] The male libertine, for whom a boy could serve as a sexual partner as readily as a woman, offers a useful example of how this system of simultaneous celebration and censure could work. As I have already argued, John Wilmot, Earl of Rochester, has helpfully memorialized this possibility in a number of poems.[19] Few would see libertine posturing as a source for "homosexual" or even homoerotic behavior.[20] By recalling the following few lines from "The Disabled *Debauchee*," in which an aging rake, in the midst of recounting tales of past conquest, gives in to a moment of nostalgia, the student of sexuality can see more then simple "homosexual" desire: "Nor shall our *Love-fits Cloris* be forgot, / When the well-look'd *Link-Boy*, strove t'enjoy,/And the best Kiss, was the deciding *Lot*, / Whether the *Boy* fuck'd you, or I the *Boy*" (37–40).[21] I quote this passage again in order to emphasize the way the "boy" functions in Rochester's fantasy. Again, the power dynamic seems what is most important, and we would not want to make any claims about Rochester's "sexuality" on the basis of this kind of remark. And just as various "cunts" in Rochester's poetry are not clearly defined by gender, so "*Boy*" here is not clearly defined by age. "*Boy*" defines social and sexual position more than it represents a sign of cross-generational desire. But surely that is not surprising when every sexual relation, as these poems suggest, is so rigidly hierarchical as to insist on power relations before any kind of desire can be articulated.[22] This is not even the kind of homosocial bonding that Eve Sedgwick describes so effectively in *Between Men*.[23] This is a sexuality of every "Man" for himself, a libertinism, as Harold Weber argues, that observes "a strict erotic demarcation between the male object of desire and the desiring male subject."[24]

Pæderasty, then, is not a pretty picture, either in classical Greece or in eighteenth-century England.[25] Throughout the eighteenth century, pæderasty often seems interchangeable with sodomy, even if the former retains its association with boys. It is less common than sodomy throughout the century, however, and it is not registered in the public imagination as a capital offense, as sodomy is. At times, though, it retains its original meaning, as in Swift's use of the term in *A Tale of a Tub* (1704) and specific references to the ancient world in David Hume and Edward Gibbon.[26]

Whenever the word is used, it is either associated automatically with master-pupil relations in school (as Swift's use suggests) or as a slightly fancier way of talking about the act of sodomy. What seems clear, however, is that throughout the eighteenth century there was no cult of pæderasty, either in the popular imagination or in fact, as distinct from the sodomitical subcultures that were regularly harassed and persecuted.

The case of William Beckford, however, suggests the ways in which the concept of sexuality was changing in the later eighteenth century. The Beckford scandal not only resulted in de facto exile and lifelong ostracism for the talented writer and musician, it also signalled a new and different understanding of male-male desire. For all the harm that came to Beckford and his paramour William Courtenay, I would claim that we can discover in this case—in Beckford's writing, in the press, and in the popular response to his situation—the beginnings of a particular kind of male homosexual sensibility. I do not mean that Beckford and Courtenay understood themselves in any way out of keeping with the grotesque way their culture saw them. I do think, however, that Beckford articulated his feelings for Courtenay in such a way that he opened a space, as it were, in which a man could identify his feelings for another male in terms that suggest the recognition of a sexual identity. The particular combination of intelligence, self-indulgence, narcissism, sensibility, and descriptive power that were Beckford's give his pæderasty a special place in the history of sexualities.

By the time of his twenty-first birthday, in 1781, Beckford had had various emotional attachments with sensitive women within his larger family circle and with adolescent or preadolescent boys both in his family and without. The length he goes to express the emotional intensity of all these affairs suggests that he is making up for their lack of actual physical involvement. What is particularly striking, even at this early stage, is the degree to which his female lovers become a part of his pæderastic enterprise. Again and again throughout these early affairs, Beckford uses a woman to bring him closer to the boy he loves. In the following letters, Charlotte Courtenay, Courtenay's aunt; Louisa, the wife of his cousin Peter Beckford; and the Contessa Orsini-Rosenberg each fill this role. Other women seem to have been somehow entangled in his love as well. The impression is one of an emotional bond that included acceptance of his "strange wayward passion."[27] Beckford seems to have needed a female friend to devote herself to him at the same time that she made herself an intermediary with the boy. As Fothergill says about the situation at Powderham, where Charlotte Courtenay was clearly devoted to him and where Courtenay was quickly capturing his heart: "to be in love with the nephew and not to be unaware of the admiration of the aunt was a situation very much to Beckford's taste."[28] What these letters demonstrate is that this was more than an arrangement of practical or emotional convenience for Beckford. The female figure, like Halperin's Diotoma, is necessary to the male-male erotic attachment: she allows it, she encourages it, she creates a space through which the man can reach out to the boy.

For example, Beckford writes to Courtenay's Aunt Charlotte, later to become the wife of his tormentor, Lord Loughborough, asking her to intercede with the boy, who has not responded to his letters:

> Surely he [Courtenay] will never find any other Being so formed by nature for his companion as myself. Of all the human creatures male or female with which I have been acquainted in various countries and at different periods he is the only one that seems to have been cast in my mold.
>
> When I first began to know him the pleasing delusion would often suggest itself of our having been friends in some other existence. You know he was never so happy as when reclined by my side listening to my wild musick or the strange stories which sprang up in my fancy for his amusement. Those were the most delightful hours of my existence.[29]

This letter goes on to tell of shared musical moments and of a friendship on which he depends for life itself. Beckford uses a vocabulary understood as erotic in the eighteenth century: "wild music" and "strange stories" could hardly be considered innocent, nor would the image of the younger and older boy "reclined" together be anything but provocative. Fothergill calls these comments "reckless," but they can only be understood as reckless if Beckford did not mean them actively to imply an intimacy outside of the bounds of social respectability. But he could hardly mean anything else: "How often has my sleep been disturbed by his imaginary cries, how frequently have I seen him approach me, pale and trembling as I lay dozing at Caserta lulled by my dear Lady Hamilton's musick and bathed in tears. . . . If anything could reconcile me to death it twould be the promise of mingling our last breaths together and sharing the same grave."[30] Far from hiding his feelings, or exposing them unwittingly, Beckford seems to threaten the boy's aunt with his own increasingly urgent desire. That he writes this way to a woman who has exposed her own deep feelings for him is more than reckless: it seems on the one hand an elaborate courtship ritual to which all his women friends have been subjected; and it seems on the other an excuse for spelling out the details of his attachment to the boy in heightened emotional detail. The presence of the woman, in other words, allows Beckford to write out his passion in terms that defy convention and create a new vocabulary for male-male desire at the same time that they mimic conventional sexual transgression. Beckford needs to write about his love because it has been silenced elsewhere, everywhere. Beckford takes the crime not to be mentioned among Christians and gives it all the emotional superstructure of "romantic friendship"; in doing so he liberates himself, as it were, from the silences that surround him.[31]

At the same time, even at this early stage, his "romantic friendship" seems to have taken on a quality that embodies the threat of social opprobrium within it. For all the poetic liberation it embodies, internalized self-hatred seems increasingly to haunt Beckford's pæderasty. Beckford's ever-more perfumed sensibility begins to seem lethal: desire implies death, brings the threat of death, becomes almost a desire for death—as Beckford's culture had taught him all too well. I resist the obvious implication of a Freudian "death-instinct," here and later, not because I do not see such a function in representations of desire in the eighteenth century but because Beckford's articulation of the attractions of death is never less than "conscious."

In a letter to the Contessa d'Orsini-Rosenberg, the wealthy widow who befriended him in Venice and was witness to his emotional attachments to various young men, Beckford writes out the details of his love for Courtenay in a way that confirms the physical expression of their love at the same time that it dramatizes the specific dimensions of his fear:[32]

From the theater, I take him to my bed. Nature, Virtue, Glory all *disappear*—entirely lost, confused, destroyed. O, heavens, that I could die in these kisses and plunge my soul with his into the happiness or the pain which must never end. Must I live in fear of a moment which must separate us again. Do not be surprised if I desire death with eagerness. Hurry, compose some sweet potion which will put all three of us to sleep, which will close our eyes without anguish, which will steal our souls away and deliver them imperceptively to the flowered fields of some other existence. . . .

Surely there is no hell for me in the other world because I am damned on earth. Do you know of a state more frightening than this which I suffer — spied upon by a thousand Arguses without hearts and without ears, constrained to abandon the unique hope that reconciles me to life, menaced at each instant, accused of the ruin of a being I adore in whom all human affections are concentrated to a point. Such is my present situation, such are the Demons that Destiny has set on my trail.[33]

Beckford, at twenty-two, has effected a link between sensibility and erotic activity that will not be fully realized until the end of the nineteenth century. To say that he is ahead of his time is only to confess that we have not understood the implications of his love for Courtenay. Pæderastic love is not idealized here. Happiness and pain are interchangeable partly because Beckford only finds happiness in pain and partly because he knows that his love brings with it the social condemnation he fears. He asks for death both as a way of preserving their moment of happiness and as a way of escaping the torment of a world that persecutes what it does not understand. At the same time he seems to want to disembody his affection and translate it into a sensuously spiritual realm. The "other existence" that he desires is as much an escape from life, from the implications of the physical, as it is a life away from the spying Arguses. It almost seems as if it would be an escape into life, into a life in which their love would be possible precisely because it would be an impossibility. If this sounds paradoxical, it is no more so than Beckford's desire itself. The "unique hope" that "reconciles [him] to life" is the hope that Courtenay will offer him a way out of this dilemma; but of course that is precisely what Courtenay can never do. That Beckford could imagine that Courtenay could be anything but a victim, either of Beckford or of his society, is a measure of his delusion. Beckford lives in his emotion, but at the same time that emotion embodies the fear of desire, the "Demons" that come to torment him from within as well as without. The sympathetic Contessa can compose the potion that will effect this transformation because she can sympathize, she can understand, she can give their love a place that exists outside of time and consequently outside of desire as well as fate. It is a place, of course, that Beckford never found.

A little over a year later he writes to Courtenay in terms that dramatize this complicated emotional stance even more vividly. The boy had scribbled a postscript to a letter written by the ever-devoted Louisa, his cousin Peter's wife, who was by now almost desperate in her love for Beckford. I quote this letter at length because it seems to me to tell the whole story of Beckford's pæderasty:

> I read your letter with a beating heart, my dearest Willy, and kissed it a thousand times. It is needless for me to repeat that I am miserable without you. You know I can scarcely be said to live in your absence. No words can express my feelings when I saw the Afft. lines you wrote in our dear Louisa's letter. At this moment I am ready to cry with joy. Do not forget me my own William. Do not forget the happy hours we have passed together. Your poor Mother loved you not better than I do. At any time I would sacrifice every drop of blood in my veins to do you good, or spare you a moment's misery. I shall never enjoy peace again till I know whether I am to be with you when I return. I am certain your Father is set against us, and will do all in his power as well as your cruel Aunt to keep us asunder; but it will be your fault, if you intirely abandon me. What have we done, Wm., to be treated with such severity! I often dream after a solitary ramble on the dreary plains near Rome, that I am sitting with you in a meadow at Ford on a summer's evening, my arm thrown round your neck. I seem to see the wilds beyond the House and the Cattle winding slowly among them. I even fancy, I hear your voice singing one of the tunes I composed when I was in Devonshire. Whilst thus engaged and giving way to a languid melancholy tenderness, two snakes start from the hedge and twine round us. I see your face turn pale and your limbs tremble. I seem to press you closely in my arms. We both feel the cold writhing of the snakes in our bosoms, both join our lips for the last time and both expire. . . . Louisa can tell you that this is not the first time such horrid dreams have haunted me. If I might interpret my vision, — and — are the Snakes, who under the appearance of prudence and affection would creep into our bosoms and sting our vitals. Why cannot we be friends in peace? Is there any crime in loving each other as

we do? You will hardly be able to read this letter: it is blotted with my tears. My William, my own dear Friend, write to me for God's sake: put all your confidence in Louisa who loves us both.[34]

This letter exposes the nature of this love affair in dazzling detail. At first, the account heightens the difference that I have articulated between "sodomy" and Beckford's male version of "romantic friendship." Moving as it does from the excitement of anticipation ("a beating heart") through misery and lifelessness, to exuberant feelings and tears of joy—all in the first few sentences—the letter comes alive with a high-pitched emotionalism that begins to suggest what Beckford's "pæderasty" has come to mean. A simple "do not forget me" becomes "your poor mother loved you not better than I do"; Courtenay's mother (recently deceased) was Beckford's friend, of course, and Beckford seems quite ready to invoke the female component of his affection even if the female, as in this case, is deceased. A Freudian reading of this attempt to express love for a boy by means of an appeal to his dead mother might suggest that Beckford was rewriting Courtenay's family romance with himself in the maternal position—a perfectly reasonable interpretation if Beckford's intention was to construct a subjectivity receptive to his "maternal" love. But Beckford also knows that a mother's love can be as brutalizing and devastating as any antagonistic force—his own mother had hardly begun her openly antagonistic campaign against him, nor had her violent affection for her son brought him anything but heartache—and he may have meant the maternal analogy as a threat. Both are implicit in his ready transition from mother to martyr, and his perfunctory willingness to "sacrifice every drop of blood" stops just short of making himself the victim of Courtenay's innocence.

Once Beckford mentions the boy's father, however, undisguised recrimination and threat follow fast upon one another, and the letter quickly turns from a love letter to a death threat. The love itself implies this hideous denouement, the letter suggests, and the boy is made to seem responsible for whatever effect paternal disapproval will finally have—"it will be your fault if you intirely abandon me"—and his pathetic "What have we done"—as if the twelve year-old could answer that question better than he—smacks either of total innocence or total disingenuousness. What begins then as the tale of music on a summer's evening and is so calculatingly disfigured as a hideous nightmare suggests not just the threat that

Beckford is sending to his young cousin but also his own deepest sense of what their affection means. The boys embrace as they are "giving way to a languid melancholy tenderness" only to find that they feel "the cold writhing of the Snakes in our bosoms." Of course, the snakes represent Courtenay's father and his aunt, but they also represent the destructive power of desire to corrupt the pure love that Beckford constantly tries to articulate when talking to the boy. It is as if he is saying that the destruction of their love is present in its very constitution; that he cannot put his arm around the boy without the snakes intruding, winding in their entrails, and finally destroying them. Beckford seems unclear as to whether it is the world outside or the world within that is most destructive.

"Why cannot we be friends in peace? Is there any crime in loving each other as we do?" The answer to Beckford's question is of course both yes and no. There is no crime in their love, or in any other that is as deeply mutual as this seems to have been. But it is a crime to defy cultural dictates in this way, as Beckford knows. By loving the boy as he does, Beckford condemns them both to a life of ignominy and shame. What Beckford has done, however, is subtly to have leveled the criminal accusation at the boy who returns his love. Courtenay is blamed here as blatantly as he will be later on. For after all, Beckford seems to say, it is the boy who causes the desire that threatens to destroy them both. At Powderham that threat was fulfilled.[35]

When the scandal first broke, Beckford thought of fleeing, but if he did start to leave the country he got no farther than Dover. He sat out the vilification of his name at home in Fonthill. That is what makes the following notice so surprising.

> Mr. — of —, &c. &C. is certainly gone post haste to *Italy!*
> Master —, the eldest, indeed the only son of Lord —, has left Westminster School, and accompanies Mr. —!
> Dr. M— D— was the gentleman who was unlucky enough to detect the late nasty flagitious business.
> Florence is the place of destination fixed on for the eccentric travellers.[36]

The hints at actual scandal are more suggestive here, and the tone of public outrage has achieved something of its vocabulary of exclusion: the terms, that is, that will keep Beckford out of polite society for sixty years.

That such a scandal would place Beckford and Courtenay in Italy is of course no surprise in the eighteenth century. Italy had already been called the *"Mother* and *Nurse* of *Sodomy"* (in *Satan's Harvest Home*) and even Beckford's friend, Sir William Hamilton, received from his nephew the following account of what had happened at Fonthill: "his promised honours will be withheld; he probably will be obliged to vacate his seat, and retire to Italy to make up the loss which Italy has sustained by Lord Tilney's death, unless he aspires to the office of G. Chamberlain to the K[ing] of P[russia]."[37] Both accounts assume that Beckford has fled, or that he has been sent away ("the destination fixed on for," etc.), and that there are witnesses to a "late nasty flagitious business." Neither assumption is correct, but each remains useful in the years to come. The term *eccentric travellers*, however, hints again at a space—however distant from the center—for two such men to occupy. Of course it is a euphemism, but is the very choice that suggests a kind of public recognition even in public censure.[38]

In the "episodes" of *Vathek*, which were never published in his lifetime, Beckford articulates a tale of pæderasty that is both elegant in its expression and chilling in its implication. In "The Story of Prince Alasi and the Princess Firouzkah," as Brian Fothergill notes, Beckford reworks his portrayal of innocent youth.[39] In this story a young boy, Firouz, becomes the obsession of Prince Alasi and leads him into a nefarious world of desire and recrimination. Notwithstanding an opportune change in the boy's gender—Firouz reveals himself later at the princess Firouzkah—Beckford's issues are not far from the surface. Fothergill makes an almost too easy connection between Firouz and Courtenay, but it seems fair to say that in the character of Firouz Beckford was looking for ways to explain the failure of his own pæderastic attachments.[40] When Firouz first appears Alasi says: "At last . . . Heaven has hearkened to my dearest wish. It has sent me the true heart's-friend I should never have found in my court; it has sent him to me adorned with all the charms of innocence—charms that will be followed, at a maturer age, by those good qualities that make of friendship man's highest blessing." This is surely an articulation of a pæderastic fantasy, the fantasy that would link desirability with inner worth. But "The Story of Prince Alasi and the Princess Firouzkah" delineates almost precisely the reverse. The more the prince feels desire for his young protégé, the more corrupt he becomes. Alasi's "innocence" is only feigned, and his influence

proves to be corrupt and corrupting. Firouz's last act of villainy is his reve-
lation of himself as a woman: no treachery in the story seems greater than
this. "What irresistible power compels me to love you," Alasi asks the boy
Firouz.[41]

This articulation of the regret inherent to pæderastic desire is as
poignant at anything in Beckford. The horror implicit in the desire for
innocence lies not in the threat that it will be fulfilled but in the realization
that it never can be. Beckford's languid refusal to do much more than look
onto a world of desire from which he is excluded, however seriously he
marks himself as a "sodomite" in later life, must be understood in this ele-
gaic account of the failure of pæderasty and the impossibility of innocent
sexual awareness.[42]

Compulsive love of a boy inherently wicked is a not quite fitting epitaph
to the affair with William Courtenay. Nor was Beckford's love of Courtenay
as beneficent as that expressed in this moral tale. Still, the tale is suggestive.
The ideal transition from love-object to friend that is celebrated in this passage eluded Beckford.[43] Firouz's ability to change gender suggests how little control one's love can ever have over another. The search for a "true
heart's-friend" may never be more than illusory. Beckford found in his own
sexuality a quality that he did not understand, that he did not trust, and that
he knew would destroy him. But he also knew that this was who he was. He
grappled throughout his life with a sexual instinct that made him a criminal in his own desire. By acknowledging it in his writing, however, he gives
it an identity, a sexual identity, which defies "grammatical" convention.
With Beckford, the pæderast becomes a part of speech.

CHAPTER SIX

Walpole's Secrets

*P*rince Volscius' boots were made of love-leather, and honour-leather, instead of honour some people's are made of friendship. (To George Montague, March 20, 1737)[1]

No writer is more elusive than Horace Walpole. The publication of forty-eight volumes of his correspondence (1937–1983) has offered a rich commentary on life in the second half of the eighteenth century. Walpole and his correspondents elaborate delightfully on questions of parliamentary politics, court intrigues, travel, European affairs, colonialism, the Gothic revival in art and architecture, auctions and masquerades, Ranelagh and other public entertainments, the opera, eighteenth-century medicine, and a carefully calculated version of private experience. Biographers have rather little to tell beyond the epistolary life that Walpole himself constructed. As a result it often seems that some particularly lurid truth is hidden beneath the surface. While one early reviewer, William Hazlitt, dismisses the letters as "gay and graceful" ("they indicate no peculiar originality of mind, or depth of thought, and are continually at variance with good taste and right feeling"), Thomas Babington Macaulay, writing some years after Hazlitt, gives this fluffiness a darker coloring that borders on the putrescent and disgusting ("as the *pâté-de-foie-gras* owes its excellence to the diseases of the wretched animal which furnishes it, and would be good for nothing if it were not made of livers preternaturally swollen, so none but an unhealthy and disorganized mind could have produced such literary luxuries as the works of Walpole").[2] This impression of a diseased dilettante, trapped in the world of luxurious overeating, also manages to suggest a kind of transgression, either Hazlitt's errors of taste and emotion or Macaulay's more serious "preternatural" swelling, and "unhealthy" mind lurking beneath the fashionable exterior. This kind of response is not unusual among readers of Walpole. Often his letters are diagnosed with an intensity that belies their glib exterior.

Readers such as Lytton Strachey complained at the bowdlerization of early editions of the Walpole letters and assumed that when an unexpurgated edition appeared various nagging questions would be answered.[3] But with later, more complete editions, the secrets recede even further. Biographers speak with authority about all that is not there. If the question turns to sex, as in Walpole's case it almost inevitably does, the answer is usually equivocal: Walpole was not a homosexual, W. S. Lewis repeatedly assures us, even if many of his letters to his friends read like love letters: "a handful of letters written in extravagant high spirits in the manner of the time are not proof [of homosexuality]"; and Ketton-Cremer, a sympathetic biographer of both Gray and Walpole, comes down in favor of a kind of gentlemanly asexuality, arguing, for instance, that the dysfunctional families that appear everywhere in Walpole's fiction and drama have little or nothing to do with his remarkable family life.[4] Even more recent critics, myself included, who think that they do see a certain figure in Walpole's carpet, are often trapped in the same quest for Walpole's "sexuality," as if it were tucked in the corner of one of his letters with all the clarity of a late-twentieth-century "coming out" speech.

Recent biographers seem to have a stake in "outing" Walpole. Walpole the homosexual makes more sense to late-twentieth-century readers than Walpole the asexual does, and even biographers who find the subject distasteful feel compelled to discuss it. What one writer calls the "subtleties of homosexual attitudes in the eighteenth century" are beyond the scope of most of these studies, and as I will demonstrate, any attempt to narrate Walpole's "homosexuality" (as if it were a feature of his bitchiness) are fraught with difficulty.[5]

'Twould have been a great satisfaction to me to have kept you longer here; My dear Lord, wherever I <am> you will always command my affections; I did not love you without thinking; and not believing you will alter, I never shall. (To the Earl of Lincoln, December 27, 1740)[6]

Perhaps all of us involved in trying to answer the question of Walpole's sexuality are asking the wrong question entirely. As I have argued throughout this study, the question of sexuality itself is a vexed one for scholars of the period. "Sodomy" and accounts of sodomitical assault have proved a crude measure of same-sex desire in the period, and both libertine and molly-house models have little to do with emotional and physical relations among men of various geographical or social backgrounds. They have least to do, perhaps, with men of feeling, if only because any expression of desire among such gentle men is at the very least deeply conflicted. In any case, same-sex desire is rarely spoken of in exclusionary terms at this time, and even when it is used to isolate individuals, it is not understood to preclude relations of a more socially orthodox kind (as the Beckford case exemplifies so forcefully). In fact, I would go so far as to claim that the homo/hetero binary is meaningless in the eighteenth century, even if the cultural advantages of sexual discriminations were just beginning to be understood. In addition, attempts to establish sexual identity itself, which was codified in the later nineteenth century and reached its political ascendancy in the 1970s, obscure more than they reveal when talking about a figure such as Walpole. Not only do his "extravagant" expressions of devotion defy attempts to uncover sodomitical practices, but his sensibility seems so utterly eroticized as to make distinctions between what is and what is not sexual almost beside the point. Horace Walpole may not hide his love for his friends, but he creates such a mutually conspiratorial mood that often it feels as if he is hiding something. He does not brood over a secret self that he dare not expose to public scrutiny, yet he creates the impression of secrecy precisely where an erotic self might be. Walpole expresses desire in so direct and unselfconscious a way that we might at first be led to believe he cannot mean what he says. But what better technique for secrecy is really available to someone like Walpole?

My dear Lord, I have read over ten times your history of Madame de Matignon's supper; you can't think how it diverted me; but I cannot find words to answer the kind things you say to me in another part of your letter. I only hope that you know how sincerely and how very much I love you and consequently how happy your goodness makes me; indeed, my Lord, it does— excessively! (To the Earl of Lincoln, October 13, 1741)[7]

The Walpole that emerges in his letters is constructed so as to exploit the assumption that there must be something beneath the surface. Twentieth-century critics are not the first to question Walpole's various male relations, nor indeed did they first suggest that in Walpole's publications there was more than met the eye. Walpole's own contemporaries raised questions about his character from time to time, and in the 1760s these muted observations became quite open and aggressive.[8] In 1764 Walpole's cousin Henry Seymour Conway was dismissed from Lord Grenville's Whig ministry as a result of a dispute in which he and Walpole were both involved.[9] Walpole's public defense of his cousin, his *Counter-Address*, raised eyebrows throughout London, and in a direct attack on Horace's masculinity, William Guthrie wrote a *Reply to the Counter-Address*, in which he notes:

> How pathetically he swells on the ingenuous modesty of the general, on his extraordinary humility, on the twenty-seven years that he served, the six regular battles he was engaged in, beside the many bye battles, or smaller actions, the heroes under whom he was formed, and the decorum which has graced every period in his fortune, if I did not recollect the unhappy situation of my Author, *C'est une affaire du coeur:* 'Tis his first love who has been so barbarously used.[10]

This discussion of the amorous features of Walpole's writing about Conway, as arch and unpleasant as it might seem, illustrates the desire for some lurid hidden truth. A French expression here helps to code Walpole's love for his cousin as erotic love. "The unhappy situation of my Author" can only refer to his gender, and Guthrie gloats with the possibility that same-sex love is the lurid secret here.

Throughout his life, however, Walpole wrote to his cousin with open expressions of love, both unselfconscious and extravagant. Even when publicly attacked in the manner just quoted, he wrote touchingly of the feelings of his "unalterable" friendship:

> I send you the reply to the Counter-Address; it is the lowest of all Grub Street, and I hear it treated so. They have nothing better to say, than that I am in love with you, and have been so these twenty years, and am no giant. I am a very constant old swain: they might have made the years above thirty; it is so long I have had the same unal-

terable friendship for you, independent of being near relations and bred up together.[11]

Walpole, who must have been hurt by the attacks on his person as well as his attachment to his cousin, laughs off the accusation by intensifying it, and he articulates the love that is a constant theme in this particular correspondence. He talks so much about this love, in fact, that no one can imagine it is anything but gentlemanly platonics. Ketton-Cremer says, for instance, that Walpole was "strongly attached" to Conway, "toward whom he felt a more consistent and lasting devotion than he was able to extend to any other person."[12] And for W. S. Lewis, this relationship is little more than a "fraternal friendship."[13] But I would argue that in letters such as this, Horace "wears the mask of truth itself."[14] The number of times that he offered Conway his entire fortune, the number of times that he interceded on his behalf, even his bitter anger at Conway's mistreatment of him, all these repeated articulations of a very special friendship begin to suggest more than simple fraternal feeling.[15] In a letter to George Montague, Walpole says that "Nature always designed [Harry Conway] for a hero of romance" (July 2, 1747).[16] Walpole's hero steps out of the fraternal and into a world of erotic intensity in these passages; Walpole does not hide his love, he celebrates it with an almost childlike wonder.

At times, Walpole protests that his cousin has never really understood his feelings and that his friendship was nothing more than an "entire friendship":

> I do not know that you feel [he says in 1781] the entire friendship I have for you; nor should I love you so well if I was not persuaded of it. There never was a grain of anything romantic in my friendship for you. We loved one another from children, and as so near relations; but my friendship grew up with your virtues, which I admired though I did not imitate.[17]

This studied articulation of a "never . . . romantic" friendship seems oddly enough structured to suggest the very thing it denies. After all, the logic of the passage suggests that the two were not involved in a romantic friendship but rather were in love. At other times, Horry's letters to Harry (their epistolary nick-names) seem however to challenge explanation and to suggest that what these two men share is a measure of intimacy that defies inter-pretation:

> I am sensible how very seldom I have written to you—but you have been few moments out of my thoughts. What *they* have been, you who know me so intimately may well guess, and why they do not pass my lips. Sense, experience, circumstances, can teach one to com-mand one's self outwardly, but do not divest a most friendly heart of its feelings. I believe the state of my mind has contributed to bring on a very weak and decaying body my present disorders.[18]

The context of this letter is variously explained. He is suffering from ill-health this summer, and the fuller description of this illness in a letter to Mason, to which Walpole's editor directs the reader in a note, sounds a note of undisguised misery.[19] Walpole adds in his letter to Conway that "You are more obliged to me for all I do not say, than for whatever eloquence itself could pen."

It seems strange to me that Walpole should express himself in this way, whatever his motivation at this time. He speaks in this letter to Conway about a conflict between outward show and inner feelings, and he articulates a the-ory of self-presentation that his journalistic contemporaries might welcome. "Sense, experience, circumstances, can teach one to command one's self out-wardly, but do not divest a most friendly heart of its feelings": Walpole seems to invoke secrecy here in an attempt to give his simple feelings the mystery that culture demands. Sensibility has articulated a theory of inner truth, and Walpole invokes it here as a way of creating the mystery of privacy. But the truth that he purports to hide is really culture's desire for a secret truth. Walpole in fact hides nothing: he refuses the dichotomy that "mask" and "truth" imply, just as his love for Conway, which is neither "friendship" nor "sodomy," defies our own homosexual/heterosexual binary.[20]

I know not how to express my joy for your uncle's success, or how to distinguish it from the general congratulations you will receive: but if you have always found my love the same, if you always knew me as glad of your good fortune when we had the Treasury, as I am now you have it, I hope you will think my friendship attached to you, not to that office. (To the Earl of Lincoln, August 23, 1743)[21]

In reading love back into the eighteenth century, critics have been guilty of a kind of cultural determinism: if the emotion is expressed across genders, an element of sexual desire is never absent, no matter how defiantly a man of feeling, say, might protest; if on the other hand, two women or two men express love for one another in terms that could be interpreted as sexual, they never are. I have written about female romantic friendship in another context, and it is possible to argue that female love works in subversive ways throughout the century.[22] What I want to consider in this chapter, however, is how male romantic friendship works at this time. What are twentieth-century readers to do with powerful expressions of love like those that appear everywhere in the writing of Horace Walpole?

As traditional a critic as C. S. Lewis reminds us that the cross-gendered affection known as courtly love did not always hold the default position in culture that it has since the English Renaissance. In *The Allegory of Love* he points out that in *The Song of Roland*, "[t]he figure of the betrothed is shadowy compared with that of the friend. . . . The deepest worldly emotion in this period is the love of man for man, the mutual love of warriors who die together fighting against odds, and the affection between vassal and lord." Lewis goes on to explain that "these male affections . . . were themselves lover-like in their intensity, their willful exclusion of other values, and their uncertainty; they provided an exercise of the spirit not wholly unlike that which later ages have found in 'love.' "[23] Lewis adds the caveat that these affections are "wholly free from the taint that hangs about 'friendship' in the ancient world," but he has already said enough to make this remark superfluous. Love between men is not foreign to Western culture, then, it exists at its very foundation. And if it required courtly love to disguise these deeper affections and cause them to be relegated to the puzzling homosocial configuration, that is only because an increasingly bourgeois culture could think of nothing more to do with male affection than to transform it into rivalry.

Throughout this study, I argue that particular men of feeling, such as Gray and West and Walpole, attempted to reimagine the emotional valence of male friendship and male rivalry and to reconceive male relations as loving. In the cases I discuss, sexual desire forms a part of that love and determines its cultural position. For me, desire and affection mean more in this context than any "proof" of particular behavior would. I would claim further that in the affection of the man of feeling, in his very sensibility, we can find a source for a sexual identity that has less to do with the libertine contempt for sexual object choice than it does with affectionate desire between men. These relations can be found in the molly houses, to be sure, and at times in the parks or the streets of eighteenth-century London, but what an educated man of feeling was able to do with his class and gender privilege was to articulate his desire in terms that reconfigured male-male affection as romantic love.

Alan Bray argues that this form of male intimacy—eroticized friendship that functions to maintain legal authority and hegemonic control—is impossible to distinguish from intimacies that are labeled sodomitical throughout the early modern period. As I have noted, Jonathan Goldberg says that "friendship and sodomy are always in danger of (mis)recognition since what both depend upon physically—sexually—cannot be distinguished."[24] Friendship and sodomy might be very different, that is, but they often seem the same. But does the difference really lie in some form of behavior? In a quality of desire? In identity? Surely "friendship" may always coexist with erotic affection; and if sodomy often excludes friendship, it does so no more or less often than heterosexual relations do. In any case, what interests me here is what happens when friendships are described as erotic and what valence that erotic quality has in discussing this intriguing chapter in the history of sexuality.[25]

Here then is the man of feeling in love: Horry's love for Harry is writ so large as to hide its intensity, and its power is disguised in the rantings of a political agitator. To the world at large his love for his cousin is an open secret, and his closet is big enough to contain an entire society in its paneled interior. Walpole's love for his friends does not suggest a sexual identity, nor does it place Horace on one side or the other of a homo/hetero divide. His writings suggest that secrets themselves are not the lurid secrets of Gothic sexuality; they are playful and arch, deeply emotional and at times acrimonious; but above all what they express is love, not of a domestic kind, unless of course we consider domestic life in as complicated erotic terms as Walpole seems to. No, this is the sexual make-up of a gentleman of feeling. It is cordial and distant. It is generous to a fault and bitter when crossed. It is endlessly articulated in the eloquence of epistolary effusion. And it passes away in the silence of a friendly heart. Of course it is possible to rewrite history in such as way as to call Walpole "queer." But in our inability to see Walpole's love as anything but a euphemistic version of itself; in our need to impose a homo/hetero binary that Walpole everywhere defies; and in our demands for "proof" of sexual desire, we are distorting the remarkably simple and notably unqueer fact of these erotic feelings: this is the love that dared to speak its name.

Oh! My dear Lord, you see how willing I am to divert myself with anything that can turn my thoughts for their real object—if I were to write what I feel, how little should my letters be filled with the foibles of other people—I should indulge my own, but as you are the person upon earth I would not have reflect on my weaknesses, I shall not give you any to consider over at your leisure—you know but too many of them, and are infinitely too good to love me with so many faults as you know I have. (To the Earl of Lincoln, August 25, 1744)[26]

Walpole's Gothic writing also turns on the question of secrecy. In *The Castle of Otranto* (1764), for instance, Prince Manfred, the prototypical Gothic villain, harbors the guilty secret that will unseat him from power and destroy both of his children. Manfred's misdeeds are politically motivated, to the extent that his lust for power is unbounded, but they are expressed in sexually transgressive ways almost too blatant to enumerate: after his son, Conrad, is crushed by a gigantic helmet that appears in the court of his castle, he attempts to seduce his son's fiancée, Isabella, in a gesture that various characters in the novel, including Isabella herself, interpret as incestuous; he also characterizes his own marriage to the chaste Hippolita as illicit in similar terms—"Hippolita is related to me in the fourth degree. . . . This it is that sits heavy at my heart: to this state of unlawful wedlock I impute the visitation that has fallen on me in the death of Conrad" (49);[27] and in order to secure arrangements for his marriage to Isabella, he promises his daughter, Matilda, to Isabella's leering father, Frederick. In the meantime, he harbors dread suspicions of Theodore, a young peasant who arrives at the castle at the time of this catastrophe, and enters a rivalry for the hand of Isabella, with whom he mistakenly imagines that Theodore is in love; and in a gesture both incestuous and sadistic, he murders his own daughter, mistaking her for Isabella as she stands in private conversation with Theodore.

I have argued elsewhere that this lurid family romance reveals something about Walpole's own sexuality and that Manfred's guilty secret can find its analogy in Horace's own privacy.[28] Without entirely disowning that argument, I would like to consider the dynamics of secrecy in this case a little more carefully. The novel of course posits a guilty secret and the grotesque consequences of hiding from the truth, and it argues that the truth will be revealed; that the true prince, in this case the charming Theodore, who turns out to be the legitimate descendent of Alphonso the Good, will emerge victorious; and that the sins of the guilty Manfred will be resoundingly punished. The resulting story has a shape that virtually defines the Gothic itself. As Robert L. Mack puts it in his discussion of the novel, "The fundamental thematic concerns of the story—the manner in which the past impinges on the present, the brutal and violent connection between sexuality and power, and the overwhelming conviction that truth will finally be brought to light—are . . . those which to a large degree are at the center of the gothic to this day."[29]

But what is "truth" in *The Castle of Otranto*? Are Theodore's historical claim and Manfred's family's usurpation of the rights to Otranto the real secrets of this text? I would argue that these putative historical "facts," and even the guilt that they help to signal, are less true than what Mack calls the "brutal and violent connection of sexuality and power." Manfred's lust could hardly be considered a "secret"; it stands out starkly on every page. Yet this is the truth that the novel reveals: this is the dark truth of family violence, sexual "abuse," and naked phallic aggression. This lurid sexual violence might be called the novel's "open secret."

Walpole's Gothic hero is a conflicted and self-contradictory figure, violent, to be sure, and sexually aggressive, but also incestuously involved: in effect, he kills both his son and his daughter and retires with his wife to quiet retirement after gargantuan family enemies rise to emasculate him. If Walpole might be seen to anticipate sexological theory, culture determines the trials and tribulations of Walpole's Manfred: haunted by the impotent effeminacy of his son and the potentially fecund aggression of his daughter, both of whom threaten his claims to unlimited power, he stalks the novel with his peculiar form of sexual aggression, naked and exposed to the contempt of all those he attempts to victimize. Both his son and his daughter are destroyed in ways that are symbolic of their affronts: as I have already mentioned, Conrad is crushed by the helmet that falls in the court of the castle to mark the beginning of the revenge, and Matilda is brutally stabbed by Manfred himself in the novel's signal scene of transgressive sexual aggression. Her murder occurs at the climax of Manfred's pursuit of Isabella:

[Manfred] hastened secretly to the great church. Gliding softly between the aisles, and guided by an imperfect gleam of moonshine that shone faintly through the illuminated windows, he stole towards the tomb of Alfonso, to which he was directed by indistinct whispers of the persons he sought. The first sounds he could distinguish were—Does it, alas, depend on me? Manfred will never permit the union.—No, this shall prevent it! cried the tyrant, drawing his dagger, and plunging it over her shoulder into the bosom of the person that spoke—Ah me, I am slain! cried Matilda sinking: Good heaven, receive my soul!—Savage, inhuman monster! what hast thou done? cried Theodore, rushing on him, and wrenching his dagger from him.—Stop, stop, thy impious hand, cried Matilda; it is my father!— Manfred, waking as from a trance, beat his breast, twisted his hands in his locks, and endeavoured to recover his dagger from Theodore to dispatch himself. (104)

The elaborate sexual fantasy involved in the gliding through the darkness of the chapel at the tomb of his deposed predecessor and discovering there his daughter in conversation with a young man, the thrill of his erotically coded blow, and the abject self-hatred of the climactic moment—all these effects help to create a Gothic primal scene. Reversing the trajectories of Freud's oedipal arrangement, Manfred has "murdered" his son so as to be free to marry his daughter (for whom Isabella has been serving as an incestuous alternative); but he is doomed to destroy her in the violence of his lust. The Walpolean subject, then, is the guilty patriarch who stamps out difference in his quest for sexual power. His incestuous sexual violence has no meaning outside the family, and his attempts to force himself on the younger generation—Conrad, Isabella, Matilda, and Theodore—are the direct cause of his dispossession. The heteronormativity of paternal power is itself the perversion here, and Walpole reminds us that the son and daughter must be sacrificed to the increasingly impotent sexual demands of the aging father.

If Manfred's villainy becomes misery before the novel's close, it is because a more telling Gothic subject cowers in the "long labyrinth of darkness" (25) beneath the castle, where the heroine Isabella flees for her life. For victimization is even more important to this novel than the abuse of power. Heightened sexual anxiety animates scenes in which Isabella,

Hippolita, Matilda, and Theodore confront Manfred, and each in her or his way seems doomed to become the victim of Manfred. The thrill of victimization is not simply a masochistic thrill, and even the most intense sexual fears are imbued with a spirit of defiance that many Gothic heroines share.

This defiance suggests a different Walpolean subject that could be said to hover over the dying form of the brutally murdered Matilda, who has been the victim of her father's lust and who uses her own brutally incestuous victimization in an attempt to reintegrate the family:

> May heaven bless my father, and forgive him as I do! My lord, my gracious sire, dost though forgive thy child? . . .—Forgive thee! Murderous monster! cried Manfred—can assassins forgive? I took thee for Isabella; but heaven directed my bloody hand to the heart of my child!—Oh! Matilda—I cannot utter it—canst thou forgive the blindness of my rage?—I can, I do, and may heaven confirm it! said Matilda—But while I have life to ask it—oh, my mother! what will she feel!—Will you comfort her, my lord?" (105).

This simple love, this wish to bring her parents back together, this act of forgiveness—all this family feeling renders Matilda's brutal victimization a central feature of Walpole's family romance. The victimized child is a martyr to paternal love. By making Matilda's death so central to his plot, Walpole makes her suffering as important as Manfred's violence. The love that Matilda expresses, the vain hope that the aggressive dynamics of family life can be transformed by her death, make Manfred's violence even more monstrous. At the same time, the gesture of rape is transformed in Matilda's suffering: she takes pleasure in the pain that in its odd way signals her father's love. But this is not a simple masochistic response to Manfred's sadism. I would see Matilda's pathetic victimization as a kind of abjection that queers the fantasy by substituting a bloody corpse for the object of sexual desire. As Theodore and Manfred fight over the bloody dagger, Matilda lies in defiance of their homosocial love-fest. The death of Matilda brings nothing but regret to this novel, and regret is the mood of the novel's close. A sexologically open reading might suggest that the regret is already implicit in the violence itself and that abjection is what the novel articulates as a Gothic identity.

The Walpolean subject finally wanders in the dissatisfaction of frustrated desire, disappointed friendship, and tepid heterosexual consummation. Bersani argues that "we have . . . become extremely sensitive to the danger of looking too closely at our fantasies."[30] He is talking about masturbatory fantasies, to be sure, but still I would argue that unless we look at the content of the fantasies that the Gothic novel offers, we find ourselves trapped in the uninteresting observations that the violence in these novels is sexual in the ways that twentieth-century sexologists permit.

One could go on to see Walpole's incestuous violence as an effect of his sexuality: a deeply felt misogyny that emerges from the family itself can hardly be excused; but it can be explained by the cultural situation that insists that identification and desire remain at odds. Suddenly we may begin to understand the role of incest in the work of both Walpole and other Gothicists such as Lewis and Beckford. They do not hate women, simply and irrevocably. They hate instead the cultural situation that turns women against themselves.

Cultural critics have suggested that the regulation of marriage ties is a restriction that serves the purposes of the patriarchy; Manfred at the very least defies such a restriction in his experiments with "perversion." In raping and murdering the women in his life, moreover, Manfred underlines the other, the forbidden desire that Conrad at first represented. If Manfred must be forced to fulfill the male role in patriarchal culture, he does so violently, with none of the subterfuge at work in the society around him. He turns the romantic fiction inside out in order to show that sexuality is always about power, and, perhaps more important, that power is always about sexuality. Silverman says that

> [t]he theoretical interest of perversion extends beyond the disruptive force it brings to bear upon gender. It strips sexuality of all functionality, whether biological or social; in an even more extreme fashion than "normal" sexuality, it puts the body and the world of objects to uses that have nothing whatever to do with any "immanent" design or purpose. Perversion also subverts many of the binary oppositions upon which the social order rest; it crosses the boundary separating food from excrement (coprophilia); human from animal (bestiality); life from death (necrophilia); adult from child (pederasty); and pleasure from pain (masochism)."[31]

I would add, of course, same-sex desire and incest to Silverman's list, and I would claim that many Gothic novels work to disrupt "the social order" in as many ways as any other works of the later eighteenth century.

Bersani argues that "sentiments and conduct we might wish to associate with love can emerge as a resistance, in the Foucauldian sense, to the violence and avidity for power inherent in all intimate negotiations between human beings." Bersani turns to Freud's "Wolf Man" for a discussion of "frictional confrontations: the real or constructed primal scene of explaining *or* correcting the terror of the dream; the presumed fear of castration leading to the repression of desire for the father; the father's vulnerability as the *child's* resistance to his fantasized violence; . . . Freud's interpretive violence against the evidence he himself records," and so on.[32] The violence in *The Castle of Otranto* is as perplexing as any Freudian case study, and Manfred's incestuous desires bespeak a fear of sexuality as terrorized and terrorizing as any primal memory. Walpole creates a family romance that both effeminizes his hero and makes him the victim of heteronormativity itself. The daughter Manfred brutally slays and the daughter he desires both teach him the meaning of his incestuous lust. If Bersani can read a scene of gay lovemaking into Freud's scene of castration, then how much easier to look for transgressive desire in the complicated permutations of Walpole's fiction: here the terrorized father and terrorizing child exist in relation to an entire family of erotic possibilities. If Freud and his sexological predecessors had looked into a broader range of literary possibility, they might have found that their own categories would never answer the complexities of sexual reality that lie outside their narrow range of vision. If we are looking for genealogies of pleasure, that is, we should never overlook the Gothic.

I have changed my mind: instead of desiring you to have done loving me, I am going to ask something much more difficult for you to comply with—pray continue loving me: I like it vastly. I could never imagine there were half so many agréments *in having a lover. You can't conceive how I regret the time I have lost.* (To the Earl of Lincoln ?1743–1744)[33]

Secret love also forms the subject of Walpole's underrated tragedy *The Mysterious Mother* (1768). In this play the heroine, the Countess of Narbonne, hides a past crime behind her haughty demeanor and challenges those who would urge her to reveal it. In spite of the fact that she performs the strictest penance, her detractors are numerous. The priest Benedict, for instance, her confessor, feels no compunction about discussing her crimes with his colleague Martin:

BENEDICT: She prays,
             Because she feels, and feels, because a sinner.

MARTIN: What is this secret sin; this untold tale,
             That art cannot extract, nor penance cleanse? (1.3.162)34

These two scheming priests seem to delight in entertaining the possibilities of murder and sexual transgression in the Countess's past, emphasizing that these are the most common types of "secret sin." A secret in their terms is doubly transgressive, in the original transgression and in its continued concealment. Their delight at the prospect of exposing her is palpable and they are confused only about the means by which to for bring her crimes into public view:

MARTIN: Then whither turn
             To worm her secret out?

BENEDICT: I know not that.
             She will be silent, but she scorns a falsehood.
             And thus while frank on all things, but her secret,
             I know, I know it not. (1.3.164)

This project occupies these not-too-pious friars until the close of the play when the secret is catastrophically revealed. In the meantime secrets will be "wormed out" by creatures such as these: power-hungry outsiders who neither understand the depth of the Countess's feeling nor comprehend what it means to her to keep her counsel. Like many attempts to pry beneath the surface, this interest is both destructive and self serving. But Benedict's almost confused "I know, I know it not" helps to articulate the attitude toward secrecy that finally renders it a cultural impossibility. Secrecy itself is open, even if the details of the countess's crimes are not. Throughout the play, the Countess must suffer a variety of insinuations that drive her to extremes of feeling:

COUNTESS: —O peace of virtue! thy true votaries
             Quail not with ev'ry blast! I cloak my guilt!

> Things foreign rise and load me with their blackness.
> Erroneous imputation must be borne;
> Lest, while unravelling the knotty web,
> I lend a clue may vibrate to my heart. (2.3.190)

She practices an even more active secrecy than Manfred. She knows herself well enough to understand that she could betray her feeling at the slightest provocation, and she knows that there is a world of watchers to expose her when she does. At the same time, the play allows its audience to suffer with the Countess and to experience the fear of exposure that she so elaborately articulates. In this way the Countess can be seen as a victim: no matter how great her guilt, it is she who will suffer. By dramatizing her suffering in this fashion, Walpole is able to build tension around the question of the secret. Far more important, however, is Walpole's ability to make the Countess sympathetic enough to render the secret less interesting than her spectacle of desperation.

Various critics have begun to articulate the importance of the secret to the construction of bourgeois subjectivity in the later eighteenth century. Andrew Elfenbein discusses Cowper's *The Task* and his letters and suggests that "Cowper's secrecy effect anticipates a 'deep' selfhood . . . that would become a nineteenth-century commonplace."[35] In Cowper's case, as Elfenbein argues, it is the effect of secrecy that is all important, not the substance it conceals, which may be only an illusion. For Elfenbein suburban consciousness itself partakes of this illusion. It is tempting to connect this secrecy effect to the homosexual closet of the twentieth century, and as Elfenbein points out, Sedgwick's *Epistemology of the Closet* helps to explain why such a connection in later nineteenth century culture would be inevitable.[36] After all, once a culture is in control of such rigid binaries as homosexual/heterosexual, the content of the secret, its truth, is in a sense predetermined. In theorizing the "open secret," D. A. Miller quotes Oscar Wilde's remark that "it is the one thing that can make modern life mysterious and marvelous. The commonest thing is delightful if only one hides it."[37] Miller adds:

> More precisely, secrecy would seem to be a mode whose ultimate meaning lies in the subject's formal insistence that he is radically inaccessible to the culture that would otherwise entirely determine him. I cannot, therefore resolve the double bind of a secrecy that must always be rigorously maintained in the face of a secret that

everybody already knows, since this is the very condition that entitles me to my subjectivity in the first place.[38]

Walpole's play, and his novel as well, suggest that the cultural implications of secrecy are already rich in the eighteenth century. And if secrecy is the precondition of subjectivity in bourgeois society, so is the guilt that goes with that secrecy and gives it shape. Manfred and the Countess both construct their subjectivity around this "double bind" of secrecy. In both cases, "everybody already knows" that sexual transgression defines them.

In *The Mysterious Mother*, the crime the Countess has been hiding is revealed after her son, who has returned, marries her ward, Adeliza. Then the inevitable incest is explained: the Countess, in grief at her husband's death, slipped into the bed in which her son's "damsel" was supposed to be expecting him. As the Countess later puts it:

COUNTESS: Yes, thou polluted son!
Grief, disappointment, opportunity,
Rais'd such a tumult in my madding blood,
I took the damsel's place: and while thy arms
Twin'd, to thy thinking, round another's waist,
Hear, hell, and tremble!—thou didst clasp thy
mother! (5.7.248)

That Edmund, her son, has just married Adeliza, the product of this union, not only compounds the incestuous implications of the plot but also underlines the seemingly inevitable consequences of secrecy. In spite of all the Countess's machinations, she discovers the marriage of the two characters that she would most like to keep apart. The Countess's "pollution" of her son and the consequences for all the characters is predictably devastating.

It is tempting to read this incest as revelatory of Walpole's own anxieties. As careful a biographer as Ketton-Cremer cannot resist this connection:

It is difficult to explain why, apart from its obvious dramatic qualities, this repulsive story should have held so much interest for Walpole. A psycho-analyst might perhaps connect his attraction to the theme of incest with his youthful devotion to his own mother, which exerted so profound an influence on his life. A subconscious urge of this sort would certainly explain both his choice of a theme and the intense feeling with which the theme was handled.[39]

A psychoanalytical critic would need far less than this literalization of oedipal desire in order to posit a sexually disturbed author, one obsessed with the peculiarities of the family romance that other writers have used to explain homosexuality. Incest eroticizes family life and renders intimate relations complex and indeterminate.[40] At the same time, it complicates notions of love in such a way that even maternal affection can seem unnatural and filial devotion pernicious. When the sin is finally named, that is, the family must cease to function as a domestic unit. If the incest taboo can be seen as a version of "heterosexual panic," then it seems here to suggest that even the most basic normative relations—between husband and wife, mother and son—can be termed, in certain situations, unnatural.

But the play tells another story as well. This same son, Edmund, who has been exiled to the crusades, has sought out his mother because he has found her letters inspiring:

EDMUND: Her letters! Florian; such unstudied strains
                 Of virtuous elegance! She bids me, yes,
                 This praying Magdelen enjoins my courage
                 To emulate my great forefathers' deeds.
                 . . . I decypher'd
                 In one her blessing granted, and eras'd.
                 And yet what follow'd, mark'd anxiety
                 For my soul's welfare. I must know this riddle.
                 I must, will comfort her.(2.1.178–179)

The Countess's letters to Edmund, that is, have resulted in his conviction both that he is loved and that the letters contain a riddle of love and anxiety that he must solve. The love that Edmund feels in the letters is of course the secret of the play itself. Far from hiding her feelings, the Countess constantly reveals them—she "wears the mask of truth," as Žižek says—and as a result her love becomes the open secret of the play. Edmund's compulsive need to solve the riddle is what undoes him, and the tragedy moves with ruthless simplicity once he arrives at his mother's forbidden home.

This speech concerns more, however, than the Countess's impending exposure. Even more compelling in this context is Edmund's very fascination with his mother's letters, his attempts to read, as it were, between the lines, and his conviction that the letters themselves articulate in their very form a riddle that he is determined to solve. He is correct to say that the blottings and rewritings that he discovers can tell him something about the Countess. He is correct as well to think that a personality can be revealed in the "unstudied strains / Of virtuous elegance." The Countess is one of the great heroines of the eighteenth century, for all Walpole's later embarrassments at his depiction of her. She emerges in her letters as an attractive, almost irresistible figure to her doomed son. What Edmund does not realize is that she has the attractions of a former lover. The riddle he reads here, that is, is the riddle of his own complex sexual make-up. Love is what emerges in these epistolary effusions: this is the "secret sin." But it is not just her secret, it is his own as well. For Walpole, the lesson is obvious. As Sir Horace Mann said in 1779, when Walpole at last allowed him to read the play, "the subject may be too horrid for the stage, but the judicious management of it by preparing the reader for the catastrophe, the sublime ideas and expressions so admirably adapted to the personages, make it a delicious entertainment for the closet."[41]

I don't express my self with as much love as I used to do, and as you know I have for you, don't wonder—Dick [Hon. Richard Edgcumbe] is here, and as he has twice perused the superscriptions of my letters, I am not sure he would not open one directed to so particular a friend of his as you are. Now, after your way of dealing with him, if he should find me very fond of you, God knows what he might suspect! He would at least burst the waistband of his breeches with the glee of the discovery—and my dear Lord, I would not for the world wrong your bed—As irresistible as he is, he shall never injure you with me. (To the Earl of Lincoln, June 22, 1743)[42]

W. S. Lewis notes that Walpole's letters to Lord Lincoln "could mislead readers who are quick to suspect homosexual relationships, but eighteenth-century men were less afraid of showing their feelings than men are today and they frequently wrote and acted in a way we should consider effeminate."[43] Lewis mentions letters to Walpole's "effeminate" friends, Horace Mann, John Chute, and George Montague, not to mention Gray and West. Like the

letters to Conway, and like the Countess's letters to her son, we could read
these letters as a riddle and imagine a hidden truth that Walpole has disguised
in near-hysterical friendliness. Or, like Edmund, we can speak the love that
the biographers, because of cultural conditioning of their own, must distort in
one direction ("high spirits") or the other ("sodomy"). But perhaps they are
only displacing their own anxieties of exposure onto Walpole.

The most important figure in this regard is Lord Lincoln, who has been
the recipient of the intense epistolary endearments that have been reproduced throughout this chapter. Timothy Mowl says that "Walpole developed his strong and enduring homosexual attachment to the Earl of
Lincoln, subsequently 2nd Duke of Newcastle, while still at Eton."[44] I fully
agree that Walpole loved Lincoln and even nursed an infatuation throughout most of his adult life. I am prepared to imagine that this love was
expressed physically—although I would be the first to admit that the evidence is slim—and that tensions surrounding the role that physical expressions of love will play in their relationship can be used to explain some
anomalies in their correspondence. But it is wrong to approach this situation, apply a notion of "homosexuality" gathered from a familiarity with
"internecine" conflict in an academic field, and then to project certain
types of "homosexual" behavior onto these figures. Walpole did not have a
homosexual code to which he could appeal, nor did he conform to other
descriptions we have of men who enjoyed the company of men—in molly
houses or other semipublic spaces. Mowl imagines such essentialized
behaviors that he can say, in all seriousness, "intelligence services are wise
to mistrust homosexuals. Being rejected by society at one level, they tend to
stand apart at others."[45] The problem with this "cold war" thinking is that it
projects a (rather silly) twentieth-century notion onto the past, and in doing
so distorts both the present and the past.

Critics such as Mowl, for all their seemingly liberal openness, see
Walpole's "homosexuality" as a vice; they understand Walpole's expression
of desire, however veiled, as predatory; and they use the secret of Walpole's
illicit loves to explain every major conflict and development in his life. This
is what essentialism can achieve. If instead of seeing Walpole's sexuality as
the figure in the carpet, we look at the letters themselves, what we see is love,
at times playful, at times demanding, but never pathological and never more
or less destructive than any love experienced by anyone in the century within
or across gender. Because Mowl believes in the "homosexual" personality, he

makes hideous misjudgments in his appraisal of Walpole. And in putting down earlier biographers who, according to him, tried to "hide" Walpole's sexuality, he merely reasserts the essentialist gesture in his own time.

Lewis says with confidence that "there is no proof that Walpole had any affairs with men or women."[46] He was not falsifying the information he had before him. What he says is literally true. If I would follow Mowl far enough to say that Walpole's friendships were erotic, that does not mean that I want to assign "homosexual" motivations to everything he does. But I would like to see these friendships for what they are. If these elaborate more-than-friendships are anything, they are "affairs of the heart." That is, they are, on the surface, deeply emotional attachments that have no analogy in the "friendships" of our own culture and only a vague similarity to the sodomit-ical relations of such contemporaries of Walpole as Beckford and Byron. Nevertheless, these are male relations of a kind that, "gay and graceful" as they are, begin to suggest the male sensibility that later in the next century would begin to cohere, not in the figure of the "homosexual" as Mowl and other twentieth-century critics caricature him but rather in the writings of Carpenter, Symonds, Wilde, and Forster.

In this study, I have shown the ways in which a variety of masculinities have functioned in a culture that was just learning how it could codify gender dif-ference and marginalize excessive behaviors; construct sexuality as a rigid binary in order to isolate the "unnatural"; and piece together identity by dri-ving a wedge between public and private discourse. If figures such as Beckford, Gray, and Walpole express love for members of their own sex, that does not exempt them from the cultural forces that were emasculating Sterne and tormenting Boswell. The love of these three men was as debili-tating and destructive as other versions of desire that were circulating at the time. The love affairs that I have described are not immune from the inequities that haunt all relations in which desire plays a part. These "loves" are the product of culture, to be sure, and they are dysfunctional to the degree that culture ensures that all desiring relationships are dysfunctional. At their worst, such male bonds have a way of solidifying power in particu-larly ugly ways. In certain circumstances, as Eve Kosofsky Sedgwick and others have argued, closeted intimacy is the very glue that holds patriarchal culture together, while it excludes women, minorities, and variously defined "others."[47]

Men have never been allowed to love one another, however, even in studies of the history of sexuality, and it is worth considering the implications of that love before charging it with the abuses of patriarchy. Usually, this suppressed and unacknowledged love between men is euphemized as heroic friendship or domesticated as fraternal feeling; ignored as physically meaningless or celebrated as spiritually meaningful; denounced as sodomy or dismissed as pæderasty. I hope I have shown that it is in fact *love*, in all the complexity of its meaning in eighteenth-century life. I hope I have also shown the ways in which this love can be threatening to heteronormative culture and how various kinds of threats and victimizations or compensations and consolations are offered to male lovers as a way of keeping them from disrupting the rigors of a procreative economy.

If the bonds between men are crucial to the smooth ordering of the sex-gender system on the one hand, and if erotic desire threatens that system, then a play like *The London Merchant* can serve as the document that embodies the contradictions of such a system and exposes the ideology upon which that system is based. Caught between love for his friend, which will save him, and love for the woman, who will destroy him, Barnwell must choose the former only to lose it in death. This is the story that is told again and again here: love between men is always already defined as loss: desire for this lost object is what defines the man of feeling and what renders him unthreatening. Gray's melancholic desire is one implicitly homophobic way of internalizing culture's rigorous demands and not threatening the status quo. Perhaps not surprisingly, the men dancing together at Mother Clap's molly house are far more threatening: they refuse to acknowledge loss and appropriate the very rituals of culture for themselves. This may in part explain why these are the men who are executed. Between these two extremes are the scandalous love of Beckford for his precocious young cousin and the "secret" love of Walpole for his darling near-contemporary one. One is excluded from society and the other is written off as a dilettante, but both of them write endlessly about their love. These loves and the others I describe are accommodating in ways that have rendered them almost invisible, and without the recent work that has been done in the history of sexuality, we might not be able to see them at all. But as much as possible we need to see them for what they are: not "homosexual" relations that we can acknowledge and celebrate but, rather, complex human relations that are fully historically determined.

Beckford, Gray, or Walpole might in other circumstances have exercised power to foster patriarchal privilege; but each of these men did more, or rather less, than their cultural privilege and elite education permitted. They loved in ways that closeted intimacy does not allow. They loved in ways that exposed their desire to resist the position into which culture had placed them. They loved in ways that made them vulnerable to feelings outside their control. In this way they can touch us, as it were, at the same time that they remind us that relations, even sexual relations, are often not primarily about sex. Love is about sexual desire, of course, but it is also about a kind of desire that reaches beyond the sexual. The loves I have described are large enough to suggest the limits of a merely physical understanding of sexuality. Often emotion determines the terms of a relationship, the context for sexual activity as well as the ground for interpersonal attachment. The emotion matters so much because it is undefined. The love between men that I have described is emotional in ways that have never been allowed. In this study I have shown just how much that can mean.

NOTES

→ ←

Introduction: Masculinity and Sexuality

1. Body Guards: The Cultural Politics of Gender Ambiguity, ed. Julia Epstein and Kristina Straub (New York: Routledge, 1991), 2.
2. The OED first recorded use of the term occurs in 1800; significantly it is a poet of sensibility, Cowper, who is first cited as using the term in describing male and female qualities of plants (OED, s.v. "sexuality").
3. Michel Foucault, The History of Sexuality, vol. 1, An Introduction, trans. Robert Hurley (New York: Vintage-Random House, 1980), 43; see also David M. Halperin, One Hundred Years of Homosexuality and Other Essays on Greek Love (New York: Routledge, 1990), esp. 26–27, and n. 52.
4. See for instance Alan Bray, Homosexuality in Renaissance England (London: Gay Men's Press, 1982), chapter 4; Gregory W. Bredbeck, Sodomy and Interpretation: Marlowe to Milton (Ithaca: Cornell University Press, 1991); Halperin, One Hundred Years, chapter 1; Cameron McFarlane, The Sodomite in Fiction and Satire, 1660–1750 (New York: Columbia University Press, 1997); Stephen Orgel, Impersonations: The Performance of Gender in Shakespeare's England (Cambridge: Cambridge University Press, 1996); G. S. Rousseau, "The Pursuit of Homosexuality in the Eighteenth Century: 'Utterly Confused Category' and/or Rich Repository?" Eighteenth-Century Life 9 (1985): 132–168; Alan Sinfield, The Wilde Century: Effeminacy, Oscar Wilde, and the Queer Moment (London: Cassell, 1994), 25–51; Randolph Trumbach, "London's

Sodomites: Homosexual Behavior and Western Culture in the Eighteenth Century," *Journal of Social History* 11 (1977): 1–33; and "Sodomitical Assaults, Gender Role, and Sexual Development in Eighteenth-Century London," in *The Pursuit of Sodomy: Male Homosexuality in Renaissance and Enlightenment Europe*, ed. Kent Gerard and Gert Hekma (New York: Harrington Park Press, 1989), 407–429. Records of sodomy trials show a very broad legal and popular understanding of the term; see *Sodomy Trials*, ed. Randolph Trumbach (New York: Garland, 1986). See also *Secret Sexualities: A Sourcebook of 17th and 18th Century Writing*, ed. Ian McCormick (New York: Routledge, 1997), esp. 49–116.

5. See Mary Poovey, *The Proper Lady and the Woman Writer: Ideology as Style in the Works of Mary Wollstonecraft, Mary Shelley, and Jane Austen* (Chicago: University of Chicago Press, 1984); see also Nancy Armstrong, *Desire and Domestic Fiction: A Political History of the Novel* (Oxford: Oxford University Press, 1987).

6. Kaja Silverman, *Male Subjectivity at the Margins* (New York: Routledge, 1992), 15–51; see also Slavoj Žižek, *The Sublime Object of Ideology* (London: Verso, 1989), 153–200.

7. See for instance Eve Kosofsky Sedgwick, *Between Men: English Literature and Male Homosocial Desire* (New York: Columbia University Press, 1985).

8. See Sir George Etherege, *The Man of Mode; or Sir Fopling Flutter* (1676); Henry Fielding, *The History of the Adventures of Joseph Andrews* (1742); William Congreve, *The Way of the World* (1700); and Frances Burney, *Evelina* (1770). For a more extensive discussion of the fop, see chapter 2, below.

9. Shawn Lisa Maurer, *Proposing Men: Dialectics of Gender and Class in the Eighteenth-Century English Periodical* (Stanford, Calif.: Stanford University Press, 1998).

10. *Spectator* 57 (May 5, 1711); see *The Spectator*, ed. Donald F. Bond, 5 vols. (1907; reprint, Oxford: Clarendon, 1961), 1:241.

11. See chapter 2, below.

12. R. W. Ketton-Cremer raised the issue of "homosexuality" in his biographies of Gray and Walpole, and Beckford's sexual proclivities were as notorious in his own age as those of Byron, who indeed was one of the first to comment on Beckford's "propensity." See Ketton-Cremer, *Thomas Gray: A Biography* (Cambridge: Cambridge University Press, 1965) and *Horace Walpole: A Biography* (Ithaca: Cornell University Press, 1964); Brian Fothergill, *Beckford of Fonthill* (London: Faber, 1979). Problematic discussions of "homosexuality" in Gray (see Robert F. Gelckner, *Gray Agonistes: Thomas Gray and Masculine Friendship* [Baltimore: Johns Hopkins University Press, 1996]) and Walpole (see Timothy Mowl, *Horace Walpole: The Great Outsider* [London: John Murray, 1996]) have been of little real help in examining male sexuality in the eighteenth

century, as my discussions of these writers make clear in chapters 4 and 6, below.

13. Sedgwick, *Between Men*, 72, 80.

14. Claudia L. Johnson, *Equivocal Beings: Politics, Gender, and Sentimentality in the 1790s* (Chicago: Chicago University Press, 1995), 11.

15. Sinfield, *Wilde Century*, 31; see also Joseph Bristow, *Effeminate England: Homoerotic Writing After 1885* (New York: Columbia University Press, 1995), 1–15.

16. The question of "friendship" in the eighteenth century is a large one that I discuss later in this introduction, as well as in chapters 1, 4, and 5.

17. See for instance: Trumbach, "Sodomitical Assaults"; Rousseau, "Pursuit of Homosexuality"; and Harold Weber, " 'Drudging in Fair Aurelia's Womb': Constructing Homosexual Economies in Rochester's Poetry," *The Eighteenth Century: Theory and Interpretation* 33 (1992): 99–118. See also Carole Fabricant, "Rochester's World of Imperfect Enjoyment," *Journal of English and Germanic Philology* 73 (1974): 338–50

18. James G. Turner, "The Properties of Libertinism," *'Tis Nature's Fault: Unauthorized Sexuality during the Enlightenment*, ed. Robert Parks Maccubbin (Cambridge: Cambridge University Press, 1987): 77–78.

19. For a discussion of the libertine figure in the eighteenth century, see Harold Weber, *The Restoration Rake-Hero: Transformations in Sexual Understanding in Seventeenth-Century England* (Madison: University of Wisconsin Press, 1986), 179–221.

20. The most complete classification of male-male sexual possibilities is that found in Rousseau, "Pursuit of Homosexuality."

21. See Halperin, *One Hundred Years*, 47.

22. Harold Weber, " 'Drudging,' " 115; see also Trumbach, "The Birth of the Queen: Sodomy and the Emergence of Gender Equality in Modern Culture, 1660–1750," in *Hidden From History: Reclaiming the Gay and Lesbian Past*, ed. Martin Bauml Duberman, Martha Vicinus, and George Chauncey, Jr. (New York: New American Library, 1989), 129–140. Weber goes on to say that "for Rochester's libertine narrators, boys and the economic underclass provide a representationally satisfying alternative to women precisely because they provide a strict erotic demarcation between the male object of desire and the desiring male subject: linkboys, porters, and grooms seem far less threatening than women, for in erecting desire on rigorously policed distinctions of power and status they assure the narcissistic triumph of a phallic power that can no longer be betrayed" (115); Rochester's play *Sodom* is also of interest in this regard; see Weber, "Carolinean Sexuality and the Restoration Stage: Reconstructing the Royal Phallus in *Sodom*," in *Cultural Readings of Restoration and Eighteenth-*

Century English Theater, ed. J. Douglas Canfield and Deborah Payne (Athens: University of Georgia Press, 1995), 67–88.

23. For an analysis of the function of misogyny within the libertine ethos, see Weber, " 'Drudging.' "

24. Samuel Pepys's *Diary*: 1 July 1663. *The Diary of Samuel Pepys*, ed., Robert Latham and William Matthews, 11 vols. (Berkeley: University of California Press, 1970–1983), 4:209–210.

25. Vincent Quinn, "Libertines and Libertinism," in *The Encyclopedia of Gay Histories and Cultures*, ed. George E. Haggerty (New York: Garland, 1999).

26. Michael McKeon, "Historicizing Patriarchy: the Emergence of Gender Difference in England, 1660–1760," *Eighteenth-Century Studies* 28 (1995): 311.

27. *Spectator* 385 (May 22, 1712); *The Spectator* 3:445–446.

28. Sedgwick, *Between Men*, 25.

29. Bray, *Homosexuality*; see also Bredbeck, *Sodomy and Interpretation*; Jonathan Goldberg, *Sodometries: Renaissance Texts, Modern Sexualities* (Stanford, Calif.: Stanford University Press, 1992); and Bruce R. Smith, *Homosexual Desire in Shakespeare's England* (Chicago: University of Chicago Press, 1991).

30. Alan Bray, "Homosexuality and the Signs of Male Friendship," *History Workshop: A Journal of Socialist and Feminist Historians* 29 (1990): 1; for a helpful gloss on Bray's comments, see Goldberg, *Sodometries*, 17–20.

31. See for instance David Veith, "Introduction," *All for Love* (Lincoln: University of Nebraska Press, 1972), xxii.

32. "Homosexual" themes are not always ignored; Vieth, for instance, argues that: "One of the several shortcomings of *All for Love* results . . . from the friendship theme. . . . Whatever Dryden's intentions were in *All for Love*, the trouble seems to be that although the Dolabella-Antony relationship provides logical parallels between these two characters, the psychological surge escapes the context of a play expressive of a civilization that has never, since classical times, really condoned homosexuality. How this homosexuality may reflect Dryden's real-life relationship with his young friend and future collaborator, Nathaniel Lee, remains unclear"; Vieth, "Introduction," *All For Love*, xxiv-xxv; see further, xxii-xxiv.

33. Eve Kosofsky Sedgwick, *Epistemology of the Closet* (Berkeley: University of California Press), 52.

34. Robert Aldrich, *The Seduction of the Mediterranean: Writing, Art, and Homosexual Fantasy* (New York: Routledge, 1993), 32, 40.

35. In this context, see ibid., esp. 13–40. Aldrich is also interesting in his discussion of Winckelmann and Platen and the cult of "Greek" erotic friendship that these men represent; see 41–69.

36. Halperin, *One Hundred Years*, 47.

37. John Boswell, *Same-Sex Unions in Premodern Europe* (New York: Villard-Random House, 1994), 53–108.

38. Ibid., 77–79.

39. K. J. Dover, *Greek Homosexuality* (Cambridge: Harvard University Press, 1978), 50.

40. Ibid., 50–51.

41. Halperin, *One Hundred Years*, 77.

42. Richard Dellamora, *Masculine Desire: The Sexual Politics of Victorian Aestheticism* (Chapel Hill: University of North Carolina Press, 1990), 24; see Arthur Hallam, *The Writings*, ed. T. H. Vail Motter (New York: Modern Language Association, 1943), 158–59.

43. John Addington Symonds, *The Memoirs of John Addington Symonds*, ed. Phyllis Grosskurth (Chicago: University of Chicago Press, 1984), 189; see Christopher Craft, *Another Kind of Love: Male Homosexual Desire in English Discourse, 1850–1920* (Berkeley: University of California Press, 1994), 45.

44. Linda Dowling, *Hellenism and Homosexuality in Victorian Oxford* (Ithaca: Cornell University Press, 1994), xiii–xiv.

45. Ibid., 8.

46. See for instance Raymond Stephanson, " 'Epicœne Friendship': Understanding Male Friendship in the Early Eighteenth Century, with Some Speculations about Pope," *The Eighteenth Century: Theory and Interpretation* 38 (1997): 151–170; see also David Robinson, "Unravelling the 'Cord Which Ties Good Men to Good Men': Male Friendship in Richardson's Novels," in *Samuel Richardson: Tercentenary Essays*, ed. Margaret Doody and Peter Sabor (Cambridge: Cambridge University Press, 1989), 167–187; and G. S. Rousseau, "Love and Antiquities: Walpole and Gray on the Grand Tour,"in *Perilous Enlightenment: Pre and Postmodern Discourses: Sexual, Historical* (Manchester: Manchester University Press, 1991): 172–199.

47. Stephanson, "Epicœne Friendship," 153–154, 155–156, 157, 158, 159.

48. Carolyn Woodward may not have said exactly what I quote her as saying. As chair of the panel, I did more fumbling than note-taking. I hope I have recounted at least the spirit of our exchange.

49. Foucault, *A History of Sexuality*: 1:103–105.

1. Heroic Friendships

1. The most interesting recent critic of Restoration heroic drama is Joseph Roach; see for instance his "'The Artificial Eye: Augustan Theater and the Empire of the Visible," in *The Performance of Power: Theatrical Discourse and Politics*, ed. Sue-Ellen Case and Janelle Reinelt (Iowa City: University of Iowa Press, 1991), 131–145; and *Cities of the Dead: Circum-Atlantic Performance* (New York:

Columbia University Press, 1996). Still among the most useful studies of Restoration drama is that by Laura Brown, *English Dramatic Form, 1660–1760: An Essay in Generic Form* (New Haven: Yale University Press, 1981); see also Robert D. Hume, *The Development of English Drama in the Late Seventeenth Century* (Oxford: Clarendon, 1976); John Loftis, *Restoration Drama: Modern Essays in Criticism* (New York: Oxford University Press, 1966); Eric Rothstein, *Restoration Tragedy: Form and the Process of Change* (Madison: University of Wisconsin Press, 1967); Eugene M. Waith, *Ideas of Greatness; Heroic Drama in England* (London: Routledge, 1971).

2. See Paula R. Backscheider, *Spectacular Politics: Theatrical Power and Mass Culture in Early Modern England* (Baltimore: Johns Hopkins University Press, 1993); Elin Diamond, "Gestus and Signature in Aphra Behn's *The Rover*," *ELH* 56 (1989): 519–541; and Kristina Straub, *Sexual Suspects: Eighteenth-Century Players and Sexual Ideology* (Princeton: Princeton University Press, 1992). Although Straub is primarily interested in a later period, her comments also have particular valence for Restoration theatrical experience.

3. See Roach, "Artificial Eye."

4. Harold Weber, "Carolean Sexuality and the Restoration Stage: Reconstructing the Royal Phallus in *Sodom*," in *Cultural Readings of Restoration and Eighteenth-Century English Theater*, ed. J. Douglas Canfield and Deborah C. Payne (Athens: University of Georgia Press, 1995), 73.

5. Weber, "Carolean Sexuality," 75.

6. For a discussion on the sexual circumstances of the Elizabethan theater, see Stephen Orgel, *Impersonations: The Performance of Gender in Shakespeare's England* (Cambridge: Cambridge University Press, 1996).

7. Kristina Straub, "Actors and Homophobia," in *Cultural Readings of Restoration and Eighteenth-Century English Theater*, ed. Canfield and Payne, 258; see also Straub, *Sexual Suspects*, 3–23.

8. Straub, "Actors," 259, 261; see also William Prynne, *Histrio-Mastrix: The Player's Scourge*, 2 vols. (1633; reprint, New York: Johnson Reprint Corporation, 1972), 1:168.

9. John Dryden, *All For Love; or, The World Well Lost*, ed. David Vieth (Lincoln: University of Nebraska Press, 1972); further references are to this edition.

10. Alan Bray, "Homosexuality and the Signs of Male Friendship," *History Workshop: A Journal of Socialist and Feminist Historians* 29 (1990): 1; for a helpful gloss on Bray's comments, see Jonathan Goldberg, *Sodometries: Renaissance Texts, Modern Sexualities* (Stanford, Calif.: Stanford University Press, 1992), 17–20. See also Eve Kosofsky Sedgwick, *Between Men: English Literature and Male Homosocial Desire* (New York: Columbia University Press, 1985); Alan Bray, *Homosexuality in Renaissance England* (London: Gay Men's Press, 1982); Gregory W. Bredbeck, *Sodomy and Interpretation: Marlowe to Milton* (Ithaca;

Cornell University Press, 1991); and Bruce R. Smith, *Homosexual Desire in Shakespeare's England* (Chicago: University of Chicago Press, 1991).

11. As I have already noted, Raymond Stephanson has posited "epicœne friendship" as an answer to these kinds of contradictions. This analysis is to a certain extent tautological. See Stephanson, " 'Epicœne Friendship': Understanding Male Friendship in the Early Eighteenth Century, with Some Speculations about Pope," *The Eighteenth Century: Theory and Interpretation* 38 (1997): 151–170

12. Christopher Marlowe, *Doctor Faustus and Other Plays*, ed. David Bevington and Eric Rasmussen (Oxford: Oxford University Press, 1995), 329.

13. Goldberg, *Sodometries*, 121, 122–123; see also Michel Foucault, *The History of Sexuality*, vol. 1, *An Introduction*, trans. Robert Hurley (New York: Vintage, 1980), 101.

14. Goldberg, *Sodometries*, 119.

15. Consider, in this context, Otway's comedy on the same theme, *Friendship in Fashion*, which was staged in 1678. Betrayal of friendship is its central theme, and it views such betrayal with contempt. See Robert D. Hume, *The Rakish Stage: Studies in English Drama, 1660–1800* (Carbondale: Southern Illinois University Press, 1983), 82–92.

16. Vieth, "Introduction," *All For Love*, xxiv.

17. Bray's essay makes this point in terms of various sixteenth- and seventeenth-century accusations of "sodomy'; for the later eighteenth century, see for instance *Satan's Harvest Home* (1749; reprint, New York: Garland, 1985), which finds cause for concern in any demonstration of affection between men.

18. For an opposing view, see Vieth, "Introduction," xxi.

19. Bray, "Homosexuality," 5.

20. Jeremy Treglown, ed., *The Letters of John Wilmot, Earl of Rochester* (Oxford: Blackwell, 1980), 232.

21. Bray, "Homosexuality," 8.

22. See Bray, *Homosexuality in Renaissance England*, 49; see also H. Montgomery Hyde, *The Love That Dared Not Speak Its Name* (Boston: Little and Brown, 1970), 44–57.

23. Straub, *Sexual Suspects*, 20.

24. Nathaniel Lee, *The Rival Queens; or, The Death of Alexander the Great*, ed. P. F. Vernon (1677; reprint, Lincoln: Nebraska University Press, 1970); further references are to this edition.

25. Lee's play and Dryden's are nearly contemporary: the latter appeared several months after the former in 1677 and was to a certain extent modeled on it. There has been some speculation concerning the personal relationship between Dryden and Lee. See Vieth, "Introduction," xxv.

26. Goldberg, *Sodometries*, 119.

27. See J. M. Armisted, *Nathaniel Lee* (Boston: G. K. Hall, 1979), 69.

28. *Cassandra: The Fam'd Romance, The Whole Work, In Five parts, Written Originally in French and Now Elegantly Rendered into English,* by Sir Charles Cotterell (London: Printed for *Peter Parker,* at the *Leg* and *Star* over against the *Royal Exchange* in *Cornhill,* 1676), 13.

29. See for instance *Cassandra,* 109, 122, 141.

30. Although there was no Restoration edition of Marlowe's *Massacre at Paris,* Lee used the work as a model for his own ill-fated *The Massacre of Paris* (1678/9); see Armisted, *Nathaniel Lee,* 94, 119–120.

31. "Lee became 'distracted' and on November 11, 1684 . . . was admitted to 'Bedlam,' the Bethlehem Royal Hospital for the Insane" (Armisted, *Nathaniel Lee,* 24). Lee remained there until spring 1688. Very little is known about the specific details of his illness.

32. Rochester, "The Disabled *Debauchee,*" l. 40; in *The Poems of John Wilmot, Earl of Rochester,* ed. Keith Walker (Oxford: Blackwell, 1984), 99.

33. Backscheider, *Spectacular Politics,* 65.

34. Armisted, *Nathaniel Lee,* 30.

35. See Goldberg, *Sodometries,* 124; see also William Empsom, "Two Proper Crimes," *The Nation* 163 (1946): 444–445.

36. See Backscheider, *Spectacular Politics,* 3–31.

37. Roach, "Artificial Eye," 143.

38. See Diamond, "Gestus and Signature," 519.

39. *Collected Works of John Wilmot, Earl of Rochester,* ed. John Hayward (London: Nonesuch, 1926), 232.

40. *The London Stage, 1660–1800, Part 1: 1660–1700,* ed. William A. Lennep (Carbondale: Southern Illinois University Press, 1965), 238, 255, 265.

41. Montague Summers, *The Playhouse of Pepys* (London: Kegan Paul, 1935), 292–296.

42. Robert D. Hume and Judith Milhouse, *Producible Interpretation: Eight English Plays, 1675–1707* (Carbondale: Southern Illinois University Press, 1985), 134; Summers, *The Playhouse of Pepys,* 292.

43. For an interesting discussion of *The London Merchant,* see Stephanie Barbé Hammer, *The Sublime Crime: Fascination, Failure, and Form in the Literature of the Enlightenment* (Carbondale: Southern Illinois University Press, 1994), 21–37.

44. Hammer, *Sublime Crime,* 37.

45. George Lillo, *The London Merchant; or, The History of George Barnwell,* ed. William H. McBurney (1731; reprint, Lincoln: Nebraska University Press, 1965). Further references are to this edition.

46. McBurney, "Introduction," *London Merchant,* xviii.

47. It is worth noting in this regard that Barnwell's parting scene with his girlfriend Maria, Thoroughgood's daughter, is stilted and almost formal. "Preserve her, heaven, and restore her peace," Barnwell says dispassionately (5.10.75).

48. Sedgwick, *Between Men*, 26.

2. Gay Fops/Straight Fops

1. Randolph Trumbach, "The Birth of the Queen: Sodomy and the Emergence of Gender Equality in Modern Culture, 1660–1750," in *Hidden From History: Reclaiming the Gay and Lesbian Past*, ed. Martin Bauml Duberman, Martha Vicinus, and George Chauncey, Jr. (New York: New American Library, 1989), 133; Susan Staves, "A Few Kind Words for the Fop," *SEL* 22 (1982): 413–428; Laurence Senelick, "Mollies or Men of Mode? Sodomy and the Eighteenth-Century London Stage," *Journal of the History of Sexuality* 1 (1990): 33–67. See also Thomas A. King, "Performing 'Akimbo': Queer Pride and Epistemological Prejudice," *The Politics and Poetics of Camp*, ed. Morris Meyer (London: Routledge, 1994), 23–50.
2. *The Second Part of the London Clubs, Containing The No Nose Club, The Beaus Club, The Mollies Club, The Quacks Club* (London: J. Dutton, 1709), 26–27.
3. See for instance Craig Patterson, "The Rage of Caliban: Eighteenth-Century Molly Houses and the Twentieth-Century Search for Sexual Identity," in *Illicit Sex: Identity Politics in Early Modern Culture*, ed. Thomas DiPiero and Pat Gill (Athens: Georgia University Press, 1997), 256–269; see also Cameron McFarlane, *The Sodomite in Fiction and Satire, 1660–1750* (New York: Columbia University Press, 1997), 19.
4. *Second Part of the London Clubs*, 27.
5. Ibid., 27.
6. George Etherege, *The Man of Mode*, ed. W.B. Carnochan (Lincoln: University of Nebraska Press, 1966); further references are to this edition.
7. Eve Kosofsky Sedgwick, *Between Men: English Literature and Male Homosocial Desire* (New York: Columbia University Press, 1985), 50–51.
8. Kristina Straub, "The Guilty Pleasures of Theatrical Cross-Dressing and the Autobiography of Charlotte Charke," in *Body Guards: The Cultural Politics of Gender Ambiguity*, ed. Julia Epstein and Kristina Straub (New York: Routledge, 1991), 142–166; see also *Sexual Suspects: Eighteenth-Century Players and Sexual Ideology* (Princeton: Princeton University Press, 1992).
9. Straub, *Sexual Suspects*, xx.
10. John Vanbrugh, *The Relapse*, ed. Bernard Harris (1694; reprint, New York: Norton: 1995), 129.
11. Straub, *Sexual Suspects*, 32–33; see also Senelick, "Mollies."
12. Straub, *Sexual Suspects*, 55.
13. Ibid., 57; see also Staves, "A Few Kind Words."
14. Straub, *Sexual Subjects*, 55; see also Trumbach, "Birth of the Queen"; and Senelick, "Mollies."

15. Straub, *Sexual Subjects*, 55.

16. See Trumbach, "Birth of the Queen," 129–140.

17. Patterson, "Rage of Caliban," 257. See also McFarlane, *The Sodomite in Fiction and Satire*, 63–68; and, Ian McCormick, ed., *Secret Sexualities: A Sourcebook of 17th- and 18th-Century Writing* (New York: Routledge, 1997). McCormick notes that "unstable and elusive, sexuality exists only as that which is read off (or against) structures that are more accessible oppositional targets" (3).

18. For the quotation from Ward, see *Second Part of the London Clubs*, 28; see also McCormick, *Secret Sexualities*, 132.

19. Trumbach, "Birth of the Queen," 138.

20. See Alan Bray, "Homosexuality and the Signs of Male Friendship," *History Workshop: A Journal of Socialist and Feminist Historians* 29 (1990): 1–19; for a helpful gloss on Bray's comments, see Jonathan Goldberg, *Sodometries: Renaissance Texts, Modern Sexualities* (Stanford, Calif.: Stanford University Press, 1992), 17–20.

21. Alan Bray, *Homosexuality in Renaissance England* (London: Gay Men's Press, 1982), 92; see also Richter Norton, *Mother Clap's Molly House: The Gay Subculture in England 1700–1830* (London: Gay Men's Press, 1992), 54–69. "Records" of these trials are to be found in *Select Trials at the Sessions-House in the Old Bailey*, ed. Randolph Trumbach, 2 vols. (New York: Garland, 1985).

22. Trumbach, ed., *Select Trials*, 2:362–372; see also Bray, *Homosexuality*, 81–90; and McCormick, *Secret Sexualities*, 73–75.

23. Trumbach, ed., *Select Trials*, 2:368; see also McCormick, *Secret Sexualities*, 78.

24. Ward, "The Mollies' Club," in *Second Part of the London Clubs*, 28; see also McCormick, *Secret Sexualities*, 132.

25. Patterson, "Rage of Caliban"; and McFarlane, *Sodomite*.

26. See Bray, *Homosexuality*, 81–114.

27. Trumbach, ed., *Select Trials*, 1:105–108, 158–160; see also McCormick, *Secret Sexualities*, 67–69.

28. *Satan's Harvest Home*, in *Hell Upon Earth: Or the Town in an Uproar and Satan's Harvest Home*, ed. Randolph Trumbach (New York: Garland, 1985), 47–48.

29. George Cheyne, *The English Malady; Or, A Treatise of Nervous Diseases of All Kinds*, intro. Eric T. Carlson, M.D. (1733; reprint, Delmar, N.Y.: Scholars' Facsimiles & Reprints, 1976), 66; 69–70.

30. See Londa Schiebinger, *The Mind Has No Sex? Women in the Origin of Modern Science* (Cambridge: Harvard University Press, 1989) and Thomas Laquer, *Making Sex* (Cambridge: Harvard University Press, 1990); see also Stephen Greenblatt, "Fiction and Friction," in *Renaissance Self-Fashioning: From More to Shakespeare* (Chicago: University of Chicago Press, 1980).

31. *Satan's Harvest Home*, 49–50.

32. Sedgwick, *Between Men*, 93.

33. For a discussion of this and other Hogarth fops in context, see David Bindman, *Hogarth* (London: Thames and Hudson, 1981), 104–118.

34. Ibid., 158–159.

35. Ibid., 152–153; see also Desmond Shaw-Taylor, *The Georgians: Eighteenth-Century Portraiture and Society* (London: Barrie and Jenkins, 1990), 67–68; and Ronald Paulson, *Hogarth: His Life, Art, and Times*, 2 vols. (New Haven: Yale University Press, 1971), 2:168–171. Paulson says that "a posturing dancing master is correcting the stance of an *Antinous* that appears much more natural than he" (170).

36. Paulson, *Hogarth: Art and Politics, 1750–1764*, 3 vols. (New Brunswick: Rutgers University Press, 1993), 3:106; see further 3:105–111. Thomas King argues that Hogarth "exaggerated the *contrapposto* stance of the Antinous beyond that of the classical sources themselves" and that "Hogarth's sketch asks us to see the difference between a 'fitting' serpentine line and the illustrated example, and to register that difference as homosexuality" ("Performing 'Akimbo,' " 30–31). This is a reasonable claim, if a slightly misleading one.

37. Philip Dormer Stanhope, 4th Earl of Chesterfield, *The Letters of the Earl of Chesterfield to his Son*, ed. C. Strachey, 2 vols. (London, 1901), 1:140.

38. Shaw-Taylor, *Georgians*, 66–68.

39. Nicola Kalinsky, *Gainsborough* (London: Phaidon, 1995), 23.

40. Warren Hodge, "When Italy Enchanted Touring Gentry," *New York Times*, December 7, 1996, p. 19.

41. *Satan's Harvest Home*, 51.

42. Brian Allen, "The Travellers," in *Grand Tour: The Lure of Italy in the Eighteenth Century*, ed. Andrew Wilton and Ilaria Bignamini (London: Tate Gallery Publishing, 1996), 52.

43. See for instance Trumbach, "Birth of the Queen," 129–141. See also Senelick, "Mollies."

44. Trumbach, "Birth of the Queen," 133–134; see also G. S. Rousseau, "The Pursuit of Homosexuality in the Eighteenth Century: 'Utterly Confused Category' and/or Rich Repository." *Eighteenth-Century Life* 9 (1985): 147–151.

45. Trumbach, "Birth of the Queen," 135.

46. Henry Fielding, *Joseph Andrews*, ed. Martin C. Battestin (1742; reprint, Middletown, Conn.: Wesleyan University Press, 1967), 312–313.

47. Battestin, ed., *Joseph Andrews*, xxiii, n. 2; 313, nn. 1, 2; see also R. F. Brissenden, *Joseph Andrews* (London: Penguin, 1985), 342, nn. 219, 220.

48. Robert Halsband, *Lord Hervey: Eighteenth-Century Courtier* (Oxford: Clarendon, 1973), 117; see 111–18.

49. Quoted in Halsband, *Lord Hervey*, 90, 102–103, 123.

50. Sedgwick, *Between Men*, 93.

51. Jill Campbell, "Politics and Sexuality in Portraits of John, Lord Hervey," *Word and Image* 6 (1990): 295–296.

52. Linda Dowling, *Hellenism and Homosexuality in Victorian Oxford* (Ithaca: Cornell University Press, 1995), 4.

53. Rousseau, "Pursuit of Homosexuality," 147; see also McFarlane, *Sodomite*, 133–136.

54. Tobias Smollett, *The Adventures of Roderick Random* (1748; reprint, Oxford: Oxford University Press, 1979), 197. Further references are included in the text.

55. McFarlane, *Sodomite*, 139–140.

56. Tobias Smollett, *The Adventures of Peregrine Pickle* (1751; reprint, Oxford: Oxford University Press, 1983), 427.

57. See chapter 4.

58. For a similar reading of Fielding's *The Female Husband*, see Terry Castle, " 'Matters Not Fit to be Mentioned': Fielding's *The Female Husband*," in *The Female Thermometer: 18th-Century Culture and the Invention of the Uncanny* (New York: Oxford University Press, 1995), 75.

59. McFarlane, *Sodomite*, 130.

60. Lee Edelman, *Homographesis: Essays in Gay Literary and Cultural Theory* (New York: Routledge, 1994), 188; McFarlane, *Sodomite*, 130.

61. "In any male-dominated society, there is a special relationship between male homosocial (*including* homosexual) desire and the structures for maintaining and transmitting patriarchal power: a relationship founded on an inherent and potentially active structural congruence" (Sedgwick, *Between Men*, 25).

62. See McFarlane, *Sodomite*, 130–131; for a theorization of masquerade in the eighteenth-century, see Terry Castle, *Masquerade and Civilization: The Carnivalesque in Eighteenth-Century English Culture and Fiction* (Stanford, Calif.: Stanford University Press, 1986), 52–109.

63. *The Pretty Gentleman: or, Softness of Manners Vindicated* (London, 1747), 9–10.

64. See Linda Dowling, *Hellenism and Homosexuality*, 1–31.

3. Sensibility and Its Symptoms

1. Laurence Sterne, *A Sentimental Journey Through France and Italy*, ed., Ian Jack (Oxford: Oxford University Press, 1984), 117.

2. Quoted in John A. Dussinger, "The Sensorium in the World of *A Sentimental Journey*," *Ariel* 13 (1982): 3; also see 3–6. See also Joseph Chadwick, "Infinite Jest: Interpretation in Sterne's *A Sentimental Journey*," *Eighteenth-Century Studies* 12 (1978/79): 198–199; and Robert Markley, "Sentimentality as Performance: Shaftesbury, Sterne, and the Theatrics of Virtue," in *The New*

Eighteenth Century, ed. Felicity Nussbaum and Laura Brown (New York: Methuen, 1987), 227–228.

3. Laurence Sterne, *The Life and Opinions of Tristram Shandy, Gentleman*, James A. Work, ed. (1759–1767; reprint, New York: Odyssey Press, 1940, 1960), 107.

4. Sensibility was not simply a male preserve. For a discussion of the female implications of sensibility, see Claudia L. Johnson, *Equivocal Beings: Politics, Gender, and Sentimentality in the 1790s* (Chicago: Chicago University Press, 1995), 1–19; Janet Todd, *Sensibility: An Introduction* (London: Methuen, 1986), 110–128; and G. J. Barker-Benfield, *The Culture of Sensibility: Sex and Society in Eighteenth-Century Britain* (Chicago: University of Chicago Press, 1992), 104–153.

5. See for instance Barker-Benfield, *Culture of Sensibility*; Judith Frank, " 'A Man Who Laughs Is Never Dangerous': Character and Class in Sterne's *A Sentimental Journey*," *ELH* 56 (1989): 97–124; Markley, "Sentimentality as Performance," 210–230; John Mullan, *Sentiment and Sociability: Language and Feeling in the Eighteenth Century* (Oxford: Clarendon, 1988); Todd, *Sensibility: An Introduction*. Any study of sensibility must also acknowledge R. F. Brissenden, *Virtue in Distress: Studies in the Novel of Sentiment from Richardson to Sade* (London: Macmillan, 1974).

6. Michel Foucault, *The History of Sexuality*, vol. 1, *An Introduction*, trans. Robert Hurley (New York: Vintage, 1980), 116.

7. Slavoj Žižek, *The Sublime Object of Ideology* (London: Verso, 1989), 26.

8. Ibid., 69; see further, 55–84.

9. Eve Kosofsky Sedgwick, *Between Men: English Literature and Male Homosocial Desire* (New York: Columbia University Press, 1985), 72.

10. Sterne, *A Sentimental Journey*, 8–13.

11. Sedgwick, *Between Men*, 72.

12. This and the following two quotations are from *A Sentimental Journey*, 51–53.

13. Frank, " 'A Man Who Laughs,' " 115.

14. This Rousseauistic revision of the Cartesian formula is an eighteenth-century commonplace. See for instance G. S. Rousseau, "Nerves, Spirits, and Fibres: Towards Defining the Origins of Sensibility," in *Studies in the Eighteenth Century, III*, ed. R. F. Brissenden (Toronto: University of Toronto Press, 1976), 139.

15. See Markley, "Sentimentality as Performance," 211.

16. See Dussinger, "Sensorium," 7–8; see also Dussinger, *The Discourse of the Mind in Eighteenth-Century Fiction* (The Hague: Mouton, 1974), 25–52; Martin C. Battestin, *The Providence of Wit: Aspects of Form in Augustan Literature and the Arts* (Oxford: Clarendon-Oxford, 1974), 267; and Mullan, *Sentiment and Sociability*, 159.

17. Tobias Smollett, *The Expedition of Humphry Clinker* (1771; reprint, Harmondsworth: Penguin, 1980), 95.

18. Ibid., 75.

19. Mullan, *Sentiment and Sociability*, 124.

20. Henry Mackenzie, *The Man of Feeling*, ed. Brian Vickers (1771; reprint, Oxford: Oxford University Press, 1970), 48.

21. Sedgwick, *Between Men*, 72, 80.

22. Michel Foucault, *The Order of Things: An Archaeology of the Human Sciences* (New York: Vintage-Random House, 1970), 62; see also Dussinger, *Discourse*, 16.

23. Mullan, *Sentiment and Sociability*, 119.

24. As Marilyn Butler demonstrates, Mackenzie himself comes to question his sentimentality, seeing it as dangerous and subversive. See *The Lounger* 20 (June 18, 1785): 172–173; reprinted in Ioan Williams, *Novel and Romance* (New York: Barnes and Noble, 1970), 328–331; see also Marilyn Butler, *Jane Austen and the War of Ideas* (Oxford: Clarendon, 1975), 21; and Frank, " 'A Man Who Laughs,' " 99.

25. See John Locke, *An Essay Concerning Human Understanding*, Peter N. Nidditch, ed. (1689; reprint, Oxford: Clarendon-Oxford, 1975), bk. 2, ch. 27, par. 17; 341.

26. See Ernest Lee Tuveson, *The Imagination as a Means of Grace: Locke and the Aesthetics of Romanticism* (Berkeley and Los Angeles: University of California Press, 1960), 27–29.

27. David Hume, *A Treatise of Human Nature*, L. Selby-Bigge, ed.; 2d ed., revised P. H. Nidditch (1739; reprint, Oxford: Oxford University Press, 1978), bk. 1, pt. 1, sec. 2, p. 8.

28. Thomas Weiskel, *The Romantic Sublime: Studies in the Structure and Psychology of Transcendence* (Baltimore and London: Johns Hopkins University Press, 1976), 18; see also Tuveson, "Locke and the 'Dissolution of the Ego,' " *Modern Philology* 52 (1955): 159–174.

29. John Sitter has characterized this uneasiness as a retreat from history; see *Literary Loneliness in Mid-Eighteenth-Century England* (Ithaca: Cornell University Press, 1982), 87; see also G. A. Starr, "Sentimental De-Education," *Augustan Studies. Essays in Honor of Irvin Ehrenpries*, Douglas Lane and Timothy Kegan, eds. (Newark: University of Delaware Press, 1985), 253–262.

30. See Barker-Benfield, *Culture of Sensibility*, 229.

31. Žižek, *Sublime Object*, 45; see also Ernesto Laclau and Chantal Mouffe, *Hegemony and Socialist Strategy* (London: Verso, 1985).

32. Markley, "Sentimentality," 213.

33. George Cheyne, *The English Malady*, ed. Eric T. Carlson, M.D. (1733; reprint, Delmar, N.Y.: Scholar's Facsimiles & Reprints, 1976), vii, 12, 133, 134.

34. For an interesting discussion of "cause and effect" in Cheyne's diagnostic work, see Mullan, *Sentiment and Sociability*, 205–207; see also Klaus Doerner, *Madmen and the Bourgeoisie: A Social History of Insanity and Psychiatry*, trans. Joachim Neugoschek and Jean Steinberg (Oxford: Blackwell, 1981), 29–30.
35. Cheyne, *English Malady*, 138.
36. Ibid., 128.
37. See for instance Roy Porter, *Disease, Medicine, and Society in England, 1550–1860 (New Studies in Economic and Social History)* (Cambridge: Cambridge University Press, 1998); Roy Porter, ed. *Patients and Practitioners: Lay Perceptions of Medicine in Pre-Industrial Society* (Cambridge: Cambridge University Press, 1985); see also Barker-Benfield, *Culture of Sensibility*, 1–36.
38. Michel Foucault, *Madness and Civilization*, trans. Richard Howard (New York: Vintage, 1965), 146; see also Mullan, *Sentiment and Sociability*, 201–240; and Doerner, *Madmen and the Bourgeoisie*, 20–95.
39. For a full account of the publication of these essays, see Margery Bailey's introduction to her edition of James Boswell's *The Hypochondriack*, 2 vols. (Stanford, Calif.: Stanford University Press, 1928), 1:3–99; for a critical discussion of *The Hypochondriack*, see Frank Brady, *James Boswell: The Later Years, 1769–1795* (New York: McGraw-Hill, 1984), 176–181.
40. Bailey, ed., *Hypochondriack*, 1:137. Further references will be included parenthetically in the text.
41. *The Ominous Years: 1774–1776*, ed. Charles Ryskamp and Frederick A. Pottle (New York: McGraw Hill, 1963), 54; *The English Experiment: 1785–1789*, ed. Irma S. Lustig and Frederick A. Pottle (New York: McGraw-Hill, 1986), 95.
42. John Hill, *Hypochondriasis: A Practical Treatise* (1766; reprint, Los Angeles: 1969), 6; see Mullan, *Sentiment and Sociability*, 208–210; for Mullan's discussion of Boswell, see 210–213.
43. Smith quoted in Mullan, *Sentiment and Sociability*, 208–209.
44. Foucault, *Madness and Civilization*, 155–156.
45. Mullan, *Sentiment and Sociability*, 235–236.
46. Doerner, *Madmen and the Bourgeoisie*, 30; Mullan questions Doerner's use of "unreason": see *Sentiment and Sociability*, 203.
47. These quotations are from *Macbeth* (3.2.36) and *Hamlet* (3.1.74).
48. See for instance Foucault, *History of Sexuality*, 103–114.
49. Žižek, *Sublime Object*, 73–74.
50. Mullan, *Sentiment and Sociability*, 213, 209; Robert James, *Medicinal Dictionary* (3 vols., London: 1743–45) s.v. HYPOCHONDRIUS MORBUS.
51. Mullan, *Sentiment and Sociability*, 209.
52. Hypocratus, *The Sacred Disease*, 18. 1.
53. William Battie founded St. Luke's Hospital in an attempt to improve treatment

of the insane in the hope of curing mental illness. He also thought that medical students should include mental illnesses in their course of study. Battie was among the first to see madness as something that depends on a "deluded imagination" for its "essential character." (Battie, A Treatise on Madness [London, 1758]; quoted in Doerner, Madmen and the Bourgeoisie, 41.)

54. Žižek, Sublime Object, 74.

55. Ibid., 74–75.

56. Ibid., 77.

57. Ibid., 75; in this context he goes on to say that "Now it is perhaps clear why woman is, according to Lacan, a symptom of man."

58. Ibid., 180–181.

59. Cheyne, The English Malady, 59.

60. See Dussinger, Discourse, 30–31; also see Foucault, Order, 46–77.

61. Shoshana Felman, Literary Speech Act: Don Juan with J. L. Austin, or Seduction in Two Languages, trans. Catherine Porter (Ithaca: Cornell University Press, 1983), 11–12.

62. Žižek, Sublime Object, 48.

63. Michel Foucault, The Birth of the Clinic: An Archaeology of Medical Perception (1963), trans. A. M. Sheridan Smith (London: Tavistock, 1973), 197; for an extended discussion of the gendering of scientific language, see also Londa Schiebinger, The Mind Has No Sex? Women in the Origin of Modern Science (Cambridge: Harvard University Press, 1989).

4. Gray's Tears

1. The texts of Gray's poems throughout this essay are those found in The Poems of Gray, Collins, and Goldsmith, ed. Roger Lonsdale (London: Longman, 1969).

2. Gray's middle-aged infatuation with Charles-Victor de Bonstettin, a young Swiss gentleman who loved Gray's poetry and found his way to Cambridge to "study," is well documented. The most interesting discussion of Gray's relations with Bonstettin remains that to be found in Jean Hagstrum, "Gray's Sensibility," in Fearful Joy: Papers from the Thomas Gray Bicentenary Conference at Carleton University, ed. J. Downey and B. Jones (McGill-Queen's University, 1974), 6–19.

3. Among the critics who have addressed Gray's "sexuality" are: R. W. Ketton-Cremer, Thomas Gray: A Biography (Cambridge: Cambridge University Press, 1965); Hagstrum, "Gray's Sensibility"; G. S. Rousseau, "The Pursuit of Homosexuality in the Eighteenth Century: 'Utterly Confused Category' and/or Rich Repository." Eighteenth-Century Life 9 (1985): 132–168; Raymond Bentman, "Thomas Gray and the Poetry of 'Hopeless Love,' " Journal of the

History of Sexuality 3 (1992): 203–22; and Robert F. Gleckner, *Gray Agonistes: Thomas Gray and Masculine Friendship* (Baltimore: Johns Hopkins University Press, 1996). Gleckner takes a lurid fascination with Gray's sexual friendships and attempts to use those friendships to make the case that Gray's poetry reveals "a struggle with Milton's ghost" that is somehow related to his struggle to reveal the terms of his "relationship with West (with some reference to Gray's friendship with Walpole and Thomas Ashton)" (8). I do not think that this study is really helpful in coming to terms with questions of sexuality in Gray or in the period as a whole.

4. For an interesting account of the place of the "Elegy" in eighteenth-century culture, see John Guillory, "Mute Inglorious Miltons: Gray, Wordsworth, and the Vernacular Canon," in *Cultural Capital: The Problem of Literary Canon Formation* (Chicago: Chicago University Press, 1993), 85–133.

5. The OED first recorded use of the term occurs in 1800; significantly it is a poet of sensibility, Cowper, who is first cited as using the term in describing male and female qualities of plants (*OED*, s.v. "sexuality"). For a discussion of "homosexuality" in the eighteenth century, see my introduction.

6. "Gray avait la gaieté dans l'ésprit et de la mélancholie dans le caractère. Mais cette mélancholie n'est qu'un besoin non-satisfait de la sensibilité," (Bonstetten, *Souvenirs* [1831], quoted in Ketton-Cremer, *Thomas Gray*, 253); see also Hagstrum, "Gray's Sensibility," 7–11.

7. Foucault, *The History of Sexuality*, vol. 1, *An Introduction*, trans. Robert Hurley (New York: Vintage-Random House, 1980), 116; see pages oo–oo.

8. Obvious exceptions include the work of: Julia Epstein, Jean Hagstrum, Claudia L. Johnson, Robert Markley, G. S. Rousseau, and Kristina Straub.

9. See for instance Nancy Armstrong, *Desire and Domestic Fiction: A Political History of the Novel* (Oxford: Oxford University Press, 1987), 48–58.

10. See Michael McKeon, "Historicizing Patriarchy: The Emergence of Gender Difference in England, 1660-1760," *Eighteenth-Century Studies* 28 (1995): 295-322.

11. "Lusit amicitiæ interdum velatus amictu,/et bene composita veste fefellit Amor," Gray wrote to West translating an Italian poem into Latin: "Sometimes Love jested, concealed in the cloak of friendship, and disguised himself in seemly attire"; see Lonsdale, ed., *Poems*, 316.

12. The phrase is from Bentman, "Thomas Gray," 203.

13. Ketton-Cremer, *Thomas Gray*, 5; see also Jacob Bryant, a contemporary of Gray's at Eton who, writing in 1798, remarks that "both Mr. Gray and his friend [Walpole] were looked upon as too delicate, upon which account they had few associates, and never engaged in any exercise, nor partook of any boyish amusement. Hence they seldom were in the fields, at least they took only a distant view of those who pursued their different diversions. Some, therefore, who were

severe, treated them as feminine characters, on account of their too great delicacy, and sometimes a too fastidious behaviour" (*Gentleman's Magazine* 35
[new Series (1846)], 140–143, quoted in Lonsdale, ed., *Poems*, 54–55).

14. William H. Epstein, "Assumed Identities: Gray's Correspondence and the
'Intelligence Communities' of Eighteenth-Century Studies," *Eighteenth-
Century Studies* 32 (1991): 276.

15. *Correspondence of Thomas Gray*, ed. Paget Toynbee and Leonard Whibley, 3
vols. (Oxford: Clarendon, 1935), 1:1.

16. Ibid., 1:5–6; 1:15–16; critics such as Hagstrum, "Gray's Sensibility"; Bentman,
"Thomas Gray"; and Epstein, "Assumed Identities," all find a dazzling array of
similarly suggestive material in the letters. It is important to remember that
even in their edited form, these letters were considered a model in the eighteenth century. See Epstein, "Assumed Identities," 278.

17. For the reference to "Miss Gray," see A. L. Lytton Sells, *Thomas Gray: His Life
and Works* (London: Allen and Unwyn, 1980), 18.

18. For another reading of Gray's letters to West and Walpole, see Bentman,
"Thomas Gray," 204–209; Bentman helpfully compares the quality of emotion in
Gray's letters to West and Walpole to that in other letters between male friends.
Žižek discusses Lacanian "lack" in terms that support this analysis of desire as loss:
"What the object [of desire] is masking, dissimulating, by its massive, fascinating
presence, is not some other positivity but *its own place*, the void, the lack that it is
filling by its presence—the lack in the Other" (*Sublime Object*, 195).

19. *Correspondence*, 1:6; Nathaniel Lee, *The Rival Queens; or, the Death of
Alexander the Great*, ed. P. F. Vernon (1677; reprint, Lincoln: University of
Nebraska Press, 1970), 38 (II.174–185).

20. Gray, *Correspondence*, 1:9; Walpole says about these lines that "One of his
[Gray's] first pieces of poetry was an answer in English verse to an epistle from
H. W." Lonsdale prints this as the first poem in Lonsdale, ed., *Poems*, 13–17.

21. Gray, *Correspondence*, 1:14–15; for a discussion of this passage, see Hagstrum,
"Gray's Sensibility," 15; see also Bentman, "Thomas Gray," 204–205; and
Epstein, "Assumed Identities," 278–279. Epstein notes the "epistolary ploy of
Gray's assuming an alternative identity in order to write about himself."

22. R. W. Ketton-Cremer, *Thomas Gray; A Biography* (Cambridge: Cambridge
University Press, 1955), 5; for "loving," see the discussion of "De Principiis
Cogitandi," below.

23. Paget and Whibley, eds., *Correspondence of Thomas Gray*, 1:87; the translation
is adapted from Lonsdale, ed., *Poems*, 308.

24. In the "Metaphysic poem," "De Principiis Cogitandi," which Gray addressed
to West in 1740 or 1741, he begins his discussion of the principles of thinking
with "touch"; see Lonsdale, ed., *Poems*, 321–32; see also Hagstrum, "Gray's
Sensibility," 13.

25. Lacan's *sinthome* is "a neologism containing a set of associations (synthetic-artificial man, synthesis between symptom and fantasy, Saint Thomas, the saint . . .). Symptom as *sinthome* is a certain signifying formation penetrated with enjoyment: it is a signifier as a bearer of *jouis-sense*, enjoyment-in-sense." Žižek insists on "the radical ontological status of symptom: symptom, conceived as *sinthome*, is literally our only substance, the only positive support of our being, the only point that gives consistency to the subject" (Žižek, *Sublime Object*, 75.

26. Toynbee and Whibley, eds., *Correspondence of Thoms Gray*, 1:158; trans. Lonsdale, ed., *Poems*, 311.

27. An interesting reading of this, the other Latin poems, and Gray's relation with West in general is to be found in Bentman, "Thomas Gray"; Bentman's discussion of the *mollitudinem* with which Gray teases West in a reference to Nonius Marcellus, and its connection to the notion of "molly," is particularly suggestive (208).

28. Lonsdale, ed., *Poems*, 57.

29. See Linda Zionkowski, who makes a similar claim for Gray's "Sonnet on the Death of Richard West," in "Gray, Marketplace, and the Masculine Poet" *Criticism* 35 (1993): 589–608; see also Paul Oppenheimer, *The Birth of the Modern Mind: Self, Consciousness, and the Invention of the Sonnet* (New York: Oxford University Press, 1989), 184. For a discussion of the flight from history in the poetry of sensibility, see John Sitter, *Literary Loneliness in Eighteenth-Century England* (Ithaca: Cornell University Press, 1982).

30. Lonsdale, ed., *Poems*, 67–68.

31. Ibid., 67.

32. See " 'The Voice of Nature' in Gray's *Elegy*," in *Homosexuality in Renaissance and Enlightenment England: Literary Representations in Historical Context*, ed. Claude J. Summers (New York: Haworth Press, 1992), 199–214; see also Rousseau, "Pursuit of Homosexuality."

33. The Gray *Concordance* (Albert S. Cook, ed., *A Concordance to the English Poems of Thomas Gray* [Folcroft, Pa.: Folcroft, 1908; reprint 1969]) lists twenty uses of *vain*—mostly in this sense of "in vain"—in Gray's poetry. It is not an exaggeration to call this mood typical.

34. Sigmund Freud, "Mourning and Melancholia," in *General Psychological Theory*, ed. Philip Reiff (New York: Collier, 1963), 164, 166.

35. See for instance Andrew Elfenbein, "Stricken Deer: Secrecy, Homophobia, and the Rise of Suburban Man," *Genders* 27 (1998). Online at http://www.genders.org/g27_stdr.html.

36. Eve Kosofsky Sedgwick, *Epistemology of the Closet* (Berkeley: University of California Press, 1990), 22.

37. Ibid., 73.

38. For a reading of the emphasis on passion and fear in this elegy, see Bentman, "Thomas Gray," 216.

39. Ibid., 209.
40. Lonsdale, ed., *Poems*, 328; translation (adapted), 332.
41. Discussions of sexuality in the poem include: Peter Watson-Smyth, "On Gray's Elegy," *The Spectator* (July 31, 1971): 171–174; Hagstrum, "Gray's Sensibility"; and Bentman, "Thomas Gray."
42. Julia Kristeva, *Powers of Horror: An Essay on Abjection*, trans. Leon S. Roudiez (New York: Columbia University Press, 1982), 1.
43. For Kristeva, "passivation, which heralds the subject's ability to place himself in the place of the object, is a radical stage in the constitution of subjectivity" (*Powers of Horror*, 39).
44. Lonsdale, ed., *Poems*, 114.
45. Patricia Meyer Spacks, *The Poetry of Vision: Five Eighteenth-Century Poets* (Harvard University Press, 1967), 115.
46. Lonsdale, ed., *Poems*, 122.
47. Kristeva, *Powers of Horror*, 140.
48. The cruelty of Gray's father is proverbial. For a useful account, see Hagstrum, "Gray's Sensibility," 12.
49. Kristeva, *Powers of Horror*, 85.
50. Toynbee and Whibley, eds., *Correspondence of Thomas Gray*, 1:209
51. For a discussion of the early version of the poem, see Lonsdale, *Poems*, 130–131, 140–141
52. Kristeva, *Powers of Horror*, 45.
53. Much has been written about this feature of the poem. See for instance Frank Brady, "Structure and Meaning in Gray's *Elegy*," in *From Sensibility to Romanticism: Essays Presented to Frederick A. Pottle*, Frederick W. Hilles and Harold Bloom, eds. (London: Oxford University Press, 1965), 177–189; Bertrand H. Bronson, "On a Special Decorum in Gray's *Elegy*," in Hilles and Bloom, 171–176; and Ian Jack, "Gray's *Elegy* Reconsidered," in Hilles and Bloom, 139–169.
54. Kristeva, *Powers of Horror*, 109.
55. "Hope trembles in the 'Elegy' because of guilt and the prospect of Judgment" (Hagstrum, "Gray's Sensibility," 10–11).

5. Beckford's Pæderasty

1. *Morning Herald*, November 27, 1784; quoted in Guy Chapman, *Beckford* (London: Jonathan Cape, 1940), 185.
2. William Beckford was born in 1760 to one of England's wealthiest families. His father was Alderman and Lord Mayor of London; his mother a strict Calvinist who did her best, especially after his father died when he was ten years old, to form a young gentleman who would rise to political prominence as his father

had. Beckford early on showed tendencies of which his mother disapproved, such as his devotion to music, his fascination with "oriental" tales, and his love of young boys. William Courtenay, born in 1768, the youngest child and heir of the 2d Viscount Courtenay (Courtenay had twelve older daughters), was known in the family as "Kitty."

3.　It is impossible to say what "really" happened at Powderham. There is little reason to think that Beckford and Courtenay were exposed in some dramatic way: Beckford himself protested that he was innocent of any wrong-doing, and he nursed a grievance against Loughborough throughout his entire life. Loughborough may only have had Beckford's letters to Courtenay. But then, what more did he need to exercise complete control over his eccentric victim? For details of the Powderham scandal, see Fothergill, *Beckford of Fonthill* (London: Faber, 1979), 163–175.

4.　To prosecute Beckford, Loughborough would have needed at least an eye-witness, which, in spite of the lurid accounts that emerged from Powderham, he seems not to have had; and he would have needed Courtenay's willingness to hand over letters and to participate in the prosecution. Records of eighteenth-century sodomy trials, such as they are, suggest no precedents for prosecuting a person of Beckford's class or social status. See chapter 2 for further details.

5.　Gregory W. Bredbeck, *Sodomy and Interpretation* (Ithaca: Cornell University Press, 1991), 146–148. See Alain De Lille, *The Complaint of Nature* (De Planctu Naturae), trans. Douglas M. Moffat (c. 1165; reprint, New York: 1908), 3; see also Alan of Lille, *Plaint of Nature*, trans. James J. Sheridan (Toronto: Pontifical Institute of Medieval Studies, 1981), 68.

6.　Fourteen was the age of consent for males at the time. See Randolph Trumbach, "Sodomitical Assaults, Gender Role, and Sexual Development in Eighteenth-Century London," in *The Pursuit of Sodomy: Male Homosexuality in Renaissance and Enlightenment Europe*, ed. Kent Gerard and Gert Hekma (New York: Harrington Park Press, 1989), 410.

7.　*Pembroke Papers* (1780–1704), p. 274; quoted in Fothergill, *Beckford of Fonthill*, 173. Lord Pembroke was writing to England at the time of the Powderham scandal; interestingly, his knowledge of the situation leads him to no conclusions about sexual roles.

8.　*Morning Herald*, December 8, 1784; quoted in Chapman, *Beckford*, 185. For a similar argument against sodomy, see *Satan's Harvest Home* (1749; reprint, New York: Garland, 1985), 50–55.

9.　Lewis Melville, *The Life and Letters of William Beckford* (London: Heinemann, 1910), 77.

10.　Ibid., 77–78.

11.　*Thraliana, The Diary of Mrs. Hester Lynch Thrale (Later Mrs. Piozzi)*,

1776–1809, ed. Katharine C. Balderston, 2d ed. (Oxford: Clarendon, 1951), 2:799, 969n; 2:969n.

12. The pæderasty of *Vathek*, obvious to readers such as Hester Piozzi, is so suffused with the twilight glow of Beckford's emotion as to defy late twentieth-century notions of child abuse and victimization. It is focused on the figure of Gulchenrouz, the only central character who escapes damnation in the novel; he does so by remaining within "the pure happiness of childhood" in which love remains unsullied by the promptings of desire. See George E. Haggerty, "Literature and Homosexuality in the Later Eighteenth Century: Walpole, Beckford, and Lewis," *Studies in the Novel* 18 (1986): 341–352.

13. See for instance Juliet Flower MacCannell, "Resistance to Sexual Theory," in *Theory/Pedagogy/Politics: Texts for Change*, ed. Donald Morton and Mas'ud Zavarzadeh (Urbana: University of Illinois Press, 1991), 64–89. MacCannell develops Jane Gallop's argument about the relation between pedagogy and pederasty from the time of Plato. See Gallop, "The Immoral Teachers," *Yale French Studies* 63 (1982): 117–128.

14. David M. Halperin, *One Hundred Years of Homosexuality and Other Essays on Greek Love* (New York: Routledge, 1990), 20–24, 54–71, and passim; see also K. J. Dover, *Greek Homosexuality* (Cambridge: Harvard University Press, 1978), 16–17, 49–54, 73–109.

15. As early as 1831 Arthur Hallam wrote his prize-winning essay on Greek love, which parallels arguments made even earlier by Percy Bysshe Shelley; see Richard Dellamora, *Masculine Desire: The Sexual Politics of Victorian Aestheticism* (Chapel Hill: University of North Carolina Press, 1990), 16–17; 24–25.

16. For a discussion of the language and imagery of Greek love, see K. J. Dover, *Greek Homosexuality*, 39–59. See also pages 11–20 above.

17. Alice A. Kuzniar, Introduction, *Outing Goethe and His Age* (Stanford, Calif.: Stanford University Press, 1996), 14–15.

18. See, for an instance of Renaissance pæderasty, Richard Barnfield, *The Affectionate Shepheard, Containing the Complaint of Daphnis for the Loue of Ganimede* (London, 1594).

19. Rochester, *Poems*, ed. Keith Walker (London: Blackwell, 1984),31. See also pages 6–11 above.

20. The most complete classification of male-male sexual possibilities in the eighteenth century is that found in G. S. Rousseau, "The Pursuit of Homosexuality in the Eighteenth Century: 'Utterly Confused Category' and/or Rich Repository?" in *'Tis Nature's Fault: Unauthorized Sexuality during the Enlightenment*, ed. Robert Purks Maccubbin (Cambridge: Cambridge University Press, 1987), 132–168; for Rousseau's account of Beckford, see p. 144.

21. Rochester, *Poems*, 99.
22. It was not only court libertines who felt this way. Randolph Trumbach alludes to the 1761 court martial in which "Charles Ferret testified that when he was awakened by the noise of the sexual exertion of Henry Newton on Thomas Finney's body, '[I] put my left hand up and got hold of both his stones fast, the other part was in the body of the boy, I asked him what he had got there, he said cunt' "; Trumbach, "Sodomitical Assaults, Gender Role, and Sexual Development in Eighteenth-Century London," in Gerard and Hekma, eds., *The Pursuit of Sodomy*, 415; see also Arthur N. Gilbert, "Buggery in the British Navy," *Journal of Social History* 10 (1976): 74–75. Gilbert also explains that "In spite of the supposed legal difficulties of proving buggery in the courts, a high percentage of purported sodomites are convicted and executed. While proof of penetration rules protected some men on trial for this offense, the navy still managed to hang more than half the men brought to trial for buggery between 1749 and 1806," (86).
23. Eve Kosofsky Sedgwick, *Between Men: Male Homosocial Desire in English Literature* (New York: Columbia University Press, 1985).
24. Harold Weber, " 'Drudging in Fair Aurelia's Womb': Constructing Homosexual Economies in Rochester's Poetry." *The Eighteenth Century: Theory and Interpretation* 33 (1992): 99–117 [115]; see also Trumbach, "The Birth of the Queen: Sodomy and the Emergence of Gender Equality in Modern Culture, 1660–1750," in *Hidden From History: Reclaiming the Gay and Lesbian Past*, ed. Martin Bauml Duberman, Martha Vicinus, and George Chauncey, Jr. (New York: New American Library, 1989), 129–140.
25. Pæderasty, of course, was implicit in accounts of male-male erotic attraction that centered on the figure of Ganymede; see for instance James Saslow, *Ganymede in the Renaissance: Homosexuality in Art and Society* (New Haven: Yale University Press, 1986); for a discussion of the "cultural translation" of the myth, see Leonard Barkin, *Transuming Passion: Ganymede and the Erotics of Humanism* (Stanford, Calif.: Stanford University Press, 1991), 8, 21–24, 29–36, 56–59. See also Bredbeck, *Sodomy and Interpretation*, 3–23; for Bredbeck's explanation of Renaissance distinctions among the terms *Ganymede*, *catamite*, and *ingle*, see 16–18.
26. In *A Tale of a Tub*, Swift mentions that his Academy will include a "large *Pederastick* school with *French* and *Italian* masters"; see *A Tale of a Tub*, ed. A. C. Guthkeltch and D. Nichol Smith, 2d ed. (1704; reprint, Oxford: Clarendon, 1958), 41. In speaking of the severe Roman punishment for same-sex activity at the time of Justinian (reigned 527–565), Gibbon notes that "a sentence of death and infamy was often founded on the slight evidence of a child or a servant, . . . and pæderasty became the crime of those to whom no crime could be imputed." See *The History of the Decline and Fall of the Roman Empire* (1776–1788;

reprint, 3 vols., London: Allen Lane [The Penguin Press], 1994), 2:839 (chapter 44). See also, David Hume, *Philosophical Works*, ed. T. H. Green and T. H. Grose (London, 1874–1875), 2: 233.

27. Beckford uses this phrase in a reverie written to Courtenay but never sent; see Chapman, *Beckford*, 55. In his essay, "Why Is Diotoma a Woman?" David Halperin tries to argue the role that femininity might play in the definition of male-male desire, and Kaja Silverman, too, talks about the "place of femininity in male homosexuality." See Halperin, *One Hundred Years*, 113–151; Kaja Silverman, *Male Subjectivity at the Margins* (New York: Routledge, 1992), 339; see also 339–388.

28. Fothergill, *Beckford of Fonthill*, 70.

29. Chapman, *Beckford*, 81–82; see also Fothergill, *Beckford of Fonthill*, 98–99.

30. Fothergill, *Beckford of Fonthill*, 99.

31. On "romantic friendship," see Emma Donoghue, *Passions Between Women: British Lesbian Culture, 1668–1800* (London: Scarlet Press, 109–150).

32. Not all of Beckford's women friends were as supportive as these. Beckford's experience in Venice was a source of serious concern to his patroness, Lady Hamilton, wife of Sir William Hamilton, envoy to Naples. Beckford could say to her, typically: "I can venture expressing to you all my wayward thoughts—can murmur—can even weep in your company" (Melville, *Life and Letters*, 98; see also Fothergill, *Beckford of Fonthill*, 93); her response was clear: "Take courage. You have taken the first steps, continue to resist, and every day you will find the struggle less—the *important* struggle—what is it for? no less than *honour, reputation*, and all that an honest and noble soul holds dear, while infamy, *eternal infamy* (my Soul freezes when I write the word) attends the giving way to the soft alluring of a criminal passion" (quoted from the *Hamilton Papers*, in Chapman, *Beckford*, 78). It is important to remember that even at the time of the scandal, Beckford's wife was present. It is perhaps because she *was* present that the scandal ever occurred. Perhaps the presence of his wife, who supported and loved him and who, if she was like any of the other women to whom he was attached, knew about his devotion to William, gave him permission, as it were, to pursue the boy during their visit there. Whatever is true, she remained faithful to him till her death a few years later.

33. Written December 1781, in French; quoted Boyd Alexander, *England's Wealthiest Son* (London: Centaur, 1962), appendix, 263–266 (my translation).

34. Chapman, *Beckford*, 135–136; dated Rome, July 1, 1782

35. There is ample evidence that Beckford was less charmed with the sixteen year-old William Courtenay than he had been with the "luscious" youth of twelve or thirteen. He wrote letters complaining of the boy's effeminacy, his interest in fashion, and his lack of attention in matters artistic or musical. After the crisis, Beckford blamed Courtenay for all that occurred.

36. *Public Advertiser*, December 1, 1784; correction of Chapman, *Beckford*, 185.

37. *Satan's Harvest Home*, 51; Hamilton quoted in Fothergill, 173, from *Hamilton Papers*, 1:95, letter 133; both characters were notorious for sexual "eccentricity."

38. Courtenay may have left Westminster School, but he did not accompany Beckford anywhere, nor were the two ever really close again. He went on to succeed his father as 3d Viscount Courtenay and later 9th Earl of Devon, and himself became notorious as a homosexual who was nearly prosecuted for his behavior. When convinced that a "jury of his peers" would not condone his activities, he "wept like a child and was willingly taken abroad on a vessel . . . and passed there under a false name." (This is quoted in Fothergill, *Beckford of Fonthill*, 178, from *Farington Diary*, 6:273.) Courtenay died in exile in 1835. Few critics or biographers have shown much interest in his later career, but some have gone so far as to blame him for Beckford's downfall. One biographer, for instance says that "in apportioning blame it is only fair to Beckford to remember that the life of Courtenay (afterwards Earl of Devon) ended, years after he and Beckford had drifted apart, in shame and moral catastrophe" (John W. Oliver, *The Life of William Beckford* [London: Oxford University Press, 1932], 196n.

39. On both *Vathek* and "The Story of Prince Alasi and the Princess Firouzkah," see Fothergill, *Beckford of Fonthill*, 128–134, 142–143.

40. Fothergill, *Beckford of Fonthill*, 142.

41. William Beckford, *The Episodes of Vathek*, trans. Frank T. Marzial, ed. Malcolm Jack (London: Daedalus, 1994), 24, 30.

42. On the question of Beckford's later sexual identification and its effect on his writing, see John Tinker, "William Beckford: The First English Homosexual" (Ph.D. diss. Stanford University, 1996), 131–182.

43. For an account of Beckford's later love affair with Gregorio Franchi, which was uniquely satisfying, see Fothergill, *Beckford of Fonthill*, 199–200.

6. Walpole's Secrets

1. *Horace Walpole's Correspondence*, ed. W. S. Lewis, 48 vols. (New Haven: Yale University Press, 1937–1983), 9:9.

2. *British Review* (May 1819); *Edinburgh Review* (October 1833); see also *Horace Walpole: The Critical Heritage*, ed. Peter Sabor (New York: Routledge and Kegan Paul, 1987), 192, 311.

3. Lytton Strachey, "Horace Walpole," *Independent Review* 2 (May 1904): 641–645; see also Sabor, ed., *Horace Walpole*, 11.

4. W. S. Lewis, *Horace Walpole* (New York: Pantheon, 1961), 36; R. W. Ketton-Cremer, *Horace Walpole: A Biography* (Ithaca: Cornell University Press, 1964), 1–7.

5. Timothy Mowl, for instance, says that "if readers suspect that a writer like myself, happily married to a second wife and the experienced father of a school-age son, has no business analyzing the subtleties of homosexual attitudes in the eighteenth century, then they are probably unaware how much homosexual activity and internecine conflict is commonplace in the world of architecture historians." See Timothy Mowl, *Horace Walpole: The Great Outsider* (London: John Murray, 1996), 7.

6. Lewis, ed., *Horace Walpole's Correspondence*, 30:6.

7. Ibid., 30:30.

8. Recently critics have suggested a connection between events in the mid 1760s and the publication of Walpole's two great literary works, *The Castle of Otranto* (1764) and *The Mysterious Mother* (1768). See for instance Robert L. Mack, "Introduction," *The Castle of Otranto and Hieroglyphic Tales* (London: Everyman, 1993), xxi–xxiii.

9. For a full account of these activities, see Ketton-Cremer, *Horace Walpole*, 198–203; see also, Mack, "Introduction," xx–xxi.

10. William Guthrie, *Reply to the Counter-Address* (London, 1764), 25; see Mack, "Introduction," xxii.

11. Letter to Conway, September 1, 1764; *Horace Walpole's Correspondence*, 38:437

12. Ketton-Cremer, *Horace Walpole*, 18.

13. W. S. Lewis, "Introduction," *Horace Walpole's Correspondence*, 37:xiv.

14. The expression comes from a discussion of the film *Another Country* in Slavoj Žižek, *The Sublime Object of Ideology* (New York: Verso, 1989): "it is impossible to maintain the coincidence of masks and truth: . . . this coincidence renders the situation unbearable: all communication is impossible because we are totally isolated through the very disclosure" (42).

15. For details of the disagreement between Walpole and Conway, see Ketton-Cremer, *Horace Walpole*, 205–207.

16. Lewis, ed., *Horace Walpole's Correspondence*, 9:50.

17. Ibid., 39:384.

18. Ibid., 339.

19. See a letter to William Mason, September 14, 1779 (Lewis, ed., *Horace Walpole's Correspondence*, 28:463).

20. Žižek, *Sublime Object*, 42.

21. Lewis, ed., *Horace Walpole's Correspondence*, 30:39.

22. See my *Unnatural Affections: Women and Fiction in the Later Eighteenth Century* (Bloomington: Indiana University Press, 1998), esp. 88–102. Terry Castle's discussion of Anne Lister's erotic attachments adds a great deal to this argument; see *The Apparitional Lesbian: Female Homosexuality and Modern Culture* (New York: Columbia University Press, 1993), 92–106.

23. C. S. Lewis, *The Allegory of Love: A Study in Medieval Tradition* (1936; reprint, Oxford: Oxford University Press, 1958), 9–10. The orientalist implications of this medieval work have yet to be fully explored.

24. Jonathan Goldberg, *Sodometries: Renaissance Texts, Modern Sexualities* (Stanford, Calif.: Stanford University Press, 1992), 119; Alan Bray, "Homosexuality and the Signs of Male Friendship," *History Workshop: A Journal of Socialist and Feminist Historians* 29 (1990): 1; for a helpful gloss on Bray's comments, see Goldberg, *Sodometries*, 17–20.

25. For a discussion of Raymond Stephanson's notion of "epicœne friendship," see pages 16–19, above. I assume that Stephanson would see Walpole as "homosexually inclined," but his concept obscures as much as it reveals about friendships such as those I am considering. See Raymond Stephanson, " 'Epicœne Friendship': Understanding Male Friendship in the Early Eighteenth Century, with Some Speculations about Pope" *The Eighteenth Century: Theory and Interpretation* 38 (1997): 151–170.

26. Lewis, ed., *Horace Walpole's Correspondence*, 30:43.

27. Horace Walpole, *The Castle of Otranto*, ed. W. S. Lewis and Joseph W. Reed (1764; reprint, London: Oxford, 1982); all parenthetical page references are to this edition.

28. See my "Literature and Homosexuality in the Eighteenth Century: Walpole, Beckford, and Lewis," *Studies in the Novel* 18 (1986): 341–352.

29. Robert L. Mack, "Introduction," The Castle of Otranto *and Hieroglyphic Tales* (London: Everyman, 1993), xvii–xviii.

30. Leo Bersani, *The Freudian Body: Psychoanalysis and Art* (New York: Columbia University Press, 1986), 41. Bersani sees this as the "counterargument" in Sigmund Freud's *Three Essays on Sexuality*. See also Michelle A. Massé, *In the Name of Love: Women, Masochism, and the Gothic* (Ithaca: Cornell University Press, 1992); and Tania Modleski, *Loving with a Vengeance: Mass-Produced Fantasies for Women* (New York: Routledge, 1988).

31. Silverman, *Male Subjectivity at the Margins*, 187.

32. Bersani, "Foucault, Freud, Fantasy, and Power," *GLQ: A Journal of Lesbian and Gay Studies* 2 (1994): 29, 31.

33. Lewis, ed., *Horace Walpole's Correspondence* 43–44. Walpole's editor says that in this letter Walpole is posing as one of Lincoln's mistresses. Perhaps, but the resonances are intriguing nonetheless. See my "Literature and Homosexuality in the Later Eighteenth Century", 343–44.

34. Horace Walpole, *The Mysterious Mother* in "Castle of Otranto" and "The Mysterious Mother", ed. Montague Summers (London: Constable, 1924). Further references are to this edition.

35. Andrew Elfenbein, "Stricken Deer: Secrecy, Homophobia, and the Rise of

Suburban Man," *Genders* 27 (1998): paras. 27–28. Online at: http://www.gen-ders.org/g27_stdr.html.

36. Eve Kosofsky Sedgwick, *The Epistemology of the Closet* (Berkeley: University of California Press, 1990), 3; see Elfenbein, "Stricken Deer," paras. 14–16.

37. Oscar Wilde, *The Picture of Dorian Gray*, ed. Peter Ackroyd (1891; reprint, London: Penguin, 1985), 26.

38. D. A. Miller, *The Novel and the Police* (Berkeley: University of California Press, 1988), 195.

39. Ketton-Cremer, *Horace Walpole*, 233.

40. For an interesting recent discussion of incest in eighteenth-century fiction, see Terri Nickel, " 'Ingenious Torment': Incest, Family, and the Structure of Community in the work of Sarah Fielding," *The Eighteenth Century: Theory and Interpretation* 36 (1995): 234–247.

41. Sir Horace Mann and Horace Walpole corresponded regularly from the time when Walpole visited Italy with Gray in 1739 until Mann's death in 1786. For this passage, see Lewis, ed., *Horace Walpole's Correspondence*, 24:517.

42. Lewis, ed., *Horace Walpole's Correspondence*, 30: 37

43. Ibid., xxvii.

44. Mowl, *Horace Walpole*, 14.

45. Ibid., 54, 64.

46. Lewis, *Horace Walpole's Correspondence*, 30: xxvii.

47. Eve Kosofsky Sedgwick, *Between Men: English Literature and Male Homosocial Desire* (New York: Columbia University Press, 1985).

INDEX

➔ ⬅

abjection: in Gray, 127–28, 131–32, 134;
    as queer in Walpole's *Castle of
    Otranto*, 163
actors as "sexual suspects," 24
Addison, Joseph and Sir Richard
    Steele: *The Spectator*, 3, 11, 176*n*9,
    178*n*27
Alain de Lille, 137, 195*n*5
Aldrich, Robert, 12, 178*nn*34–35
Alexander, Boyd, 198*n*33
Algarotti, Francisco, 70
Allen, Brian, 185*n*42
Althusser, Louis, 2
androgyny: man of feeling and, 83–85
Antinous, Emperor Hadrian and, 64
apprentice's role in *The London
    Merchant*, 39
aristocracy: and masculinity, 4, 10;
    pathologization of, 59–60
Armisted, J. M., 181*n*27, 182*nn*29–31&34
Armstrong, Nancy, 176*n*5, 191*n*9

Backscheider, Paula, 23, 35, 180*n*2,
    182*nn*33&36
Bailey, Margery, 189*n*39
Baker, Thomas: *Tunbridge Walks*
    (1703), 69
Banks, John, 23
Barkin, Leonard, 197*n*25
Barker-Benfield, G. J., 187*nn*4–5,
    188*n*30, 189*n*37
Barnfield, Richard, 196*n*18
Barnwell, George: ballad of, as source
    of *The London Merchant*, 39
Batoni, Pompano, 65, 69
Battestin, Martin C., 70, 185*nn*46–47,
    187*n*16
Battie, William, 189*n*53
Beckford, Louisa, 143, 147; love for
    Beckford, 147
Beckford, Margaret (William's wife),
    138
Beckford, Peter, 143

4th Earl of: advice concerning dress, 64, 185*n*37

Cheyne, George: *The English Malady* (1733), 60, 95–99, 104, 108, 109, 184*n*29, 188*n*33, 189*nn*34–36, 190*n*59

Chute, John, 170

Cibber, Colly, 51–52; and masculine masquerade, 51–52; *Love's Last Shift* (1696), 51; as Lord Foppington (in Vanbrugh's *The Relapse*) and Sir Novelty Fashion (in *Love's Last Shift*), 51–52

Clarke, Thomas (Restoration actor), 38–39

classical tradition in eighteenth-century culture, 11–20

Collins, William, 119

Congreve, William: *The Way of the World* (1700), 3, 176*n*8

Conway, Henry Seymour, 154–60, 200*n*11; dismissal from Whig ministry, 155

Cook, Albert A., 193*n*33

Cotterell, Sir Charles: translation of *Cassandra* (1661), 33, 182*nn*28–29

Courtenay, Charlotte, 143–44

Courtenay, William, 138, 143; blamed by Beckford, 149, 198*n*35; and the character Firouz, 150; family, 194*n*2; later life, 199*n*38; role in Powderham Affair, 136

courtly love, 158

Cowper, William, 175*n*2

Cozens, Alexander, 139

Craft, Christopher, 15, 179*n*43

cross-dressing in Restoration drama, 23

cultural determinism in discussions of love in the eighteenth century, 158

Death as ultimate Other for Gray, 131

Dellamora, Richard, 15, 179*n*42, 196*n*15

desire: and inaccessibility, 114; articulation of in Gray's "Elegy," 132; expressed within closet-like framework, 123. *See also* male-male desire

Diamond, Elin, 23, 37; and the concept of "theater apparatus," 24, 182*n*38

Dicks, John: sodomy trial of, 58

Doerner, Klaus, 102, 189*nn*38&46

dominant fiction, 2–3

Donoghue, Emma, 198*n*31

d'Orsini-Rosenberg, Contessa, 145

Dover, K. J.: on Greek love, 14, 179*nn*39–40, 196*nn*14&16

Dowling, Linda, 15, 16, 73, 179*nn*44–45, 186*nn*52&64

Dryden, John, 23, 28, 29, 31, 35, 38; *All for Love* (1677), 24–30, 38, 178*n*32, 180*n*9, 181*n*25; *Aureng-Zebe*, 23; *The Indian Emperor*, 23, 36; and orientalism, 23

Duffus, George: sodomy trial of, 58

Dussinger, John A., 81, 186*n*2, 187*n*16, 188*n*22, 190*n*60

Edelman, Lee, 77, 186*n*60

effeminacy, 44–80; in dress, 44, 45–48; and male-male sexual desire, 53; and monstrosity, 16; and sexual object choice, 44; and sexuality, 44; sodomy and, 61

effeminate sodomites described, 19

Elfenbein, Andrew, 167, 193*n*35, 201*n*35

Empson, William, 182*n*35

epicœne friendship, 18. *See* Stephanson, Raymond

Epstein, Julia, 1, 175*n*1, 191*n*8

Epstein, William H., 192*nn*14&21

erotic friendship, 11–20; and cultural

"other" is viewed, 37; as love, 18–20; as luxury, 4; as open secret of sensibility, 114

man of feeling, 4, 27; as alienated bourgeois subject, 86; as andogynous, 84; and the body, 81–95; and class-transgression, 89; and erotics of benevolence, 90; and family, 83; feminization of, 114; and gender-transgression, 89; as masturbatory, 83–84; as narcissistic, 84, 92; as passive and self-involved, 86, 90; and reconfiguration of desire, 90

Mann, Sir Horace, 170–71, 202n41

Margaret Clap's molly house: 1726 raid on, 55

Markley, Robert, 186n2, 187n15, 188n32, 191n8

Marlowe, Christopher: *Edward II*, 26–28, 32–33, 36; *Massacre at Paris*, 182n30; as source for Lee, 34

masculinity: and aristocarcy, 10; as a cultural construct, 1–6, 10; cultural function of, 172; as defined in Restoration theater, 31; social construction of, 60

masculinity: straight, collapse of, 110

masochism: and masturbatory fantasties, 163–64; in Walpole, *The Castle of Otranto*, 163

Mason, William, 116, 157, 200n19

masturbatory fantasies: in Gray's "Elegy," 130; and masochism, 164

Maurer, Shawn, 3, 176n9

McBurney, William H., 41, 182nn45–46

McCormick, Ian, 176n4, 184nn17–18&22–24&27

McFarlane, Cameron, 2, 53, 75–77, 175n4, 183n3, 184n25, 186nn53&59&62

McKeon, Michael, 10, 11, 178n26, 191n10

melancholy, 86; in Gray's *Elegy*, 114–15, 172–73; in *The London Merchant*, 40; and madness, 105

Melville, Lewis, 195nn9–10, 198n32

mercantile culture: in *The London Merchant*, 39

middle-class intellectual, 4

middle-class morality, 115; and erotic friendship in *The London Merchant*, 42

Milhouse, Judith, 38, 182n42

Miller, D. A., 167, 168, 202n38

misogynism: in *The Rival Queens*, 35

mock marriage as mockery of social structure, 57–59

molly/mollies, 2, 5, 19, 173, 193n27; arrest and execution, 55–59; and love, 57; and mock Christening, 57; not fops, 53; as threat, 57

molly house, 54–59; as "coherent social milieu," 55; penetration and, 56; physical description of, 56; and subcultural identification, 58; as threat to heteronormative culture, 59

molly house accounts, 54–59; as history or fiction, 54; and sexual identity, 55

Montague, George, 156, 170

Mouffe, Chantal, 94

Mowl, Timothy, 171, 172, 176n12, 200n5, 202nn44–45

Mullan, John, 89, 92, 100, 101, 104, 105, 187n5, 188nn19&23, 189nn34&38&42–43&45, 189nn50–51

Nickel, Terri, 202n40

Noble Savage in Dryden, 36

Norton, Richter, 184n21

Sedley, Sir Charles, 9; as character in Etherege, 10; sexual performance, 9
Select Trials at the Sessions-House in the Old Bailey: sodomy trials in, 54–59, 184nn21&23&27
Sells, A. L. Lytton, 192n17
Senelick, Laurence, 183n1, 183n14, 185n43
sensibility: and arbitrary language, 91; as cause of madness, 82; and control of bodily functions, 82–83; dangers of, 101; and desire, 82; and elitism, 102; and eroticism in Beckford, 146; as fissure in bourgeois ideology, 103; as ideological fantasy construction, 94; language of, 87; and mind-body duality, 87; as morbid, 100; pathologization of, 100; and physical response as symbolic, 86; and physical response as symptomatic, 86; politics of, 109; and putrefaction, 87; and sexuality, 81–110; as a symptom, 83; as source of goodness, 81, 82
sentimentalism, 5; code of, 92
sexual identity: source in men of feeling, 159
sexual sensibility, 114
sexuality (male), 1, 2, 175n2; cultural construction of, 3, 172; defined, 191n5; and gender as fluid concepts, 3; Gray's, as expressed in the "Elegy," 130; and power, 27
Shakespeare, William, 189n47; as source for Lee, 34
Shaw-Taylor, Desmond, 64, 185nn35–38
Silverman, Kaja, 2, 5, 164, 165, 176n6, 198n27, 201n31
Sinfield, Alan, 2, 5, 175n4, 177n15
Sitter, John, 188n29, 193n29

Smith, Bruce, , 178n29, 181n10
Smith, William, 100
Smollett, Tobias, 74–76, 78, 94–95; *The Adventures of Peregrine Pickle* (1752), 75, 186n55; *The Expedition of Humphry Clinker* (1771), 87, 95, 188n17–18; *Ferdinand Count Fathom*, 78; grotesque fops in *Peregrine Pickle*, 75; homophobia in *Peregrine Pickle*, 78; *Roderick Random* (1748), 69, 74, 186n54; sodomitical scene in *Peregrine Pickle*, 76; Strutwell as predatory sodomite in *Roderick Random*, 74; Whiffle and Simper as male-male couple in *Roderick Random*, 74
Societies for the Reformation of Manners, 55
Sodom, 31; and male-male desire, 24; and misogyny, 31
sodomite: as figure in comedy, 51; in *The Relapse*, 51–52; Italians and Catholics as, 55
sodomy, 2; as an affectional system (in *Roderick Random*), 75; compared to pederasty, 141; effeminacy and, 61; and friendship, 159; and the Grand Tour, 69; as measure of same-sex desire in the eighteenth century, 154; as political, 25–27, 30–31; as regime in *Edward II*, 24–25
sodomy trials, 53; keyhole testimony in, 58
Song of Roland, The (*La Chanson de Roland*, c. 1100), 158
Spacks, Patricia Meyer, 128, 194n45
Starr, G. A. , 188n29
Staves, Susan, 45, 52, 183n2, 183n13
Stephanson, Raymond: and epicœne friendship, 16–19, 179nn46–47, 181n11, 201n25

Sterne, Laurence, 4, 88, 91, 94, 172; *A Sentimental Journey* (1768), 81, 83–84, 91, 95, 102, 186*n*1, 187*n*10; *Tristram Shandy* (1759–67), 81, 187*n*3

Strachey, Lytton, 153, 199*n*3

Straub, Kristina, 1, 23, 24, 31, 51, 52, 175*n*1, 180*nn*2&7–8, 181*n*22, 183*nn*8–9&11–12&13–14, 184*n*15, 191*n*8

Summers, Montague, 38 , 182*n*41

Swift, Jonathan, 47, 142–43, 197*n*26

Symonds, John Addington, 15, 16, 172, 179*n*43

symptom: as kernel of enjoyment, 83; as pathology, 107; as sinthome, 106; theory of, 104, 106–108

Tinker, John, 199*n*42

Todd, Janet, 187*n*4

Trumbach, Randolph, Jr., 2, 45, 48, 49, 53, 54, 69, 175–76*n*4, 177*nn*17&22, 183*nn*11&14, 184*nn*16&19&21–23&27, 185*nn*43–45, 195*n*6, 197*nn*22&24

Turner, James Grantham, 6, 177*n*18

Tuveson, Ernest, 92, 188*nn*26&28

Vanbrugh, Sir John: *The Relapse* (1696), 51–52, 183*n*10

venereal disease: dressing room as metonymy for, 47

Vere Street scandal, 137

Vieth, David, 29, 178*nn*31–32, 181*nn*16&18

Voltaire: and socratic love, 13

Waith, Eugene M., 180*n*1

Walpole, Horace, 4, 5, 13, 19, 71, 76, 113, 116, 118, 135, 152–72, 174; *The Castle of Otranto* (1764), 160–65, 200*n*8, 201*n*27; *The Castle of Otranto*, abjec-

tion as queer in, 163; *The Castle of Otranto*, family romance in, 160; *The Castle of Otranto*, incestuous sexual violence in, 162; *The Castle of Otranto*, masochism in, 163; *The Castle of Otranto*, sexual transgression in, 160; *The Castle of Otranto*, secrecy in, 161; *The Castle of Otranto*, victimization in, 162; *The Castle of Otranto*, violence of male role in patriarchal culture, 164; as Celadon, 116–17; *Correspondence*, 152–60, 199*nn*1&4, 200*nn*6–7&13, 200*nn*16–18&21, 201*n*26&33, 202*nn*41–42&45; *Counter-Address*, 155; describes love for Conway, 155; disagreement with Conway, 200*n*15; as diseased dilettante, 152–53; early friendship with Gray, 116; and elitist education, 16; friendships, loving, 154–60, 171; and Gothic writing, 160–70; homosexuality and, 153–54, 170–72; incest in, 164–70; invoking secrecy, 157; and later gay writers, 172; masochism and masturbatory fantasies, 164; *The Mysterious Mother* (1768), 165–70, 200*n*8, 201*n*34; *The Mysterious Mother*, incest in, 168; *The Mysterious Mother*, secret sin in, 166; as queer, 159; secrets and, 152–70; sexuality of, 152–60

Ward, Ned, 46, 47, 54, 59; "The Beau's Club," 45, 183*nn*4&6; "The Mollies Club," 45, 53, 57, 184*nn*18&24; fictionality of his account, 46; *The London Clubs* (1709), 45, 183*n*2

Watson-Smyth, Peter, 194*n*40

Weber, Harold, 6, 8, 24, 177*nn*17&19&22, 178*n*23, 180*nn*4–5, 197*n*24

Chris Straayer, *Deviant Eyes, Deviant Bodies: Sexual Re-Orientation in Film and Video*

Edward Alwood, *Straight News: Gays, Lesbians, and the News Media*

Thomas Waugh, *Hard to Imagine: Gay Male Eroticism in Photography and Film from Their Beginnings to Stonewall*

Judith Roof, *Come As You Are: Sexuality and Narrative*

Terry Castle, *Noel Coward and Radclyffe Hall: Kindred Spirits*

Kath Weston, *Render Me, Gender Me: Lesbians Talk Sex, Class, Color, Nation, Studmuffins . . .*

Ruth Vanita, *Sappho and the Virgin Mary: Same-Sex Love and the English Literary Imagination*

renée c. hoogland, *Lesbian Configurations*

Beverly Burch, *Other Women: Lesbian Experience and Psychoanalytic Theory of Women*

Jane McIntosh Snyder, *Lesbian Desire in the Lyrics of Sappho*

Rebecca Alpert, *Like Bread on the Seder Plate: Jewish Lesbians and the Transformation of Tradition*

Emma Donoghue, editor, *Poems Between Women: Four Centuries of Love, Romantic Friendship, and Desire*

James T. Sears and Walter L. Williams, editors, *Overcoming Heterosexism and Homophobia: Strategies That Work*

Patricia Juliana Smith, *Lesbian Panic: Homoeroticism in Modern British Women's Fiction*

Dwayne C. Turner, *Risky Sex: Gay Men and HIV Prevention*

Timothy F. Murphy, *Gay Science: The Ethics of Sexual Orientation Research*

Cameron McFarlane, *The Sodomite in Fiction and Satire, 1660–1750*

Lynda Hart, *Between the Body and the Flesh: Performing Sadomasochism*

Byrne R. S. Fone, editor, *The Columbia Anthology of Gay Literature: Readings from Western Antiquity to the Present Day*

Ellen Lewin, *Recognizing Ourselves: Ceremonies of Lesbian and Gay Commitment*

Ruthann Robson, *Sappho Goes to Law School: Fragments in Lesbian Legal Theory*

Jacquelyn Zita, *Body Talk: Philosophical Reflections on Sex and Gender*

Evelyn Blackwood and Saskia Wieringa, *Female Desires: Same-Sex Relations and Transgender Practices Across Cultures*

Marilee Lindemann, *Willa Cather: Queering America*

Andrew Elfenbein, *Romantic Genius: The Prehistory of a Homosexual Role*